JOHN CLAYTON

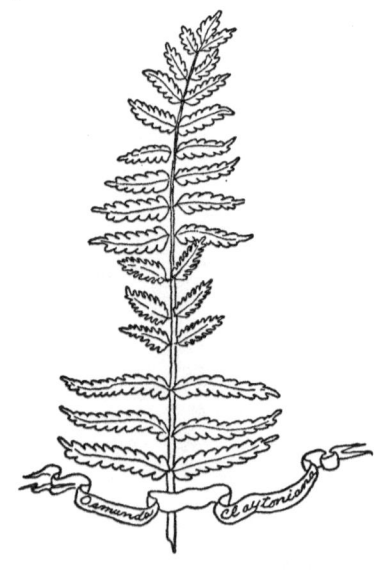

PIONEER OF

THE UNIVERSITY OF NORTH CAROLINA
CHAPEL HILL

JOHN CLAYTON

AMERICAN BOTANY

*by Edmund Berkeley
and Dorothy Smith Berkeley*

COPYRIGHT © 1963 BY
THE UNIVERSITY OF NORTH CAROLINA PRESS
Manufactured in the United States of America

PRINTED BY THE SEEMAN PRINTERY, DURHAM, N. C.

THIS BOOK WAS DIGITALLY PRINTED.

To our long-suffering children and friends, who have patiently put up with our tendency to live in the eighteenth century, this book is gratefully dedicated.

ACKNOWLEDGMENTS

The most pleasant part of writing this biography has been our association with many old and new friends, who have been very generous in their assistance and encouragement. Dr. Conway Zirkle, Professor of Botany, University of Pennsylvania, urged us to undertake the work, and has contributed much to its completion. A generous grant from the American Philosophical Society assisted us in spending the summer of 1961 abroad seeking material unavailable in this country. A grant from the Faculty Research Fund of The Woman's College, University of North Carolina, helped with other expenses. Dr. Joseph Ewan, Professor of Botany, Tulane University, gave us access to his excellent personal library, and the benefit of much assistance and advice. Dr. Earl G. Swem and Mr. Herbert L. Ganter of The College of William and Mary, have helped in innumerable ways. Mr. John Jennings and Mr. William M. E. Rachal, of the Virginia Historical Society, gave continual help and encouragement. All of the following people have given much appreciated help in one way or another: Mr. Charles Adams, The Woman's College; Miss Lynette Adcock, Mrs. Rutherfoord Goodwin, and Dr. Thad W. Tate, Colonial Williamsburg, Inc.; Mrs.

viii *Acknowledgments*

Gertrude D. Hess, the American Philosophical Society; Dr. W. B. McDaniel, 2nd, College of Physicians, Philadelphia; Dr. David C. Mearns, Library of Congress; Dr. Robert W. Hill, New York Public Library; Miss Mattie Russell and Mrs. Virginia R. Gray, Duke University; Mrs. Hugh Keane Dabney and Mrs. James Bland Martin, Gloucester, Virginia; Dr. Francis Harper, Chapel Hill; Dr. Edwin C. Mack, City College of New York; Mr. Mangum Weeks, Alexandria; Mrs. Robert H. Davis, Jr., Richmond; Dr. Bayly Turlington, University of the South; Mr. Hughes Bridges, Norfolk; Edmund Berkeley, Jr., Sewanee Military Academy; and finally, Mrs. Junetta Hill, who struggled so successfully with the typing of the final draft of the manuscript. We should also like to especially thank the staffs of the following libraries: Virginia State Library; the Historical Society of Pennsylvania; the Virginia Historical Society; the Library Company of Philadelphia; the Academy of Natural Sciences, Philadelphia; The Woman's College of the University of North Carolina; the University of North Carolina; Dartmouth College; and The University of Virginia.

We are particularly indebted to the patience and cheerful assistance of Mr. Thomas O'Grady, General Secretary, The Linnean Society of London. Mr. Paul D. A. Harvey, Assistant Keeper, Department of Manuscripts, and other members of the staff of the British Museum were unceasingly helpful. Dr. J. E. Dandy, Keeper of Botany, Dr. William T. Stearns, Miss P. I. Edwards, Librarian, and Miss Julie Nokes, Botany Department of the British Museum (Natural History) were of great assistance. Miss W. D. Coates, Registrar, National Register of Archives, gave us some excellent suggestions. To Mr. Taylor Milne, Librarian, and the staff of the Institute of Historical Research, University of London, we are indebted for many hours of peaceful, uninterrupted work in their open stacks. Among the many in Great Britain whom we wish to thank for their generous help are: Mr. I. Kaye, Librarian, The Royal Society of London; Mr. E. A. P. Hart, Librarian, Inner Temple Library; Mr. Kirkwood, and his assistants at Somerset House; the staff at the Public Record Office; Dr. W. G. McKenzie, Chelsea Physic Garden; Dr. S. M. Walters and Dr.

Acknowledgments

J. S. L. Gilmour of the Botany School, and Mr. J. C. T. Oates, Assistant Librarian, University of Cambridge; Miss Hermia M. Clokie, Botany Department, and the staff of the Bodleian Library, Oxford University; Lord Denham; Messrs. R. Davidge, C. C. Hubbard and E. Milne-Redhead, The Herbarium, Royal Botanic Garden, Kew; Mr. Felix Hull, Maidstone; Mr. Peter Walne, Berkshire Record Office; Mr. C. P. Finlayson, Keeper of Manuscripts, University of Edinburgh; and Professor A. C. O'Dell, of the University of Aberdeen.

For their courtesy and assistance, we should also like to thank Dr. Wilhelm Odelberg, Director of the Royal Society, Stockholm; the staff of the library of the Karolinska Institute; and Dr. Gustaf Holmgren, Keeper of Manuscripts, University of Uppsala.

We are grateful to Dr. P. C. Boeren, Keeper of Manuscripts, and to Dr. E. Hulshoff Pol, Classics Archivist, of the University of Leiden for their interest and help; also to Dr. Maria Rooseboom, Director of the National Museum for the History of Science, Leiden, and Dr. M. E. Kluit, of the Library of the University of Amsterdam. Dr. Frans Verdoorn and Miss de Vries, of the Institute of Biological History at the University of Utrecht, were exceedingly kind and helpful.

Unpublished Crown-copyright material in the Public Record Office, London, has been reproduced by permission of the Controller of H. M. Stationery Office.

And to all those people who have generously given permission for us to quote, we express our most sincere appreciation.

The drawings of plants associated with Clayton and his contemporaries, scattered throughout the text, are by Dorothy Smith Berkeley.

CONTENTS

Acknowledgments	vii
I. Which John Clayton?	3
II. The Clayton Family	7
III. Life in Virginia	22
IV. English and North American Botany, 1650-1750	41
V. Gronovius, Linnaeus and the *Flora Virginica*	58
VI. The Middle Years	71
VII. Recognition by the Natural History Circle	94
VIII. Clayton's Travels	110
IX. "Flora Virginiana Claytonii"	128
X. Years of Harvest	146
XI. Clayton's Contribution	173
Appendix "Flora Virginiana Claytonii": Notes by Ellis	183
Notes	193
Bibliography	218
Index	229

JOHN CLAYTON

I
WHICH JOHN CLAYTON?

There is nothing we want so much as a Biographica Botanicorum; the old were very negligent in that: there are any of which we hardly know any other thing but the name; nay, if we seak yet to the history of their life, we are obliged to pick up here and there a word in the writings of their contemporary's; . . . I have already got the history of Mr. Bartram's life; of Clayton I hope D. Gronovius will give out his vitae historiam.

Peter Kalm to Cadwallader Colden,
January 4, 1751[1]

In the British Museum is a collection of some five hundred plants gathered in Virginia over two centuries ago, and still of great value to present-day botanists in the interpretation of Linnaean species of North America. Among the elegantly mounted specimens is *Claytonia virginiana* L., named for John Clayton, the American botanist who made the collection. An esteemed contemporary of John Bartram, Mark Catesby, Peter Collinson, Benjamin Franklin, and Carolus Linnaeus, Clayton is remembered today for his part in the publication of the first important *flora* of British North America. This book, the *Flora Virginica*, was compiled by John Frederick Gronovius and published at Leiden in two parts, in 1739 and 1743; a second edition, enlarged and corrected, was published in his father's name by Laurens Theodore Gronovius at Leiden in 1762.

Despite this important contribution to science, the details of Clayton's life are little known and much of what has been written about him is fragmentary and inaccurate. As Peter Kalm feared, Clayton's career can be reconstructed only from bits and pieces of the correspondence of his friends, twenty-six of his own letters, and some curt official documents: if Gronovius ever sent the "vita" of Clayton to Kalm, it is now lost. Standard biographical reference works have confused him with his namesake, the Reverend John Clayton, who belongs to a much earlier period, and was only distantly related. The Reverend John and Clayton's grandfather, Sir John, were both members of the Royal Society of London. The botanist does not appear to have been a member, but has frequently been cited as being one. One noted present-day historian has credited him with the title of his father, John Clayton, Attorney-general of Virginia. There has been definite misunderstanding of the character of the family background from which he came. Even in his own day he found it necessary to correct a prominent contemporary who evidently thought him to be a "self-made man."

Another source of confusion concerning Clayton was introduced by one of his most ardent admirers, Benjamin Smith Barton. This University of Pennsylvania professor was so impressed by the *Flora Virginica* that in 1805 he wrote an article in the *Philadelphia Medical and Physical Journal*, of which he was founder and editor, entitled "Memorandums of the Life and Writings of Mr. John Clayton, the Celebrated Botanist of Virginia." This has been our only biography of Clayton and is, on the whole, good, but contains some error. Then in 1812, Barton undertook to produce a new *Flora Virginica*, which would incorporate all of the 1762 edition with extensive additions by Barton. He never completed this project but did publish some seventy-four pages of it.

Even Thomas Jefferson contributed to misunderstanding of Clayton in his frequently quoted comments in the *Notes on the State of Virginia*:

There is an infinitude of other plants and flowers, for an enumeration and scientific description of which I must refer to the

Flora Virginica of our great botanist Dr. Clayton, published by Gronovius at Leyden, in 1762. This accurate observer was a native and resident of this state, passed a long life exploring and describing its plants, and is supposed to have enlarged the botanical catalogue as much as almost any man who has lived.[2]

Jefferson mistakenly refers to Clayton as a native of Virginia. Clayton was born in England in the fall of 1694.[3] Neither the day nor the exact location of his birth are known. It is true that he spent much of his life in Virginia, certainly from 1720 until his death in 1773. It has often been stated that he accompanied his father there in 1705, but no record has been found which establishes this as a fact. On the contrary, there is considerable reason to believe that even more of his early life was spent in England, and it is there that we must seek the factors which influenced him.

The Claytons themselves have contributed to the difficulties of biographers by their persistent use of the names John and Jasper in many generations and on many branches of the family tree. One of the botanist's descendants, Jasper S. Clayton of Chesterfield County, Virginia, might have been able to clear up some of the confusion, for he had one of the botanist's letter books, other papers, and some of his library, including his autographed copy of Catesby's *Natural History of Carolina*. These were seen by Dr. W. G. Stanard, president of the Virginia Historical Society. He copied one of Clayton's letters which he later published. When he returned about 1906 to study the letter book further, Clayton was dead and his books and papers had vanished. Dr. E. G. Swem made an unsuccessful attempt to locate them in 1929. The authors renewed the search with the same result in 1958. As a result of litigation after Jasper S. Clayton's death, his land, "Hawkhurst," named for the town near which the botanist's English estate was located, passed to his niece, Rowena Clayton Reams. Some of the land is still in the possession of her children. One of these, Mr. Arthur S. Reams, recalls vague memories of a fire which destroyed "the home place" early in this century, but he is unable to recollect whether this was before or after the death of his great-uncle. Likewise, he is uncertain about the number of household effects which were saved at that time. Property, other than the land, apparently went to Jasper S. Clayton's widow and second wife, Cleverine Knight Clayton, and her child, born near the time of her husband's death. All attempts to locate Mrs. Clayton or her child have failed.

The records of Gloucester County, of which Clayton was Clerk from 1720 until 1773, are entirely lost for this period. Manuscripts left by Clayton when he died were destroyed by fire. Thus it has been necessary to seek information about him in many places. The search has been, on the whole, productive, but many items of information are still lacking. Though there are many references to Clayton in letters of his friends, few of Clayton's own letters have been found. Fortunately, copies of the wills of both Clayton and his father, long thought to be lost, turned up a few years ago among the Jennings' papers brought back from England by the late Ambassador Alexander Weddell. These have provided a great deal of useful information about the family. Perhaps this volume may serve the purpose of bringing to light in some unexpected place additional letters or other biographical data.

II
THE CLAYTON FAMILY

The earliest member of the Clayton family in England who definitely exerted a tangible influence on John, was his great-grandfather, Jasper. Property which he acquired descended to John and furnished part of his income for many years. Jasper was a younger son of William Clayton of Oakenshaw, Yorkshire, and, having little prospect of inheriting substantial family property, went into business in London.[1] Both his father and older brother, John, were barristers, members of the Inner Temple. Nothing is known of Jasper's youth, but he became a prosperous haberdasher, with a place of business on Lombard Street in the early 1620's.[2] Lombard Street was then, as it is today, a bustling exciting place, important in the financial world. Jasper's property was at numbers 24 and 25, at the northeast corner of Nicholas Lane.[3] It was rebuilt by his widow, Dame Mary Clayton, following the Great Fire which destroyed all of this part of the city. The land, now owned by The Royal Insurance Company, lies in the Parish of St. Edmund the King.

On May 1, 1624, Jasper Clayton married Mary, daughter of William Thomson. The latter's address is given in one record as Tinmouth Castle, Northumberland, and in another, as St. Catherine Creechurch, London.[4] Possibly both were correct, certainly the latter was, since Mary referred to it as her birthplace, in her will. The Thomsons were evidently a family of some education, as Mary's nephew, Dr. Jasper Thomson, was a Fellow of Magdalene College, Oxford.[5] Mary and Jasper probably lived for a time at the place of business on Lombard Street. As their family grew and Jasper's business prospered, they acquired property elsewhere, and made their home in the fashionable suburb of Parson's Green.[6] Among their neighbors were Lord Mordaunt and the Earl of Peterborough, famous for his gardens.[7] According to Jasper's will, the six surviving Clayton children were Mary, Rebecca, John, Prudence, George, and Andrew.

In addition to that previously mentioned, Jasper acquired property at Stepney, in Middlesex, and extensive holdings in Kent. The latter included, among others, the manors of Teston and Pettlesdon; lands in Appledore Marsh and Kennerton; the manor of Morehouse and other lands at Hawkhurst; Staplehurst and the presentation of the church there; and Frittendon. All of these he purchased from Sir John Baker.[8] One of these properties is of especial interest to our study. Jasper, in his will, wrote: "I give and bequeath unto my sonne John Clayton and the heyres male of his bodie lawfully to be begotten, upon and under the Condition hereafter mentioned, all those my Landes, Tenements, and Hereditments lyeing and beinge in the Parrish of Hawkhurst in the Countie of Kent Called or Knowne by the Name of the Mannor of Morehouse." It was this property which was eventually inherited by the botanist and was willed by him to one of his sons.[9]

As his business prospered, Jasper took an increasingly important part in the life of the city. He was one of the Commissioners for Langbourne Ward for the collection of the levies to be used for the defense of the Kingdom in 1648.[10] On September 9, 1651, he became an Alderman, representing Bridge Ward.[11] It is probable that he was one of the many who helped to finance Charles II's return to the throne in 1660, for in that year he was knighted on July fifth. He did not long enjoy this honour, as his death came only a few months later. His will was probated October 1, 1660. Sir Jasper directed that he should be "buryed in the parish Church of Edmund the Kinge in Lombarde Streete in London in case I happen to die in that parish." Evidently he did so, for his widow in 1690 directed in her will that she "be buryed in Christian buriall in the parish Church of St. Edmund, Lombard Streete in the vault where my dearly beloved husband lyeth buryed which is under the Reader's pew." Sir Jasper further directed "that nothinge shall be spent for vayne glory and I will that noe silk mournings shall be worne att my buriall: and that as small charges as convenientlie may shall be Expended thereabouts."

Jasper's will would seem to have made very adequate provision for his large family. In the Common Serjeant's Book at the Guildhall, in London, are several accountings of the estate. The inventory for June, 1662, showed the gross worth as 25,404 pounds, 4 shillings, 8 pence. One particular phrase of the will is of especial interest. In leaving the bulk of his estate to his wife, Jasper added that he was "confident of her faithful Dealings with her Children and Myne." Unfortunately, Dame Mary's "faithful Dealings" with her Children were called into question by her daughter, Prudence, not long after her father's death. She started a series of legal actions against her mother, and later against Dame Mary's executors and other members of the family which continued for nearly fifty years.[12] These eventually involved the botanist's father, as executor of his grandmother's will. Dame Mary died in February, 1692, and was buried on February 17.[13] From her will comes a picture of Clayton's great-grandmother as a rather forbidding matriarch, well-accustomed to controlling the family purse-strings, her children, and her grandchildren.

The botanist's grandfather, Sir John Clayton, seems far more likely than Sir Jasper to have influenced him, but in less tangible ways. There is every reason to believe that he saw much of his grandson during the botanist's formative years. Fortunately, more is known about him than about Sir Jasper, and he led a colourful and interesting life. He matriculated at King's College, Cambridge, in Lent of 1648-49.[14] It is likely that he prepared for the University at Eton, but few of the school's registers for the seventeenth century have survived. His younger brother, Andrew, was a student there in 1661-2. The Court of Aldermen, acting as guardians for the minor children after Sir Jasper's death, ordered that Andrew be withdrawn from "Eaton School and put to board with Mr. Rich writing Master to be instructed in writing and accompts to prepare him to be placed out apprentice for his future good."[15] Sir John was admitted to the Inner Temple in 1649, becoming a barrister in 1656.[16]

Sir Jasper Clayton not only left his children well provided for financially, but also socially. Even Dame Mary must have approved of Rebecca's marriage to Robert Paston, who later became Earl of Yarmouth.[17] Rebecca and Paston were married sometime prior to 1651.[18] Paston and her brother John were either already close friends, or soon became so. They eventually quarrelled, but were closely associated for many years. Sometime around 1664, Sir John married Alice Bowyer Buggins, widow of William Buggins of North Cray, County Kent, who had left her an income of three hundred pounds a year. Her parents were Sir William Bowyer, baronet, and Margaret Weld Bowyer, daughter of Sir Humphrey Weld.

John Evelyn, in his diaries, made a number of references to both Clayton and Paston. Thus, on December 30, 1656, he noted, "Dined with me Sir William Paston's sonn, Mr. Henshaw & Mr. Clayton."[19] These four men were quite close friends, despite some differences in their ages. Thomas Henshaw[20] and Evelyn had spent a year traveling together in Italy. Whatever other interests they may have shared, the four men certainly had a common one in science, especially in alchemy. All four men were among the Original Fellows of the Royal Society.[21] Evelyn's *Sylva* was the first book published under the aegis of that group. John Clayton was proposed for membership September 11, 1661, and admitted October 9th, while Paston was admitted on New Year's Day of the following year.[22] At least two other men among the Original Fellows were later associated with Clayton in various ways and are thought to have influenced his son and grandson. These were the well-known Sir Christopher Wren and the less-known Sir Thomas Nott (1606-1681).

For the wealthier English gentlefolk, the Continent was a magnet in the seventeenth century. They not only travelled there, but spent long periods of time, forming small islands of English society in foreign cities. It was considered *de rigeur* for anyone with ambitions at court to have travelled abroad. Thus, it is not surprising that soon after John Clayton inherited extensive land holdings from Sir Jasper, he joined the travellers. On April 8, 1663, he wrote to Paston from Florence: "As soon as the snow is dissolved on the Alps, I mind to cross them for France, and so directly to Paris, where I will spend my time 'till next winter, and then for England; there I hope to serve you with gusto . . . I can say but little of my travels than what I have told you, only the entertainment of the Holy Week at Rome. . . ." In reference to their common interest in alchemy, he told Paston with mock solemnity that he had purchased secrets reputed to "have been found in a book hidden in the bottom of a well, inclosed in soldered lead, and after that a marble cover; the title of the book, Phoenix Hermetica, with a clovis and six wedges, three of gold, three of silver, made by the same process."[23]

Clayton went to Paris as planned, and was dallying there on November fourteenth. He had not only been to church that stormy day, but had heard Lady Mordaunt, his Parson's Green neighbor, read at length from "The Duty of Man."[24] By February, he was back in England and apparently continuing to lead a gay life. On February sixth, Paston wrote to Rebecca: "Yesterday at your brother's lodging, supped the Breame's family, and some of the Boye's; we had the Duke of Richmond there and his fidlers and stay'd up till three in the morne."[25]

On November 17, 1664, John Clayton was knighted at Whitehall.[26] It was probably in this same year that he married Alice Bowyer, although the date is not known. Their eldest son, another John (father of the botanist), was born in 1665.[27] The Bowyers lived at "Denham Lodge" in Buckinghamshire.

Sir William Bowyer was a member of Parliament for twenty years, 1659-1679. He is said to have assisted Dryden in his translation from Vergil. The Virginia Claytons maintained a correspondence with their Bowyer relatives for many years.[28] Whether or not Sir John and Lady Clayton made their home with Dame Mary at Parson's Green when they were first married is not clear.[29] Their son, Jasper, was born there in 1675, as was a daughter, Charlotte, in 1678. A daughter, Elizabeth, died there in 1686, but the parish registers make no mention of two other daughters, Alice and Mary.[30]

In spite of the diversions of a growing family, Sir John seems to have continued his interests in chemistry. In June, 1669, he wrote to Paston, now living at "Oxnead":[31] "I have taken pity and consideration upon your marrow, and have ordered a stuff suit for you, which is done by this time, and shall be sent by the first opportunity, least you should fall away to an Alderman's thumb ring before I see you . . . The chemical glasses sure are come safe by this time, and the glass bottles with stoples which will perfect the experiment I so much long after."[32] Paston also discussed alchemy in his letters to Henshaw. Perhaps all of them may have been influenced by another Original Fellow of the Royal Society, Robert Boyle.

Sir John's activities were certainly not all frivolous. He was practising law[33] and also became involved in certain business ventures. One of the latter was originally a joint undertaking with Paston and Sir Thomas Osborne,[34] for the construction of possibly the first English light-houses and channel buoys at various places along the coast. This maritime venture involved Clayton for some years, but Paston and Osborne seem to have dropped out of the picture.[35] Sir John also maintained his contacts in France, for he was able to "arrange a settled correspondent at Paris" for his nephew William Paston and his tutor, who were traveling on the Continent in 1671.[36]

There are many references to a quarrel between Clayton and Paston in the latter's correspondence, of which the following is typical. On July 31, 1676, he wrote to Rebecca: "As to what you write me concerning your mother I am very glad she is to send to you. pray present my duty to her, and also to Sr John. I should very well approve you should both ask for his wife & children, & even bee civill to him—butt to have any thing to doe with him is butt to betray orselves. I told you before it would come to a whining story and that he thinks reasonable to purge all his falsehoods by contempt, now by his particularity that we were fallen out that he might not more bee troubled with us. for my part I am resolved to have nothing to doe with him far than speaking to him & eating & drinking with him . . . I hate and abhor ye remembrance of his ingrateful returns to me."[37]

In spite of family dissension, Sir John continued to make a name for himself. He was chosen steward for the "reader's dinner" at the Inner Temple in 1675.[38] In August, 1676, he was dining at John Evelyn's with Lord Halifax; Sir Thomas Meeres, who was one of the Commissioners of the Admiralty; Mr. Slingsby, who was the Master of the Mint; Mr. Henshaw and others.[39] His name appeared on a list of those who enjoyed "protections," when the House of Lords was considering withdrawing all of these except those registered in the Clerk of Parliament's office. On December 27, 1690, his "protection" was recalled by his sponsor, the Duke of Northumberland, third son of Charles II by the Duchess of Cleveland.[40] Perhaps the clearest indication of his social position is the fact that he was one of the Gentlemen of the Privy Chamber under William III, as Paston had been under Charles II.[41]

One of Clayton's fellow members of the Gentlemen of the Privy Chamber was the artist, Sir Godfrey Kneller, who was then at the height of his popularity as a court painter. Kneller painted Paston's portrait about 1676 or later, and also members of Sir John's family some time in this period. These Kneller portraits were seen in the home of the botanist's son a century later, but have since disappeared.[42]

Evidently Alice Clayton maintained the family home at Parson's Green while Sir John was attending to his affairs at Hampton Court. Possibly his mother felt that he spent too much time there. At any rate, Dame Mary's will gives the impression that she lacked faith in his judgment, financial and otherwise. She left the property intended for his family to the Bowyers in trust for his wife. She further directed that two of Sir John's children seek the approval of their Aunt Rebecca, "Countess Dowager of Yarmouth," and their uncle, Sir William Bowyer, before entering into any marriage agreement. She named her grandson, John, rather than her son, as one of her executors.

The botanist's father followed the family tradition of studying law. He was admitted to the Inner Temple on the 16th of June at the age of seventeen, after preparation at Eton.[43] On September 29 of the following year he matriculated at Trinity Hall, Cambridge.[44] He was called to the bar in 1691,[45] and apparently practised law in England for the next twelve years, although little has been learned about his activities during this period. He maintained chambers at the Inner Temple, for the records of the Temple show that on February 1 and 3, 1693, orders were issued "fore the attendance of John Clayton, to makeing a disturbance created by a blackamore belonging to Harcourt Goodrick, lodging in Clayton's Chambers, and for the removal of Goodrick."[46] In future references, we shall call him "Mr. Clayton," to distinguish him from his son, the botanist.

If we are correct in believing that the botanist grew up in England, then he presumably would have seen something of his father's family. His Uncle Jasper made a very successful career of the Army, and they would not have been likely to see much of each other, since much of his military duty was overseas. He probably did know Jasper's wife, Juliana, and their children, Juliana, John, Jasper, and Charlotte. A copy of a letter which he wrote to Charlotte in 1737 was in existence in the 1890's but has since been lost. It was addressed to "Fern Hill Park" in Cranbourne, near Ascot.[47] Jasper bought this house in 1706 and it is still standing.[48] Jasper had a brief acquaintance with the Colonies through a tour of duty in Canada. Later, he served as Commander of the English forces in North Britain.[49] In 1726, he was promoted to Lieutenant General, and appointed Governor of Gibraltar. He was killed in the Battle of Dettingen in 1743.[50] One phrase from his will gives a rather stern picture of the botanist's soldier uncle: "I give and bequeath to my very undutiful and lost daughter, Juliana, the reputed wife of Peter Hooper, who was my servant 1/ & no more."[51]

Mr. Clayton's sisters were Elizabeth, Alice, Charlotte, and Mary. Elizabeth died young. Alice married Henry Symonds, a great-nephew of her father's friend, Sir Christopher Wren. Symonds was Clerk of the Works at Hampton Court under William and Mary. Wren had been ordered to design extensive renovations and additions to the palace,[52] and Symonds directed the work of some four hundred men engaged in carrying them out. This work extended over quite a period of time, and might well have been viewed by the botanist as a boy in the company of either his grandfather or his Uncle Henry.[53]

Charlotte Clayton, the botanist's aunt, married John, Baron Lovelace, of Hurley.[54] Lord Lovelace was a colonel in the army, when he was appointed Governor of New York and New Jersey in 1708, an office which had earlier been held by his grandfather, the first baron. Lord Lovelace and several of his children died within a few months of their arrival in New York. Charlotte and her two surviving children, Martha and Nevill, returned to England. Martha later married Lord Henry Beauclerk, grandson of Charles II and Eleanor Gwyn.[55] The botanist's Aunt Mary was unmarried in 1713 when her mother's will was written. LeNeve's *Knights* states that she married one Thomas Strickland.

Clayton's great-grandmother, Dame Mary, died just two years before his birth. His father, Mr. Clayton, as his grandmother's executor, promptly found himself involved in the long litigation of his Aunt Prudence over her father's estate, which continued at least until 1707. His uncle, Sir William Bowyer, co-executor with him of Dame Mary's will, "refused to prove ye same or any waie to intermeddle or concerne himself with the execution thereof."[56]

In Prudence's suit of 1707, both Sir John Clayton and his son, Mr. Clayton, are said to have left England. The former is accused of having made over his estate to Sir William Bowyer in trust for his wife and children, and of having sold some houses for two thousand pounds, with which to abscond and so defraud his creditors. Prudence did not know whether he was alive or dead, only that he had gone to "some remote place unknown" to her. Likewise, the son was accused by his aunt of having "absconded for many years & lately gone into Maryland or some other part beyond the seas."[57] There is no further record of Sir John. No will has been located. He may very well have left England at this time. With the death of William III in 1702, and Anne's succession, a new group came into favour at Court. William's favourites were left to fend for themselves, and Sir John may have thought it expedient to leave the court and perhaps the country. Dame Alice referred to herself as his widow when she wrote her will in 1713.[58]

Mr. Clayton *had* left England prior to 1707. His presence in Virginia as early as 1705 is well authenticated. He was, at that time, Secretary to the newly appointed lieutenant-governor, Edward Nott.[59] The date of his leaving England is not known, but it was probably not until 1705. The lieutenant-governor and his party arrived in Virginia on August 11th of that year. The Clayton connection with Nott might be explained in several ways. If this Edward Nott was the son of Sir Thomas Nott, an Original Fellow of the Royal Society, then Sir John Clayton had known him for many years. Sir Thomas had served as a Gentleman of the Privy Chamber in 1682, concurrently with Robert Paston. Like the Claytons and the Pastons, Sir Thomas was an ardent royalist. He had three sons: Thomas, Roger, and Edward. Sir John might also have brought influence to bear through George Hamilton, Earl of Orkney. Nott was Hamilton's deputy, the latter acting as Virginia's Governor for thirty years without ever visiting there. His wife, Elizabeth Villiers, mistress of William III, was a sister of Sir Edward Villiers, later the Earl of Jersey. He was a member of the court of William III at the same period as Sir John.[60]

It is interesting to speculate that Sir John Clayton might have accompanied his son to Virginia, but there is no evidence to support it. Both men seem to have left their families in

England. Dame Alice died there in 1718.[61] Nothing is known of the botanist's mother, except that her name was Lucy.[62] It is strange that in all of the many references to her husband and her three sons in Virginia records, none has been found to Mrs. Clayton. There would seem to be two likely, but unsubstantiated, explanations: one would be that when Mr. Clayton left, she remained in England to educate her sons, and never accompanied them to Virginia; another, that she may have died soon after her youngest son, Thomas, was born, and the children may have been raised by their grandmother, Dame Alice, or other relatives.

The botanist's youngest brother, Thomas, was born in 1702. He was christened at St. Mary's Church, at Walton-on-Thames, a suburb fifteen miles from London.[63] Among the church's records the entry of Thomas Clayton's baptism may still be seen, but the parish registers include no other items concerning the Claytons. We have no way of knowing whether they were living there at the time, or possibly merely visiting. John was, at that time, eight years old, and the third brother, Arthur, somewhat younger. His date of birth is not known. John had only the two brothers and no sisters.[64]

Whether or not Mr. Clayton accompanied Nott on the voyage to Virginia, he was there in November of that year (1705), for his name appears on an endorsement of a petition to Nott at that time.[65] In January, 1706, he was appointed Register of the Court of Admiralty.[66] It was just as well that Mr. Clayton was establishing his personal career, since Nott only lived a year after his arrival in Virginia. In 1707, Mr. Clayton acted as the Virginia Attorney-general's assistant in a case involving the Tuscarora Indians, who had murdered a man named Pate.[67] In the next few years, he acted as attorney for a number of prominent men, including William Byrd II, Robert ("King") Carter, John Custis, Benjamin Harrison, and Micajah Perry. In 1710, he was made a "member" of the College of William and Mary, and Clerk of the powerful Committee of Propositions and Grievances.[68]

When the new lieutenant-governor, Colonel Alexander Spotswood, finally arrived in Virginia four years after Nott's death, he appointed Mr. Clayton as a mediator in a dispute between North Carolina's newly appointed lieutenant-governor, Colonel Hyde, and the deputy-governor, Colonel Cary, in 1711. Spotswood wrote to Cary, "I have chosen him because of his great moderation and eveness of Temper which redr him very fitt for managing an affair of this nature, and on whose Truth I can depend for a faithful full and impartial relation of what you shall charge him with."[69] Spotswood was well satisfied with the manner in which Mr. Clayton carried out his assignment, and it is not surprising to find him writing the Board of Trade March 9, 1713: "Mr. Thomson, who for some years past was Attorney General of this Colony, died at the beginning of last month, and I have commissionated in his place Mr. John Clayton an English gentleman and a barrister-at-law, who has as fair a character as anyone I ever knew of that profession."[70] Mr. Clayton held this position for the remainder of his life, along with many other offices. He was the first Justice of the Peace for James City County, was elected to the House of Burgesses many times,[71] and was Judge of the Court of Admiralty in 1718, succeeding John Holloway. In appointing him to this office, Spotswood made the following remark, "I believe, I need make no apologies to their Lord'ps for my appointment of Mr. Clayton to the Judge of that Court, since, besides his being the King's Attorney General here, everyone who knows him will allow him the Character of a very honest Gent'n."[72] That the foregoing estimate of Mr. Clayton was one rather generally held may be seen from the following comment made a few years later by another of the most influential men in Virginia, Robert Carter, who wrote to Colonel Page, December 5, 1727: "Were I to give my opinion impartially for a person to make up the breach of Colonel Harrison in the Council and to fill up his place as a judge, I can think of no person so properly qualifyed as Mr. Clayton. All mankind must allow we want such a man in the Court . . . & I fancy the Attorney hath very good interest both by his own relations & Mr. Perry who pushes strong where he's harty."[73] Carter adds that he holds this high opinion of Mr. Clayton despite the fact that he has just opposed Carter successfully in England, representing Virginia's case against the Proprietors of Northern Neck, for whom Carter was agent.

Mr. Clayton was not only popular in official circles, but in the social life of the Colony as well. When away from court, he was no longer the precise, dignified man of law, but showed the gay spirits and jolly companionship exhibited by his father years before. He enjoyed cards and convivial drinking, and was not above all-night sessions of such pleasures. In a letter, he mentioned a present of "arrack" from London, which "was last night drunk by some of the best company in Virginia."[74] From contemporary accounts, it would seem that there were few prominent Virginians whom he did not know well. Above all, Mr. Clayton was loyal, as his good friend Spotswood discovered. As was usual for those who represented their Majesties' Government, Spotswood was the target for innumerable attacks by bellicose and powerful Virginia planters, attacks which culminated in his removal from office. From 1715 on, Mr. Clayton defended his friend against many accusations, with strongly worded legal testimony forwarded to London.[75] He did this in spite of the fact that many of his close friends were among those who opposed Spotswood. Strangely enough, his actions apparently did nothing to alienate such men.

Perhaps Spotswood's most vigorous opponent was William Byrd II, with whom Mr. Clayton had a long and enduring association. He was also one of Mr. Clayton's friends who might have interested his son, John, in botany. Mr. Byrd was intensely interested in natural history and was, at twenty-two, one of the few Virginia members, if not the only one, of the Royal Society of London. In 1706, he wrote to Sir Hans Sloane in London: "This Country where fortune has cast my Lot, is a large field for natural inquirys and this much to be lamented; that we have not some people of skil and curiosity among us. I know no body here capable of making very great discoverys."[76] Mr. Clayton and Mr. Byrd may have known each other in England, where Byrd was educated and studied for the bar, as well as working for some time in the offices of Perry and Lane, Merchants.[77] If the two had not met in the

Inns of Court, they could have become acquainted at the offices of the Virginia merchants, since Mr. Clayton acted for many years as a legal counsel in the Colony for the well-known Micajah Perry.[78] Byrd and Clayton worked together on the settling of Nott's estate,[79] and from that time on there are many allusions to their friendship in Byrd's diaries.[80] Mr. Clayton was a frequent visitor at "Westover," Byrd's home, famous for a library said to be the finest of its time in the colony. There the two men enjoyed innumerable games of billiards, piquet, bottles of wine, and perhaps even "fricasse of possum." There, too, were held many gay parties which, no doubt, Mr. Clayton enjoyed even if the "conversation with the Ladys, like Whip Syllabub, was very pretty but had nothing in it!"[81] Mr. Clayton lent Mr. Byrd a horse on occasion and kept him informed of whatever occurred in Williamsburg.

Perhaps the most enthusiastic botanist among Mr. Clayton's friends was Mrs. Byrd's brother-in-law, John Custis, who noted in his letter-book, "I have retained Messrs. Holloway, Randolph & Clayton who give me encouragement as all Lawers will do & tell me I am in no danger."[82] He had inherited vast landholdings from his father, whom Swem describes as being "one of the wealthiest men of his time in Virginia."[83] His real enthusiasm in life was his garden, of which he said in a letter to Peter Collinson: "I have a garden inferior to few if any in Virga."[84] Custis carried on a long correspondence with Collinson beginning in 1734, concerning seeds and plants which the two men exchanged over a period of years. Of all of Mr. Clayton's friends and acquaintances, the one who had the most profound influence on John Clayton was Mark Catesby. So important was his contribution, it will be discussed in detail in a later chapter.

Unlike the majority of his friends who lived in the country, Mr. Clayton lived in Williamsburg itself. If he had not done so before 1714, he was required to live there as Attorney-General.[85] At that time, the Virginia Capital consisted of approximately two hundred houses and a population of a thousand persons, both Negro and white. Most of the inhabitants were tradesmen, only ten or twelve "gentlemen's families" living there permanently. Mr. Clayton's home was in a most convenient place for a lawyer at, or near, the corner of Francis Street and the Capitol, on either Lot 26 or Lot 27. If it was on the first, it is possible that his home may have been what is now known as the Nelson-Galt house, one of the oldest in Williamsburg—an unpretentious, but charming, white clapboard, with roof of cedar shingles, set in a quiet garden. This house was built some time before 1718 by William Robertson, but little is known of its history until it was bought by William Nelson in 1749.[86] It seems likely that this was "home" for the young Claytons, when they first came to Virginia after completing their education.

Whether they made their home with their mother, their grandmother, or some other relatives after their father left for Virginia, there can be very little doubt that John Clayton and his brothers remained in England for some years. Much of this time was spent in school, but they would have had abundant opportunity to become well acquainted with the many relatives and friends of the family during the holidays. It is likely that they visited the family land holdings in Kent. All facets of London life at the beginning of the eighteenth century would have been quite familiar to them by the time they joined their father at Williamsburg.

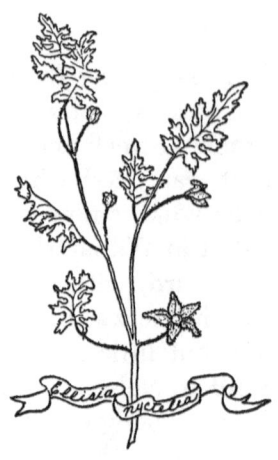

III
LIFE IN VIRGINIA

John Clayton, in a letter to Linnaeus some thirty years after his arrival in Virginia, apologized, "Pardon my inexperience in the use of the Latin language, since I have lived so long in these rich regions without practice and without conversation with learned men that I have almost forgotten the learning of my youth, such learning as you believe spontaneous."[1] While no educational records have been located concerning John and Arthur Clayton, it is definitely known that the third brother, Thomas, attended Eton for two years before matriculating at Pembroke College, Cambridge.[2] He remained at the University six years, commencing Bachelor of Medicine in 1726. It seems most unlikely that the youngest of the family would have received more schooling than his two older brothers. There was a Clayton (Christian name unknown) at Eton in 1707 who might easily have been the botanist.[3] There is also every likelihood that he attended Cambridge, for that too was in the family tradition. His father, grandfather, and great-great-grandfather, as well as his brother, Thomas, were Cambridge alumni. When the time came, he even planned to send his oldest son there.[4] There is an oblique confirmation of Clayton's Cambridge education. It was the custom of former students who left England, to send specimens and seeds to their old professors. In the Cambridge Herbarium there were specimens of Pteridophytes from North America, sent by "Dr. Clayton."[5]

The designation "Dr." before Clayton's name, brings up a much debated question. Not only did Thomas Jefferson and many others give him this title, but so did Laurens Gronovius in the second edition of the *Flora Virginica*. The majority of the botanist's contemporaries and friends referred to him as "Mr. Clayton," but he was also called "Capt." and even "The Honourable."[6] Although the *Flora Virginica* gives many instances of the medicinal uses of various plants, this emphasis on drug possibilities was customary for the period. It can be argued both ways: that such medicinal properties were amplified because of Clayton's medical training, or that his study of plants had aroused an interest in gaining some knowledge of medicine. Peter Collinson probably described the situation correctly when he said that Clayton had "made Physik some of his study, but only for his own & Familys Use."[7] It is far more likely that Clayton had made a study of law. There was a long family tradition for the eldest son, John, to become a barrister. The office of Clerk of Court would require at least some legal training and is normally held by lawyers today. Legal training in Virginia was somewhat informal at this time; so much so, that Mr. Clayton and John Holloway were appointed in 1732 to serve as "examiners" of persons wishing to practice law.[8] John and Arthur might well have read law under their father's direction after coming to Virginia.

The earliest documented evidence for Clayton's residence in Virginia consists of an entry in the vestry book of Petsworth Parish, Gloucester County, Virginia, on October 20, 1720, in which he is listed as Clerk of the County Court.[9] He was, at that time, twenty-six years old. Since most of the records for Virginia's Tidewater in the eighteenth century have either been lost or destroyed, this date is not necessarily significant. He may well have been in Virginia for a number of years before becoming Clerk of Court. It seems most likely that

Clayton had joined his father as soon as he had completed his education in England, which would place his arrival in Virginia about 1715. There was a Clayton there in 1715, who might well have been the botanist. John Fontaine, a twenty-two year old Huguenot refugee, had come to Virginia in May of that year, with the purpose of acquiring land on which to settle. He spent almost six months in Williamsburg before starting on November 9 on a visit to the interior. Since a "Mr Clayton"[10] accompanied him on his travels, there has been some speculation that this might have been the botanist. The attorney-general's family seem to have been the only Claytons living in Williamsburg at that time. It is highly unlikely that the lawyer went with Fontaine, as he was then fifty years old, suffering from gout, and had just started upon the duties of a new and demanding office. It is much more likely that his oldest son, who was about the same age as Fontaine, went with the latter on the leisurely trip to Germana, Spotswood's colony of German miners in Spotsylvania County. If Clayton did indeed go with Fontaine, it may well have been his first view of the exciting frontiers which lay beyond the comparative civilization of the Tidewater area.

If "Mr. Clayton," Fontaine's companion, was the botanist, it might even be conjectured that he was also one of the "Knights of the Golden Horseshoe," those men who accompanied Spotswood on his expedition in 1716. This exploration was to open up Virginia frontiers hitherto little considered for colonization because of ignorance of the Blue Ridge mountains and what lay beyond. It succeeded in opening up the Great Valley of Virginia, but the roster of the expedition is still in doubt. Ten of the twelve "gentlemen" have been more or less identified, mainly from Fontaine's *Journal*, but the other two as well as many of the "scouts" and soldiers are still unknown. Lt. Governor Spotswood was intimate enough with the Claytons for an invitation to join this group to have been justified on that alone, and Fontaine, of course, led the expedition. Clayton certainly collected plants in this area later.

John Clayton succeeded Peter Beverly as Clerk of Gloucester Court,[11] a position which he held for fifty-three years.

According to a Williamsburg physician, Dr. Galt, writing some thirty years after Clayton's death, the botanist had worked in Beverly's office prior to that time. Clayton's brother, Arthur, held a similar position, being the first Clerk of Hanover County.[12] Because there were few such offices available to young men, clerkships were undoubtedly more sought after then than they are today. Before 1722, they were appointed by the Secretary of the Colony, but it was remarkable that Mr. Clayton was able to obtain two such posts for his sons, although the Secretary at that time was John Carter, III, of "Shirley." It was his father, Robert, who held such respect for Mr. Clayton.

County clerks in eighteenth-century Virginia were responsible, as they still are, for the records of the courts, the filing of wills, land surveys, and other such documents. The clerk was paid in tobacco and it was, on the whole, a lucrative post as can be seen from the following schedule of fees:

Entry of order	8 lb.
Oath taken in court	5 lb.
Recording verdict of jury	10 lb.
Recording surveyor's report and filing	20 lb.
Recording deed	50 lb.
Recording lease	30 lb.
Commission of administration (for estate not over value of 100 lb.)	150 lb.
Commission of administration (for estate not over value of 10 lb.)	100 lb.
For every day's attendance in court	100 lb.[13]

In addition to court fees, there was a small income from furnishing the church with a list of the titheables.

Although the use of tobacco as currency was prevalent in Virginia, there were two great weaknesses in this practice. The first was that its value continually fluctuated and a payment equal to two pounds in currency one month could easily drop many shillings in exchange the next. The second argument against its use was the temptation to defraud. There were many grades of tobacco and, unless the hogsheads were opened and closely examined, an inferior product could be substituted for a better one. This Clayton found to his cost:

"I recd also the account of my 19 hhds of Tob'o by Capt Lilly, which proved muchly below my expectation, but for the future I will take a little more pains in examining the quality of the Tobaccos paid me at the Warehouse before they are shipped."[14]

The Gloucester County clerkship should have been a considerably more profitable one than that of Hanover. The county, which had been established in 1651, included in Clayton's time the entire peninsula, an area of some 164,000 acres. Hanover was larger, with 40,000 more acres, but could boast only 1,941 titheables to the 3,421 in Gloucester.[15] Although the duties of the clerk of court of the wealthiest Virginia county may have been onerous at times, there was one tremendous virtue to that office. Since there was no stipulation that the clerk be present each day, a deputy could serve in his place. This comparative freedom was ideal for Clayton and gave him the opportunity for extended collecting expeditions as well as field trips in his own area. The present courthouse and gaol for Gloucester County were built during Clayton's tenure as Clerk of the Court. The former was built in 1766, and the latter some time before 1754.[16] Whether or not they were built on the site of the earlier buildings which burned is not clear. It is also uncertain whether the clerks maintained their offices in the courthouse or in their homes. General William B. Taliaferro favored the latter view: "The office of County Clerk or Clerk of the Court, in the early period of the country was one of the most important and responsible in the Colony—for there were no public Clerk's offices, the records being kept at the private residence of the officers."[17] In any event, much of Clayton's official business, during the last years of his life, was carried on in the same courthouse which is in use today. It is a typical eighteenth-century brick structure, dignified by tall, white columns—one of several buildings located in the comparative quiet of the walled town square.

Gloucester Court House, which is the actual name of the town, was a small village and is not a large place today. The finer houses then, as now, were along the rivers. Social life may have been less gay than that of Williamsburg, but Gloucester was not without amusements. There was racing at Seawell's Ordinary almost every Saturday, and sometimes as many as three consecutive days of the sport. The prizes were sufficiently generous to attract many contestants, with purses of thirty pistoles.[18] In addition there were card and dice games as well as the ubiquitous cockfights.[19] For the men, superb hunting and fishing were available whenever time permitted.

There were fewer opportunities for amusement for the ladies, but all enjoyed walking and riding. Church was a weekly meeting place for neighbors, and there were always house guests from other areas. Families enjoyed card games and dancing in their own homes, and looked forward to their visits to Williamsburg, when the General Courts were in session. There they met old friends who lived at too great a distance for casual visiting. They enjoyed shopping, formal balls, and even the "theatre" when the townspeople and the young gentlemen from the college presented "Cato," or some other play.

Gloucester rumors have persisted through the years that the old courthouse was located at the end of the lane which leads to the North River plantation, "Elmington." This belonged to Major Henry Whiting, who had married Anne, daughter of the Peter Beverly, whom Clayton had replaced as Clerk. Major Whiting, a doctor and planter, was, at one time, a member of the powerful Council.[20] It is not surprising, in view of Clayton's close relationship to Beverly, and the general propinquity, that he fell in love with one of the Major's daughters, Elizabeth.

The twenty-eight-year-old Clayton and Elizabeth Whiting were married in Ware Church in 1723.[21] This gracious old church of tawny brick, shaded by a magnificent grove of trees, still stands little changed from Clayton's day. Adjoining it is an ancient graveyard with wall of mellowed brick. This was the church which the Claytons attended throughout their lives. While there are many notes of payments to "Cap Clayton" or "Cap. John Clayton" for the titheing lists which he furnished to the church, Clayton's name never appeared as vestryman nor churchwarden on the parish records. Nevertheless, Governor Page described Clayton as "a strict, though not ostentatious, observer of the practice of the Church of England; and seemed constantly piously disposed. I have heard him say, whilst examining a flower, that he could not look into one, without seeing the display of infinite power and contrivance, and thus he thought it impossible for a BOTANIST to be an ATHEIST."[22]

The Whitings were not only a family of wealth and background, but were connected to many of the other prominent Virginia families. They took an active part in the life of the colony. Clayton's brothers-in-law, Beverly (godfather of George Washington) and Thomas, distinguished themselves as burgesses, justices of the peace, and councillors. Another brother, Francis, "migrated to Shenandoah Valley." Elizabeth Clayton's sister, Catherine, married John Augustin Washington, uncle of the first president, and lived at "Highgate," not far from the Claytons' home.[23]

It is difficult to form any clear picture of Elizabeth Clayton, since her husband's only remaining reference to his wife was in his will, where he stated that he wished to be buried at her side. There emerges a tantalizingly hazy portrait of her, if she was represented by the initials "B.C." (Betty Clayton?) in the orders which Clayton sent to his London agents during the last few years of his life.[24] As far as is known, there were no daughters or daughters-in-law with these initials then living at home. Although in her sixties at that time, Betty Clayton's taste in dress illustrates the charm and utter femininity of an eighteenth-century Virginia lady: a "Flowered Blue Sattin Bonnet," a black silk one, "Striped & Sprigged Muslin," flowered calico, blue and white printed linen, an Indian fan and one with ivory sticks in a case, bolts of ribbon and feathers of egret, a French wax necklace and earrings. Betty Clayton's predilection for shoes was demonstrated by orders for ten pairs in one year: four pairs of calf skin pumps, two of green leather, three of black and one of white satin. This seemingly inordinate love of footgear was tempered by the fact that orders came infrequently. Likewise, she displayed a weakness for gloves shown by orders of five or six pairs at a time: white, coloured, and French kid, as well as "warm black silk mittens." She was more restrained in regard to stockings, seldom desiring more than three or four pairs a year, of fine thread or cotton, but perhaps these were supplemented by some knitted at home. Except for stays and a black "Brussels" [lace] petticoat, undergarments did not appear on the lists, as they, too, must have been made at home. Elizabeth Clayton was still very conscious of style. In the event that a sample of "fine cotton material" could not be matched, she wished another of "fashionable" colour. She ordered a stylish "Woms pastel Stomacher," a "fashionable Breast Flower," and a "Tortoise shell comb to keep up the hair." Although her favourite colours were blues and greens, she satisfied a youthful craving for gaiety with orders for red and white Cambric pocket handkerchiefs. Strangely, the orders seldom included any warm clothing. Heavy materials probably were woven from the thread spun from the plantation's own wool, and furs could be procured locally.

As far as Elizabeth Clayton's interests are concerned, aside from fashion, the only hints are from orders for embroidery thread and cat gut. It may be concluded from these that she shared the popular recreation of fine sewing, and had some talent in music. The latter may have been inherited by her grandsons, for a visitor in their home speaks of "a Roman Catholic Scotch fiddler," who lived with the family and taught violin to the sons, a bare five years after Clayton's death.[25] As Mrs. Clayton's orders cease with the 1771 invoice, it can be inferred that she died some two years before her husband.

The exact location and name of the Claytons' home in Gloucester has been a matter of considerable debate. The question might seem to have been settled when a marker was erected in 1950. "Many months of painstaking research on the part of Miss Georgia Mogford, a member of the Mathews County, Virginia, Garden Club, culminated Saturday afternoon, October 14, 1950, when a wrought iron marker to John Clayton (1693-1773) was unveiled. This took place at Windsor Farms near Soles where he resided for more than fifty years while serving as Clerk of Court in Gloucester County."[26]

Despite the erection of this marker in Mathews, a new county made from part of the old Gloucester, there are some who question that it is accurately placed. Since that time, the botanist's will has been discovered, which seems to indicate a different location, and one authority favors still another spot. Clayton referred to "horned pond weed," growing on the shore of the Pianketank River "juxta hortum meum."[27] If his garden was in the vicinity of his house, this would place it in an area quite different from those now projected and one similar to that mentioned by Dr. John Dunn (1862-1934) in his reminiscences to a friend. Dr. Dunn, a Richmond oculist and Clayton enthusiast, spent many pleasant hours following in the botanist's footsteps, later writing "I see the little river Pianketank that runs by Clayton's, and I see, too Winsor Road on which stood this garden, marked now by traces of brick wall."[28]

Clayton does not, in any of his letters which have been located, refer to his home as "Windsor," "Windsor Farms," "Windsor Castle," or any other name. The letters are headed either "Gloucester," or "Gloucester Court House." Hargreaves implied that John Clayton's son, Jasper, was living in his father's old home. He referred to it as "Windsor Castle," and credence can be given to this statement since Jasper did inherit his father's home, although there is no way of knowing whether he lived there or remained in his own.[29] John Bartram visited Clayton's home in 1739,[30] and again in 1760, but his references to the trips are of little help in pinpointing its location. It is unfortunate that, with the exception of a surveyor's book, no Gloucester official records of this period survive. Without such confirmation, it cannot be stated categorically that "Windsor" was Clayton's home, although there seems every likelihood that it was.

Description of both the land and the house at "Windsor," are a matter of record; although the owners of adjoining lands had probably changed since Clayton's day, as the following description was written in 1808:

beginning at the corner of Marables land on the side of the highland branch thence East of Dances corner, thence along Dances line East to Sam Hodges corner thence East along said Hodges line to the main road thence north along said road to Sadlers corner thence along Sadlers line to corner three standing in Poplar Neck thence south 34½ West to a corner marked gum of this land, Andrew Van Bibbers land thence North 67½ West 236 Poles to a marked white gum tree on the side of F. Whiting's meadow thence along said meadow to the mouth of the branch dividing said Whitings and Claytons land and thence up said branch to the beginning place.[31]

The central portion of the house, twenty-four by sixteen feet, was two-storied, the first story being of brick and the second of wood, with ten dormer windows. On each side of the main house were one-story wings of wood, seventeen by sixteen. As the lower floor of the central section was several feet below ground, it must not only have been cool in the summer, but have caused the whole building to fit well into the landscape.[32]

Whether or not the family lived at "Windsor," there are reasons for believing that they lived rather well. Certainly this was true during the later years of Clayton's life, as can be inferred from his orders to the Nortons in London. The firm of Flowerdewe and Norton was started in the eighteenth century. In 1740, twenty-year-old John Norton came to Virginia to superintend the company's interest there. He married, raised a family, and remained for many years. When business finally necessitated his return to England, his oldest son, John Hatley Norton, was left in charge of the Virginia office. The firm which had then become John Norton & Sons, survived for many years, until after the American Revolution. Fortunately, for the present day historians, nearly all of the later Norton papers were preserved.[33] Although Clayton, like his father before him, had for a time entrusted his business affairs to Micajah Perry's firm, from 1768, and perhaps earlier, the Nortons handled them.[34]

The relationship between the Nortons and their Virginia customers was a delightful one, which is quite apparent from their letters, whether scolding or chatty. For John Norton,

Clayton had a very "real affection and regard." Having the younger Norton as the Virginia representative assured the customers of a much more personal touch, aside from the fact that the Nortons were related to so many of the Virginia families. When Clayton went to Yorktown to supervise the loading of his hogsheads, he could discuss his problems directly. The Nortons' services to their customers went far beyond the sale of their tobacco. They filled the planters' orders for all sorts of goods, often from merchants outside of London, and even outside of England. Specific materials were to be matched, clothing of exact sizes procured, and newspapers and magazines included. Sometimes, their clients requested that errands be performed, as when Clayton asked that a letter be personally delivered to a friend. They acted as bankers, honoring bills of exchange. One of these Clayton drew up for two hundred pounds, payable to a Francis Willis, Jr. Since such notes were interchangeable with, and used as, currency, they often passed through many hands before they were redeemed. This particular one, drawn in 1773, was still around twenty-three years after Clayton's death.[35]

As might be expected in transactions made at a distance of three thousand miles and a considerable lapse of time, there were errors and misunderstandings in connection with the London orders. It is astonishing that more mistakes were not made. Sometimes the goods were slow in being unloaded from the ship when they arrived, resulting in some spoilage. A book of Clayton's was packed in a box directed to Thomas Nelson, a Council member, living at some distance. When he discovered it, he "very politely" sent it to Clayton. There were losses of individual items: a basket of roots, and a keg of ironware which were never found. Credit for the latter was duly entered on Clayton's account. Mistakes in the orders occurred, and goods were unsatisfactory. Clayton seldom voiced any criticism, but twice he could not resist it. In 1768, he wrote to John Norton: "I am not much given to complaining or finding fault but hope you'l excuse my mentioning a few articles among the goods which were not quite agreeable, the shoes were not from Greshams, as I desired, but from Davis, and proved so bad that ⸺ part of my family cannot wear them, the Catochu [Terra Japonica, an extract made from an East Indian plant, used as an astringent], not of what I wanted but nothing but Japan earth in powder, the thing I meant is a preparation of Japan earth, made with mush and perhaps some other ingredients into very small lozenges pointed at each end, and should be put into a Phial, also stoppered. in the Trunk with some of my things was one box of London Magazines w'ch I never had the last Thought of sending for, however I only mention this, with [out] any view to be credited for the price of one because I made a present to a friend, but only that no more of that sort may be sent for the future."[36] Four years later, his disappointment again had to be expressed: "I received your Favour of the 22nd of February last also another by Capt Robertson, with Invoice of my Goods, which were a most Tedious while in coming to me after the Ship arrived, & when opened there were several articles so bad as not to be of any use first the piece of White Callico was quite Rotten, my shoes were so small that I was obliged to give 3/ a pair to boot in Exchange with them for Shoes to wear. The box of Anderson Pills had no more than 12 Pills in it, whereas it ought to have been full. The Cambrics were bad at the Price, & several other articles too tedious to mention."[37]

The Norton invoices give a fascinating picture of the dependence of Virginians upon England for an incredible variety of goods. Because John Clayton exported an average of fifteen hogsheads of tobacco annually from 1767-1773, in addition to the rents from his "Morehouse" property, he could well afford the rather extravagant orders which he made in the last years of his life, and there is no reason to believe that he could not do so as a young man as well. From these invoices, it may be gathered that the Claytons' home was well-furnished. For the downstairs, Clayton ordered two Scotch carpets (one twelve by fifteen, the other nine by seventeen), two coarse "spotted" rugs, a "hangeable Persian," a square "neat" mahogany table with a drawer and one "passable plain Mahoghany teatable," and six "strong Mahoghany chairs with Spanish leather bottoms." In the summer the chairs and sofas were covered by the coolness of blue and white Holland slipcovers. On the walls, hung the family pictures done by Sir Godfrey Kneller which Mr. Clayton had brought from England. Artificial illumination was a problem which Clayton hoped to solve efficiently by requesting "1 tin chamber Lamp contrived so as to be used 12 hours without hoisting up wick or refilling," and ordering thirty pounds of "small Rust candles as long as they are made" and desiring them to "keep alight for the whole night."

The dining room appurtenances apparently equalled the elegance of those of the parlor: pastel wine glasses, "double flint cut glass cans in cut-frames," Queen's china, green glass cans, flat plates and small dishes of pewter and "Earthern tortoise shell plates." Although the flatware ordered was of buckhorn, the family also had silver. The china was blue and white, and included "2 pairs of men's China drinking mugs." Kitchen supplies, being more or less unbreakable, were not ordered in such quantity: two saucepans of tin with covers, and two others with wooden handles on the covers, two "Brown glazed," a large fryingpan and a "Small Brass Kettle to hold 4 Gallons." Few furnishings may have been needed for the kitchen, but orders for groceries were huge. Almost every invoice stipulated cheese by the hundred weight and sacks of salt from Mr. Backhouse of Liverpool. Most of the staples, as well as fruits, meat and vegetables, were raised on the plantation, but some came from England: sugar, both single- and double-refined, rice, coffee, tea, chocolate, oatmeal, olive oil, sago, and vinegar in an "iron bound cask." Pepper, mace, nutmeg, cloves, and other spices were imported as well as raisins and capers. The last item enjoyed great popularity with the Claytons, one order alone being for eight pint bottles. Delicacies included Spanish olives, currants, orange peel, twenty-five pounds of Pistachio nuts, twenty boxes of dried figs, peppermint water, and five boxes of chocolate almonds!

Madeira wine graced the Claytons' table, as well as beer for which they ordered large quantities of hops. The wine came from either Dr. Hill's House, or Lamarr and Company, of Madeira. It was expensive, thirty-three pounds a pipe, to which was added seven and a half pounds in charges for freight and duties, making a total close to forty pounds. The Nortons had it shipped when convenient, and paid the charges, putting it on the Clayton account. There was sometimes a comedy of errors. In March of 1771, Clayton had ordered a pipe, but to his consternation invoices came for two. When in Williamsburg attending court, he mentioned the matter to young John Hatley Norton, who assured him that the mistake would be rectified. When the second pipe arrived, Norton relieved Clayton of it, and credited his account, but the matter was mentioned many times in the correspondence. A year and a half later, Clayton was still muttering to the older Norton, "You made a great mistake in ordering me a Pipe of Wine, from Madeira, so soon after the Receipt of the other." It was finally discovered that it was not the Nortons' fault at all, the mistake having been made in Lamarr's House.

Clayton's library was kept well supplied with writing materials: three reams or quires of "cheap writing paper," three thousand "good Quills" or sometimes "Dutch quills," sealing wax and wafers, a "Flat Mahoghany Ruler about 18 inches long," three pounds of ink powder at a time, and glasses in pewter stands for the ink. The walls were lined with well-stocked bookshelves, although the extent of Clayton's library can only be judged by indirect references and casual remarks in letters, and by the books appearing on the Norton orders. Hargreaves wrote "The family is good, for one of their Ancestors was a Bishop (I think Jasper's Grandfather) I saw some of his works in Jasper's library but have forgot what they were."[38] These books were probably: *Introduction to the Jews* and *Defence of the Chronology of the Hebraic Bible*, published in Leiden in 1747; *Dissertation on Prophecies*, 1749 and *Defence of the Old and New Testaments* (in three parts, 1752, 1754, 1757). They were written by Robert Clayton, Bishop of Clogher and Cork, son of the Reverend John Clayton. As mentioned in Chapter I, the relationship between the two families of Claytons was quite distant and there is no actual evidence of a friendship. On the other hand, Clayton's grandfather, Sir John, may well have met the Bishop's father at the Royal Society. There is also every likelihood that he and Mr. Clayton read the minister's reports on Virginia which were published in the *Transactions* of the Society not too many years before Mr. Clayton left for the New World. Since the botanist owned the bishop's writings, it might seem likely that they corresponded. Unfortunately, most of Bishop Clayton's personal correspondence has disappeared.[39] Two other works, with a religious flavour, appeared on the invoices: *Sermons on several occasions* by Thom. Ashton, and "The Collects epistles & Gospels & reading Psalms bound up together in Morocco in a little Pockett Volume." Naturally, many of the works in Clayton's library were volumes pertaining to natural history, but the invoices do record *Poems* by Nobody and *Georgical Essays*.

Clayton's biological books were in several languages in addition to English: French, Greek, and the international scientific tongue, Latin. Particularly in the field of botany, his collection must have been an outstanding one. In thanks to Linnaeus, Alexander Garden wrote in 1757: "Since any of my letters to you can have come to your hands, I have received many marks of your esteem, and last by Captain White, I had your invaluable and truly grand present of the *Hortus Cliffortianus*. I never saw this superb and inestimable work before; neither do I believe there is another copy in America, unless one which Mr. Clayton has in Virginia."[40] Linnaeus' writings were well represented in the Clayton library and the botanist wrote the Swedish author in 1748: "Your works, especially *Hort. Clif.*, *Gen. Plan.*, and *Fl. Lap.*, are beside me night and day."[41] There was John Bartram's 1751 *Journal* bound in with Stoerke's *Description of East Florida*, Rauwolf's *Flora orientalis*,[42] edited by J. F. Gronovius, Mark Catesby's *Natural History of the Carolinas*, and Theophrastus' *Enquiry into Plants*.[43] In August of 1772, Clayton ordered copies of two of Adanson's books in the original French: his treatise of the Baobale and his *Famille des Plantes*. A year later, Clayton wrote to Norton, "Sir, I was sadly disappointed in not receiving Adanson's family of plants & must intreat the favour of you to try once more to procure it. You may very well remember in the life time of my good friend Mr. Collinson, you sent me some of Linnaeus' works in Latin, w'ch were printed either in Holland or Sweden and I imagine some Booksellers of yr acquaintance in London, who correspond with those of the same calling in Holland or Paris, could safely get this book from any part of Europe."[44]

Clayton suffered similar disappointment with the several magazines which the Nortons procured for him. In a postscript he testily remarked "No Magazines or Supplements are come to hand yet altho Mr. Fontaine has rec'd from you his for April last."[45] On the whole, the delivery must have been fairly regular, considering the number supplied. Clayton "subscribed" to two journals, Bartavius' and Baldwin's. Of the latter, he once remarked that it "had almost the whole month of January missing." Magazines were often slow to be received in Virginia, and Clayton could not forbear a certain impatience: "the two last Magazines I have had the pleasure to receive from you were for April 1773 and should now be very glad to have perusal of some of later dates."[46] *The Gentleman's Magazine,* to which he subscribed, was of particular interest, as it covered a wide range of topics current in England. There was a section which dealt with the social scene: marriages, births and deaths, military and clerical promotions, and court appointments. As Clayton's relatives frequently appeared in these lists, he was able to keep up with the various members of the family who were poor correspondents. There he read of the death of his cousin Nevil, who had been appointed a Gentleman of the Bed Chamber in 1735, the year before he died: "Nevil Ld. Lovelace, Baron of Hurley, Bucks. (only surviving son of John Ld. Lovelace, who . . . dyed Governor of New York 1708) left only a Sister, one of the Maids of Honour to her Majesty, so the Title is extant [sic]."[47] The marriage of his cousin Martha to Lord Henry Beauclerk took place June 25, 1739, when the bride was thirty-seven.[48] *The Gentleman's Magazine* for July, 1743, had a long article on the deployment of his Majesty's forces at the battle of Dettingen, in which his Uncle Jasper was mentioned at some length.[49] Uncle Jasper's son, Colonel Clayton's marriage was noted in 1745, with the additional information that Miss Buck, the bride, was worth £20,000.[50] The magazine also had articles on the English political scene and the Colonies, as well as reviews of books, epitomes of the *Transactions of the Royal Society* and like groups on the Continent. Many letters appeared on varying subjects and, at least twice, Collinson submitted portions of Clayton's letters to him, which were published. In addition to the English papers, the Claytons must have subscribed to the local newspaper, *The Virginia Gazette*, published in Williamsburg. Although their friend, John Custis, declared it only recorded such items as "lost spaniels and who has the pox,"[51] nevertheless it kept the county people *au courant* to city life, and the doings of their neighbors and distant friends. News of many members of the Clayton family appeared on its pages from time to time.

Among the Norton invoices were the endless replacements needed to keep a large household functioning: bed cords, a firkin of Crown soap, coarse and fine sifters, large clamps for "House Brushes," padlocks and cupboard locks, staples, corks, "clothiers' cards," starch, salt petre, and "Rotten stone" or pumice. There were many orders for window glass cut to specific sizes. To assure the jauntiness of the coachman a new postillion cap and chaise whip were listed, and one "Small Seal skin Trunk w'th Brass Lock" for the family when they travelled. Many medicines were ordered from England to augment the local supply of herbs and medicinal plants: green myrrh, an Arabian plant used as an antiseptic; ipecac; laudanum, gentian root, from which a stomach tonic was made; Chinese rhubarb, a purgative; balsam, an ingredient of cough syrups; angelica stalks, and many others.

From the huge orders for textiles and sewing supplies, an idea of the extent of the operations in the plantation's sewing rooms can be estimated. Not only did the major portion of the family's wardrobe have to be made there, but also clothing for the household servants and field hands. Almost every order included sixty to seventy yards of "white cotton for Negroes." But even larger amounts were necessary for bedding: eighty-two yards of sheeting was ordered at one time, supplemented by forty yards of "Irish" sheeting. Several invoices stipulated as much as eight pieces of linen at varying prices from one and a half shillings to two and a half shillings. Since a piece is the equivalent of twelve yards, this meant that almost one hundred yards was ordered at a time. A good-sized family such as the Claytons required many shirts, innumerable napkins, table-cloths, and curtains. This certainly would not have been an inordinate amount. The forty-eight yards of white calico on one order may have been made into aprons and caps, and the same amount of lawn undoubtedly became undergarments and children's clothes. In every order, there appeared great quantities of thread: brown, white, and "coarse shoe thread," as well as binding, tape for aprons and bolts of ribbon. Buttons came by the half gross: "white shirt buttons," metal "coat" buttons, brass buttons. Pins were ordered either by the thousands or by the pound: sometimes six thousand, at other times four pounds. "White Chapel needles" in assorted sizes came in hundreds. There was a multitude of materials for the family's clothes: book muslin, scarlet swanskin, drugget, shammy skin for the breeches, blue Durrance, Tabby and shalloon,[52] and "sky blue parsons." Often, the orders included items for grand-children or daughters who were still at home, or who lived nearby. These were mainly for shoes and gloves, but sometimes included "stays to measure," "cloak trimmed with fur," a "bondlace girl's cap, handkerchief and Tucker," or "a mother-of-pearl necklace and ear-rings."

John Clayton's plantation consisted of four hundred and fifty acres, for which the quitrent was eleven shillings three pence. He was also taxed a pound for the four "wheels," or carriages, which he owned.[53] In addition, there was a "Parish and County levy" or tithe. In 1770, there were 19 persons on whom a tithe was levied in his household. The extent of his farming operations can be gauged by requests for such things as: fifty yards of canvas, six felling axes, two dozen broad and one dozen narrow hoes, a dozen milk pans, large quantities of nails, fish hooks and lines for trout, drum and perch, hempen rope, saddles, and bridles. It is probable that

Clayton raised a good deal of tobacco on his land. He shipped large quantities to the Nortons, rather more than he might be thought to have received in payment of fees as a clerk. He maintained a substantial balance on the Nortons' books despite the extensive orders for goods which he sent. This was in contrast to the many Virginians who were perennially in debt to the London agents. "In this year (1773) the list of Virginia debtors to the house of John Norton & Sons of London carries 398 names whose outstanding accounts amount to £63,856/ 7/5."[54] Besides tobacco, Clayton raised cattle, sheep, hogs, horses, and most of the food needed on the plantation. This latter was no small undertaking, for there were at least fifty to sixty persons to be fed three times a day. These included the slaves, on which he depended for farm and domestic labor. Of these, he had a considerable number, as he disposed of thirty-four by name, and others not named, in his will. They were comparatively expensive, when viewed as a farm necessity, the average couple selling for fifty-four pounds.[55] As cash was a rare commodity with the planters, it took a man many years, and a family often several generations to collect an adequate labor force for a large plantation. Thus Clayton's slaves represented a considerable investment.

John and Betty Clayton had eight children, five boys and three girls. True to family tradition, the eldest son was named John, which made him the fourth in direct line. He was born not many years after his parents' marriage, probably in 1725 or 1726.[56] The other sons were William, Jasper, Robert, and Thomas. Robert and a sister, Mary, died young. The two surviving daughters were Catherine, probably named for her mother's sister, Mrs. John Washington, and Lucy, named for Clayton's mother.

IV
ENGLISH AND NORTH AMERICAN BOTANY, 1650-1750

John Clayton as an amateur of botany was a colonial offshoot of the great European scientific movement that had been growing since the early years of the seventeenth century. Whether or not his interest in natural history was acquired before or after he arrived in America, and despite the certain influence of Mark Catesby and William Byrd in Virginia, Clayton's roots were in England and Europe, specifically in the Royal Society of London.

The Original Fellows of the Royal Society, including Sir John Clayton, were enthusiasts with interests more helter-skelter than scientific, but over the next thirty years, men like Isaac Newton, Robert Boyle, Martin Lister, Christopher Wren, John Ray, and other serious students, established sound scientific foundations for the Society. Early topics of discussion usually dealt with animal physiology and physics, but in 1667 John Ray was elected to membership and, with his inspiration and that of Dr. Nehemiah Grew, botany became one of the

Society's favorite subjects. Over the years, this interest of the group had a great and lasting influence on the growth of this branch of science.[1] Thus, John Clayton indirectly became one of the legatees of his grandfather's fellow members, Grew and Ray. Grew (1641-1712), plant anatomist and Cambridge graduate, studied medicine at the University of Leiden. He was particularly concerned with the study of sex in plants,[2] a controversial subject which was to engage Clayton and some of his contemporaries in lively debate over a half century later.

John Ray was born in 1627 and died in 1705, when Clayton was still a schoolboy. His system of plant classification was widely used—Clayton first used it, before he was indoctrinated, for better or worse, into the Linnaean one. Ray was the son of a blacksmith who was sent by an unknown benefactor to Cambridge (at the same time Sir John Clayton was there) where he received both his bachelor's and master's degrees. Ray remained to teach at Cambridge until 1662, when his fellowship was withdrawn because he refused to bow to the Act of Uniformity. In the forty odd remaining years of his life he made many field trips in the British Isles and on the Continent, often with his friend, Francis Willoughby, the ornithologist. Ray published a number of books, mainly botanical, but some on other aspects of natural history. One of his last books, the third volume of *Historia Plantarum*, published in 1704, was of great importance to American botany. It included plants collected by the Reverend John Banister, William Vernon, and David Krieg. Much of the work of these men, who explored parts of the mainland of America, was lost, but it was due to Ray that even fragments were preserved.

John Ray had seen some of the curious plants discovered by these men in the garden of Henry Compton (1632-1713), the "Maecenas of botany."[3] A younger son of the second Earl of Northampton, Compton relinquished a military career in 1660 to enter the ministry. Within twelve years of his ordination he became a bishop: first of Oxford, then of London. Fortunately for botany, there were serious differences between the Church and London's bishop. As a consequence, Compton was relieved of his clerical duties, but not of his bishopric.

To fill his idle hours, he decided to further develop his gardens at Fulham Palace, not far from Parson's Green. With the assistance of his expert gardener, George London, plants were sought all over the world. As a result, the gardens were famous for their huge collection of exotic plants. There were numerous visitors, both from the British Isles and abroad, to see these strange imports, and it would be surprising if Clayton, as a youngster, had not spent some time there, since the gardens were so near to his grandmother's, and perhaps his, home.

Compton's garden did much to stimulate botanical interest and, in order to insure a continuous flow of unique specimens, the bishop did not hesitate to use the offices of his calling. He appointed ministers to various colonies, having considered perhaps more carefully their qualifications in natural history than their clerical aptitudes. Among these was the Reverend John Clayton (1657-1725)[4] who went to Jamestown shortly after his ordination in 1684 under Compton's auspices. The two years which he spent there are the basis of his articles on Virginia, previously mentioned, and the subject of a dissertation on the Indians to his friend, Dr. Grew.[5] Bishop Compton had been singularly perceptive in his appointment of the Reverend John Clayton. Whether the Fulham Palace Gardens benefited from his Virginia sojourn is not documented, but he was not only a "curious" man, but one well able to evaluate most of what he saw. An Oxford graduate with a master's degree, he had been well trained in various branches of science. Before he went to Virginia, he had performed anatomical experiments with Dr. Allen Moulen,[6] and he had a definite knowledge of physics and chemistry as well. In the latter, he was encouraged by his friend, Robert Boyle. Thus, this Clayton was able to set down his lengthy observations on the Virginia scene with some authority and, in so doing, gave to England the first fairly complete account of that Colony from the viewpoint of a natural historian. Henry Compton was extremely gratified by the labours of another such recruit, the Reverend John Banister, whom he sent to Virginia about the same time and whose indefatigable collecting supplied not only the gardens of Fulham Palace but those of other patrons who had augmented the bishop's assistance to Banister. In addition to the *Catalogus Plantarum in Virginia Observatarum* (1686) and his writings which were included in Ray's book, some of Banister's scattered observations are still extant. As was the custom, too, several were incorporated by authors into their own writings without acknowledgment.

Another London garden, based on more utilitarian motives, was the Chelsea Physik Garden on the Thames Embankment, named for the manor from which the garden's three and a half acres were originally leased.[7] It was established in 1673 by the Society of Apothecaries for the cultivation of the medicinal plants upon which they depended for their cures. Their first curator, John Watts, sent James Harlow, one of his gardeners, to Virginia about the same time Bishop Compton's ministers were there. Harlow forwarded to Watts many parcels of plants which had possible curative virtues. Watt's hothouse, heated by hot water pipes, was an innovation far in advance of his day. The value of the garden lay, however, not only in its research capabilities, but in an even more practical application since it served for the training of the apothecaries themselves. Most interesting of all, Chelsea Garden not only survives today but has an active laboratory, library, and experimental garden used by the same Society of Apothecaries and other botanists. High brick walls, some of which date back three centuries, insure a comparative quiet along the paths bordering beds where ordinary plants jostle rare and unique ones from all over the world. Some of the trees are very ancient, one having been given by Mark Catesby.

Chelsea Garden's survival through the centuries is due, in part, to the gift of Sir Hans Sloane (1660-1753),[8] one of the many young men who have studied there. Many years after his training there in drug plants and chemicals, as an eminently successful and wealthy physician, Sir Hans acquired the Manor of Chelsea. In 1722, realizing that the Society of Apothecaries could not afford to buy outright the land leased from him, he presented it to them for a five pound annual rent. He further stipulated that the Society send dried specimens of fifty new plants from the Garden, mounted and named, to the Royal Society each year. This custom continued throughout the forty years demanded by Sloane and it accomplished much in stimulating botanical interest among the members. Sloane ordered presses and cabinets, still in use today, to be made for the Apothecaries's books, which had been augmented by John Ray's library left to them by Isaac Rand (superintendent 1724-1743). In the center of the garden, a fine statue of Sir Hans by John Michael Rysbrack (completed in 1737), contemplates this peaceful retreat now in the center of London, which he helped to preserve. Chelsea Garden's importance to the economy of the United States has never been really recognized, for it is little known that the first cotton introduced into this country was grown from seed sent by a later superintendent, Philip Miller, in 1732.[9]

Sloane's benefaction to the Apothecaries was only one of his many contributions to botany. Born in Ireland, of Scotch descent, he continued his English medical studies on the Continent in 1673. First, he studied in Paris at the Hospital de Charité, supplemented by botanical instruction under Tournefort at the Jardin des Plantes. He continued from Paris to Montpellier, the famous centre of French medicine and botany, pausing on the way to take his M.D. at the University of Orange in southern France. This was necessary for Protestants, who were often refused degrees at Paris or Montpellier. The latter city lived up to all of Sloane's expectations. There he met and knew intimately M. Magnol, the botanist in whose honour the *Magnolia* was named. After a year's stay, Sloane returned to London. His excellent European training obtained for him the sponsorship of the prominent Dr. Thomas Sydenham. At the same time, Sloane's former friendship with John Ray developed into a lifelong intimacy. Ray encouraged the younger man's botanic tastes, and was as delighted as Sloane when the latter received the appointment as personal physician to the Duke of Albemarle in 1687. Sloane accompanied the Duke, who was the new governor, to Jamaica, and remained there until shortly after the Duke's death a year later. To his medical duties, Sloane added untold hours in a study of the island and in making a natural history collection, which included eight hundred plants, the majority unknown. This tremendous work was the basis for his *Natural History of Jamaica,* published many years later.[10] These fascinating volumes, with their illustrations and lively accounts of animal and plant life, were undoubtedly used as a model by Sloane's protégé, Mark Catesby. Shortly after returning to England, Sloane resumed his private practice. He was highly successful in his profession: well-liked, kind, and fashionable, he eventually became one of Queen Anne's personal physicians.

Sloane's ardor for natural history lasted throughout his life. He enjoyed a friendship with most of the English men of science of his day, and corresponded with collectors and botanists all over the world. His home became a fabulous museum, with remarkable accumulations of geological, botanical, and zoological specimens, as well as a renowned library which included 42,000 printed books. A detailed description of these and of his valuable gems appears in a delightful account of a visit made to Sir Hans in 1748 by the Prince and Princess of Wales.[11] In 1725, Benjamin Franklin, studying printing in England, offered Sloane an asbestos purse from New England. Sir Hans bought the curio (although he did not cherish it, and eventually gave it away) after inviting the young man to his home to view his museum.[12] In order to insure that his collections, library, and irreplaceable correspondence should be preserved for the delight and instruction of future generations, Sir Hans in his will appointed a number of trustees who were instructed to arrange a sale of Sloane's treasures for £20,000 to the Crown, the Government, or the Royal Society. After Sloane's death, the Crown having refused to become the purchaser, the English government, by means of a lottery, raised the funds necessary to buy the collections,[13] and thereby founded the British Museum. Sloane was an active member of the Royal Society for over fifty years. He served as Secretary for nineteen years and as President for fourteen. His energy and enthusiasm did much to infuse vitality into the Society when it was most needed.

Sir Hans also belonged to a less formal organization, the Temple Coffee House Botany Club, which he may have founded on his return from Jamaica, about 1689. Botanical discussions and display of specimens took place at the weekly meetings on Friday nights. Letters from distant correspondents were read and in good weather there were occasional field trips. A roster of members included, at one time or another, such men as Dr. Martin Lister, John Watts, Dr. Leonard Plukenet, Dr. Grew, William Sherard, and the three apothecaries, Samuel Doody, Samuel Dale, and James Petiver.

James Petiver (1663-1708)[14] accomplished much for botany, not so much from his study and research as from the immense collecting web with which he covered the world. He attempted to enlist practically every man leaving England as ship's surgeon or captain, traveller or coloniser. Friends suggested acquaintances in far places who might be willing to assist him. For thirty years a steadily increasing flow of botanical specimens was received at his shop in Aldersgate Street, London. Although this necessitated a vast correspondence, Petiver was even more generous with his time and specimens. In various annual publications of his own, he made these collections available to interested scholars. After his election to the Royal Society in 1695, he felt that he could speak with more authority, sometimes promising his correspondents that their important specimens might be exhibited before this august body. Petiver did not hesitate to employ similar bait by encouraging his collectors with intimations of their public recognition in print, and he was scrupulous in giving credit for the sources of the plants which appeared in his *Centuries*. He often supplied the collecting materials, such as paper and bottles, complete with detailed printed instructions for their use. This long activity resulted in Petiver's collections being larger than any up to that time. At his death, Sloane bought them, and some are still to be seen at the British Museum.

Petiver's friends numbered almost all the great in the English botanical world. Through some of them he was introduced to the young Virginian, William Byrd, who had remained in England after completing his education and being admitted to the Middle Temple. Byrd lost no time in introducing another correspondent to Petiver, the Reverend John Banister, for whom he, as well as Bishop Compton, acted as a patron.[15] Banister's letter to Petiver (1690-1) approving a plan to publish his communications yearly is the only survivor of what is thought to have been a brief correspondence. It has been conjectured that the Temple Coffee House Botany Club partially subsidized Banister, but there is no proof. Banister was killed while collecting on the Roanoke River the following year.

Byrd became Petiver's enthusiastic ally in the Royal Society. At the meeting on November 10, 1697, he made a motion that the members send someone to make a complete study of Virginia natural history, suggesting that the Society pay the man's passage and a salary of twenty-five pounds a year. Accordingly, William Vernon, a Cambridge graduate, was sent in January of 1698. He only remained until the following fall—the reason for his departure is not known—but in those few months he was able to make a large collection, not in Virginia, but rather in Maryland where he landed. The Reverend Hugh Jones, who had been quite openly ordained a priest for the specific purpose of collecting plants,[16] also collected in Maryland. A third man, Dr. David Krieg, a German who had boarded with Petiver for some time when he first came to England and a member of the Botany Club, went to Maryland in 1698 for several months. On his return he brought many drawings as well as specimens. Parts of these three men's collections were those preserved by John Ray. Why their collections were in Maryland rather than Virginia is not clear, but the brevity of their stays may have limited their collecting.

When Byrd's father died in 1704/5, he returned on short notice to Virginia, later writing Petiver to offer his services to the Royal Society. Petiver lost little time in suggesting that Mr. Byrd send him specimens, enclosing "3 Tables of Virginia Plants, most of them Mr. Banister's drawings." In spite of this, and two subsequent letters, Petiver never persuaded Byrd (or his Negroes, as he helpfully suggested) to collect for him, although Byrd carried on a lively correspondence with Sloane for many years.[17]

Petiver had several correspondents in the Carolinas, the most knowledgeable being John Lawson, the immediate predecessor of Mark Catesby in this area. Except for one letter prior to 1709, Lawson's surviving letters to Petiver were written in 1709 and later, after Lawson had returned to London from his first stay in Carolina.[18] While in London, he met Petiver and George London, Bishop Compton's gardener; on recommendation of a petition of the North Carolina Assembly to the lords proprietors, he was appointed surveyor-general of North Carolina; he saw his book, *A New Voyage to Carolina*, through the press and it was published in 1709.[19] Lawson sailed that winter for the colonies, armed with Petiver's many supplies and drugs, and Ray's tract on Banister's plants. For two years he sent collections of wild life to his friends, Petiver and London. He planned a most ambitious work, covering all phases of Carolina botany, agriculture, medicine, zoology, geology and paleontology. In 1711, Lawson and Edward Mosely met the two Virginians, Philip Ludwell and Nathaniel Harrison, in order to establish the disputed Virginia-Carolina boundary line. At the same time, Mr. Clayton was sent by Spotswood to arbitrate between Colonel Hyde and Colonel Cary, and Lawson and Mr. Clayton met. In fact, Lawson asked the favour of the lawyer to carry a letter for him.[20] In September of this same year, Lawson was killed by the Tuscarora Indians. Petiver's death seven years later marked the end of his particular group, though their influence was felt for many years to come and a few men, like Sloane and William Sherard, were carry-overs. In this new century, the ranks of botanists, both amateur and professional, were to be augmented almost unbelievably, and botany itself was to enjoy what might be called a Golden Age.

Despite the keen interest in the subject in England and in Europe, the flow of information concerning American flora had been maddeningly slow, and surprisingly few plants, possibly one hundred and fifty species, were introduced into England during the seventeenth century.[21] The next century was quite another story. By then the Colonies were so well established that the struggle for actual survival was no longer the prime concern. There was now time for further exploration to the west of the immediate seaboard, and another new plant world was opened up. Those of the Old World who were unable to take part in the great adventure were understandably eager to see and read about the fascinating discoveries of the New. The Royal Society had done much to stimulate this natural curiosity and the collection of foreign plants was no longer limited to the botanists and the apothecaries. It became an absorbing hobby for the wealthy merchants and the nobility. Their gardens were large and elaborate, and often included greenhouses and hothouses for the cultivation of tropical plants. These men encouraged the colonials to send them seeds and plants of all sorts. As the Atlantic crossing often took several months, many plants died. Rats often ate them, or the sailors stole them; they died from the sea water and from poor packaging, in spite of being placed in bog moss and matting; and the masters of the ships forgot to give orders to water the plants or were unwilling to waste their precious fresh water. Seeds arrived in much better shape. They were sent in gourds, small bottles, and even snuff boxes of silver and tortoise shell, carefully sealed with varnish. Grasses were packed in old linen in glass canisters, with camphor added to discourage insects. Such merchants as Peter Collinson, who was a gardener himself, often attended to the actual mechanics of importation for their wealthy friends. Probably the majority of the rich patronized the many nursery-gardeners around London. These men had enjoyed a prosperous business for many years, as Collinson attested when describing his visits to them with relatives, as a child, at the beginning of the century:

I often went with them to visit the few nursery-gardens around London to buy fruits, flowers, and clipt yews, in the shape of birds, dogs, men, ships, etc. For these Mr. Parkinson in Lambeth was very much noted and had besides a few myrtles, oleanders, and other evergreens. This was about the year 1712. At that time Mr. Wrench, behind the Earl of Peterborough's at Parson's Green, near Chelsea, famous for Tulip-Trees, began the collecting of evergreens, Arbutus, Pollyneas & from them came the gold and silver Hegehog-Holly, being accidental varieties from the Hedge-Hog variety of the common Holly. He gave rewards to encourage people to look out for accidental varieties. . . . He and Parkinson died about the year 1724. Contemporary with them were Mr. Darby and Mr. Fairchild, they had their gardens on each side the narrow alley leading to Mr. George Whitemore's at the farther end of Hoxton. As their gardens were small they were the only people for Exotics, and had many stoves and greenhouses for all sorts of aloes and succulent plants.[22]

These nursery gardens prospered immensely due to the new interest, and the importation of rare plants became an important branch of their business. Like Collinson, John Clayton must certainly have visited some, if not all, of these gardens as a boy, or even as a young man. It is not unlikely that he made his home at Parson's Green after his father went to Virginia. The gardens of Mr. Wrench would have been as difficult for him to miss as those of Bishop Compton at Fulham Palace.

Competition was exceptionally keen among the amateur gardeners to whom expense was seldom a factor. Towards the end of the eighteenth century, emphasis was placed on elaborate landscaping complete with grottoes, waterfalls, mazes, gazebos, and other delightful elaborations with which to titillate the eye, but at the beginning, rare plants and extensive collections were most popular. Because of this, it was necessary to engage not only well-trained gardeners, but often botanists to oversee their operations. Thus, seldom has a hobby of the wealthy resulted in so many benefits to knowledge as eighteenth-century gardening. Foremost, of course, was the study of the many unknown plants which resulted in old systems of classification being considered outmoded and new ones devised. A peripheral effect was the experimenting in acclimation for these strange imports, and the beginnings of plant ecology. The employment of the botanist in such matters was actually a generous subsidy for research. The scientist not only had a superb and meticulously maintained garden for his studies, uninterrupted by teaching duties, but he was paid a salary usually more generous than that offered by the universities. Moreover, he was practically guaranteed that the results of his research would reach the learned world in the form of a printed book, in order to enhance the fame of his employer's garden. Sometimes the work would be illustrated by a famous botanical artist, thus giving employment to these men and, at the same time, insuring that the book had far more value than one which depended solely on mere verbal description for use in identification. In fact, all books pertaining to natural history began to enjoy a very ready sale.

Two outstanding botanists are typical examples of this patronage system. The first was the well-known Carolus Linnaeus, of whom more later. He was employed by George Clifford, a wealthy banker and merchant of Amsterdam, to not only act as his personal physician, but to catalogue his garden as well. The latter duty resulted in the *Hortus Cliffortianus*, illustrated by the brilliant artist George Dionysius Ehret. The second man was the German botanist, Johan Jakob Dillenius (1687-1747) who had been brought to England by William Sherard[28] to help him complete his *Pinax*. This was interrupted by Sherard's death and his brother, James, a very wealthy apothecary, employed Dillenius to catalogue his Eltham garden. This labour resulted in two large books, which Dillenius illustrated with his own engravings. Sherard published these in 1732 at his own expense, later giving the botanist all the remaining books and the plates, which Dillenius eventually sold to a Dutch book-seller for three hundred pounds. After the publication of the *Hortus Elthamensis*, Peter Collinson wrote:

Mr. James Sherard saw with much concern the contemtible appearance of the public Physik or Botanic Garden at Oxford Covered with common plants very few rare ones no good Green House or Stoves, no salary settled for a Professor—Which had long been a discredit to that opulent University—when even the least in Europe had It's Garden and It's Professor with an ample provision for his maintenance. To remove so great a neglect Mr. James Sherard endowed a Professorship with one Hundred Pounds per Annum— And in order to Establish the Garden on a more respectable footing He generously proposed to give it his Collection of Plants provided the University wou'd build a good Green House and Convenient

Stoves for their reception. In Testimony of his regard for his friend Dr Dillenius, he promoted him to be the first Sherardian Botanic Professor at Oxford.[24]

A beneficiary of this wave of botanic enthusiasm was the Apothecaries' Garden, now under the aegis of Philip Miller (1691-1771), whose *Gardener's Dictionary* was a standard botanical reference work in the eighteenth century. Miller had been trained by the well-known amateur collectors, James Sherard and Lord Petre (1713-1742, the eighth Lord Petre), and did them, and himself, much credit. It was not only his writing which gave lustre to his reputation, but his incomparable gardening skill. With seeds of curious plants sent by his world-wide correspondents, he transformed Chelsea Garden into one of outstanding stature, which was said to excel all others for its great variety of plants.[25]

Very few of the naturalists in England and on the Continent who were interested in North American flora and fauna were able to go there and see its wonders for themselves. A notable exception was Mark Catesby, a nephew of one of John Ray's philological friends, Nicholas Jekyll.[26] This great naturalist and gifted artist, first came to Virginia in 1712, at the age of twenty-eight. He accompanied his sister, Elizabeth, who was joining her husband, Dr. William Cocke, graduate of Queen's College, Cambridge. Dr. Cocke had arrived in Virginia with Governor Spotswood in 1710.[27] Like Mr. Clayton, who enjoyed a close friendship with Spotswood, he was an intimate of the influential William Byrd, who was an old school-fellow of his. Cocke's excellent connections certainly helped to make things pleasant for his brother-in-law, Mark Catesby, regardless of any introductions he may have had on his own. Catesby had inherited some property from his father, and while his means were probably limited, he seems to have been able to avoid undertaking any remunerative occupation at this time. He spent the next seven years in Virginia, except for a short voyage to the West Indies in 1714. These years seem to have been largely devoted to observing the plants and animals of the region. He did do some collecting of plants and seeds for friends in England, and some drawing.

His great work, however, came later. At this time, he made extended visits to people such as William Byrd, and took advantage of any opportunity to explore the region and study its plants and animals. Byrd, with his wide interests, must have been the ideal person to advise Catesby.

Another man whom Catesby met early in his Virginia stay was the lawyer, Mr. Clayton, father of the botanist. Soon after Catesby's arrival in Virginia, he spent three weeks visiting Byrd at "Westover." He went there on May 24th and remained until after June 14th. On June 4th Byrd recorded, "We and 11 people at dinner and Mr. Clayton among them."[28] Catesby and Mr. Clayton had almost certainly seen each other frequently in Williamsburg and must have continued to do so throughout the former's seven years' visit. Dr. Cocke's position as Secretary of State and Mr. Clayton's as Attorney-General would have necessarily insured that the two men met often in their governmental duties.

As suggested above, Catesby may well have met Mr. Clayton's son John, whose presence on the Spotswood expedition is probable. In any case, their correspondence of fifteen years later seems more intimate than one which developed without a previous face-to-face friendship. In 1719, Catesby returned to England and remained there until 1722, when he returned to North America, but not to Virginia. He went this time to Charles Town in South Carolina, financed by a group of men in England, who had commissioned him to make extensive studies and drawings of the plants and animals of the region. This group was organized primarily by William Sherard, and included Sir Hans Sloane.[29] The project was also endorsed by the Royal Society. Catesby remained in Carolina until 1725, when he went to the Bahama Islands. He returned to England in 1726. Richard Pulteney credits Catesby with the discovery of 171 plants, 9 quadrupeds, 111 birds, 33 amphibia, 46 fish and 31 insects.[30] The remainder of his life was devoted to the writing of his *Natural History of Carolina*, two large folio volumes describing the zoology and botany. Although the books are now scientifically *passé*, Catesby's lively drawings, most of which were executed from life, still have charm. Catesby did his own engraving, and the plates in the original edition were either coloured by him or under his supervision. His written descriptions were chatty and readable. In the eighteenth century, the books were a sensation. Here were volumes where the wonders of the New World could actually be seen. *The Natural History* had an almost unrivalled popularity throughout the century, and went into many editions after Catesby's death, both in England and abroad.[31] The only difficulty Catesby encountered from the first was the enormous expense involved in such an undertaking, and the consequently high price of twenty guineas for the two books. To counteract this, he conceived the idea of publishing installments of twenty plates, with the accompanying text, which could be sold for a reasonable two guineas.[32] This had the additional factor of providing a fairly steady income, while he worked during the twenty years required to complete this ambitious project. He used such parts as an annual exchange with John Bartram for the plants which he sent.[33] In gratitude for Clayton's assistance Catesby presented him with an autographed copy.

Peter Collinson also helped Catesby. He lent him enough money, without interest, to enable him to continue with his project.[34] He also introduced him to the Royal Society in 1729, where he exhibited the first twenty plates of Volume I of his book. In 1732, he was elected to membership, and through the years was an enthusiastic addition to the company. There, too, Catesby met many prominent men and through them extended his interests and relationships not only in England but on the Continent. He became a part of the international natural history circle, a loose confederation which included such men as Sloane, Ehret, Philip Miller, Linnaeus, Isaac Lawson, and John Frederick Gronovius.

In the course of completing his *Natural History*, Catesby from time to time needed to have plants sent him from Virginia. At least three of these included are credited by him to Clayton. Although Clayton may have sent plants earlier, the first one recorded was the "*Magnolia flora albo*," or *Magnolia acuminata* (L.) which was sent to England in 1736.[35] A

Stuartia, sent in 1742, arrived in excellent condition and delighted Catesby by blooming in his Fulham garden in May.[36] The third plant mentioned was the *Hamamelis*, or Witch Hazel, which was even more fascinating in that it displayed its unique quality by being in bloom when it arrived in December.[37] In Catesby's *Hortus Europae Americanus*, a more modest work than the *Natural History* and one devoted to the adaptation of American plants to English gardens, Catesby described the attributes of this curious plant further: not only did it survive the coldest winters, but it always bloomed at Christmas. It was difficult to propagate by layering, but could easily be grown by seed, if one remembered it took two years for germination.[38]

Catesby was also indebted to Clayton for an ornithological specimen. The description which accompanied it is one of the only three known Clayton observations outside the field of botany. Mr. Catesby's subject was the Whip-poor-Will:

This bird I have mentioned in the Addenda to this Volume; but having since received two of them from Virginia, it has enabled me to exhibit the figure of it, and also to add to the description of it some remarks sent me by Mr. Clayton, concerning it, as follows:

"The Whip-poor-Will is not so large as the Bird called here the East-India Bat, i. e. Caprimulgus; but in shape and colour of the feathers, it very much resembles it; having also at each side of its mouth, three or four stiff black hairs like those of a horse's main, two or three inches long. These Birds visit us about the middle of April, from which time, till the end of June, they are heard every night, beginning about dusk, and continuing until break of day; but it is chiefly in the upper or western parts that they are so very frequent: I never heard but one in the maritime parts, Altho my abode has been always there; but near the mountains, within a few minutes after sun-set, they begin, and make so very loud and shrill a noise all night, which the echoes from the rocks and sides of mountains increase to such a degree, that the first time I lodged there I could hardly get any sleep. The shooting them in the night is very difficult, they never appearing in the day-time. Their cry is pretty much like the sound of the pronounciation of the words Whip-poor-Will, with a kind of clucking noise between every two or three cries, and they lay the accent very strong upon the last word Will, and least of all upon the middle one.

"The Indians say these Birds were never known till a great

massacre was made of their country-folks by the English, and that they are the souls of departed spirits of the massacred Indians. Abundance of people here look upon them as Birds of ill omen, And are very melancholy if one of them happens to light upon their house, or near their door, and set up his cry (as they will sometimes upon the very threshold) for they verily believe one of the family will die very soon after. These Birds, as I have been credibly informed, breed exactly as the Goat-sucker before mentioned, which is thus: They lay only two eggs of a dark greenish colour, spotted and scrawled about with black, in the plain beaten paths, Without the least sign of any nest, upon which they sit very close, and will suffer a very near approach before they fly off."[39]

V

GRONOVIUS, LINNAEUS AND THE FLORA VIRGINICA

Unfortunately, no correspondence between Catesby and Clayton seems to have survived, but they did correspond extensively. Not only did Clayton send plants to Catesby, but Catesby also did favours for Clayton. The most important of these was his introduction of Clayton to Dr. John Frederick Gronovius (1690-1762), of Leiden. In addition to his medical practice, Gronovius, son and grandson of professors of the classics,[1] held public office as Senator, and was an active student of natural history, publishing at least three works of his own in the field,[2] and assisting in the publication of others. Apparently at the suggestion of Catesby, who was himself too involved in his own work to be of much assistance, Clayton began sending to Gronovius large numbers of dried plant specimens for identification as early as 1735, if not earlier.[3] These plants, many of which were unknown, could not have reached him at a more auspicious time. On August 30, 1735, Gronovius wrote to his English friend, Dr. Richard Richardson:

"You will remember that, at the time you arrived here in town, you met at Mr. Lawson's a gentleman from Sweden, that went the same night to Amsterdam, where he is printing his Bibliothecam Botanicum. His name is Carolus Linnaeus . . . I don't believe that since the time of Conrad Gesner there has been such a like or that was so learn'd in all parts of Natural History as he; and that not superficial but to the bottom."[4]

Linnaeus (1707-1778)[5] is the man generally credited with ushering in the era of modern botany. At the time he went to Leiden, he was only twenty-eight years old. Nevertheless, he had something of a reputation in Sweden, and he came to Holland armed with many manuscripts, the result of eight years' intensive work. When he left there after three years, he had seven publications to his credit, and his name was well-known in many parts of the world. Before coming to Holland, he had studied medicine at the University of Uppsala, and later instructed students in botany. Two aspects of this science seemed most unsatisfactory to him: the existing systems of classifying and naming plants. In 1730, he had written a monograph on the sex of plants, entitled romantically the *Introduction to the Floral Nuptials*. In this, he proved as fact the long-held theory that plant reproduction was based on the sexes as in animals. This study gave him the idea for a very simple system for plant classification, which could be used by the tyro. He divided the plant kingdom into twenty-four classes, based on the number of stamens, and sixty-seven orders based on the number of pistils. The outline of this so-called "Sexual System" of classification he gave in his *Systema Naturae* and further expounded in *Genera Plantarum*, whose manuscripts he took with him when he left Sweden. Although this system was highly artificial, it has been considered by some superior to any previous one. Linnaeus' lasting fame, however, rests on the binomial system of nomenclature which, while it was not entirely original with him, he firmly established. It is used to this day in zoology as well as in botany. Writing to the Swiss physiologist Haller[6] June 8, 1737, he said "Botanists seem to me never to have touched upon nomenclature as a subject of study, and therefore this path of their science remains still unexplored."⁷ It was more than fifteen years until he actually expounded his theory of using merely two words to name a plant, the genus and species names, in *Species Plantarum.* The 1753 date of publication of this book is generally considered the beginning of modern botany.

In 1732, Linnaeus made an expedition to Lapland, where he made extensive plant collections which later became the basis for his *Flora Lapponica,* published in 1737. It was there he acquired the dramatic Lapp costume and "magic" drum which appear in his best-known portrait, and which astonished the good burghers of Amsterdam when he sometimes walked their streets in full regalia. Not long after his return, in 1735, Linnaeus went to Holland to take his medical degree at Harderwijk. He defended his thesis and passed his degree within a week's time, proceeding to Leiden for visits with the famous Dr. Herman Boerhaave[8] and Dr. Gronovius. He showed the latter his *Systema Naturae,* which so impressed the Dutch doctor that he persuaded a friend to join him in financing the publication of these tables. This friend was Isaac Lawson, a Scotchman, who was studying medicine at Leiden. On the 19th of December, the two men wrote to Sir Hans Sloane:

Sir

Some months ago came to this city Dr. Carolus Linnaeus from Sweden, a person very well known by his knowledge of Natural History: for which reason he was sent by the Royal Society of Upsala to Lapland, where he hath discovered several things not before known, which possibly ere long will be published. He was so kind [as] to communicate to us his Systema Natura, which we sent to the press at our own expense, with an intention only to have a few copys; but at the request of Several friends we were determined to communicate it fully (judging it might be agreeable) to the Learned World. Wherefore we take the Liberty to present You a copy, & request you will also make the other acceptable to the Royal Society, of which you are deservedly president

Sir

    Your most obedient & Humble Servants
     Joh. Fred. Gronovius
     Isaac Lawson[9]

The *Systema Naturae* consists of only seven large folio sheets, and is exceedingly rare today. As is the case in any new approach in scientific methods, Linnaeus' system was the subject of much controversy and it was not at first widely accepted. Three years after publication Gronovius wrote to Dr. Richardson: "I now send you all the rest of Linnaeus' works, in which you will find great learning, and many curious remarks. Most of your triflers in Botany dislike his method, and particularly his *Critica*, because they do not understand him; especially some of his characters, of which a great number are illustrated by examples to be found in his *Hortus Cliffortianus*. I assure you, Sir, it was by his principles alone that I could reduce several of your Virginian plants to their proper genus, which till now could not be referred to any class. . . ."[10]

"Triflers in Botany" were not the only ones who disagreed with the brash Swedish scientist on the subject of classification. Linnaeus had become well aware of this on his visit to England in 1736, where he had been sent to procure some rare plants for Mr. Clifford,[11] whose employ he had just entered. There he met Philip Miller, who wrote to Dr. Charles Alston at the University of Edinburgh a year later: "There is a very learned gentleman in Italy, who is examining all the plants he can collect into his private garden by Linnaeus's characters, and he writes me that more than half he has yet examined are false. I do suppose he will publish his notes. I have gone a great way in remarks of this kind my self, and am fully convinced of this, that he has never view'd the growing plants. When Linnaeus was in England, he spent some days at Chelsea, but the whole was spent in viewing dried plants, tho' it was in July when the plants were in the Garden in their greatest perfection."[12] Likewise, Dillenius accorded Linnaeus the same treatment at first, being extremely haughty and disagreeable to the visitor. But, as so often happened, Linnaeus' unique charm soon won over the professor, who not only kept him there a month, but also offered to share his salary with him if he would agree to remain permanently.[13]

Linnaeus remained in Holland until 1738, by which time seven of his books had been published under the auspices of his friends, Dr. Gronovius and Professor Johan Burman of Amsterdam. During this period he became a very close friend of Gronovius. They were fellow members of a club which met every Saturday in winter to discuss matters of scientific interest—an organization similar in character to the Temple Coffee House Botany Club. With Linnaeus representing natural history and Gronovius botany, the membership also included Lawson for history, Bartsch and Kramer for chemistry, the Prussian Lieberkuhn with his microscopes, and a man for medicine. The meetings often acted as a research laboratory for the testing of Linnaeus' method and its application not only to plants, but in attempts to reduce zoological and mineralogical specimens to some sort of order. Gronovius wrote of this group "Last winter we had an exceeding fine club every Saturday with Lawson, Van Swieton and some other gentlemen, being Linnaeus our president. We examined one time the minerals, another day flowers of plants and so insects and fishes."[14] Among some of the plants studied were those sent by Clayton. But it was not only during the meetings that Linnaeus assisted Gronovius in classifying the plants. Although extremely busy, he still found time to give the Dutchman a great deal of assistance in studying not only the original eighty specimens but many others which Clayton sent later. The importance of this fact to present-day botanists is discussed in a later chapter.

Although Gronovius and Clayton corresponded for almost twenty years, none of the letters seems to have survived. Fortunately, time has been kinder with the Linnaean-Gronovian correspondence. It is through these letters we can understand the close botanical bonds between England and Holland which, in this one instance, resulted in a long and fruitful relationship between an English colonial and a Leiden doctor. Gronovius had visited England in 1718, where he met Sherard and other botanists. After returning home, he started a large English correspondence, which he continued enthusiastically, and beneficially for all concerned, through the years. This was further encouraged by the fact that his brother Abraham, librarian of the University of Leiden, had also spent some time in England, where he made many friends.[15] Gronovius' interest in American plants had been aroused several years before Clayton's plants reached him. Philip Miller's protege, William Houstoun, had collected plants in Georgia and New England in 1733. He died in that year and his last letter directed that his patron divide his American plants among his friends. Gronovius wrote to Linnaeus that Miller intended to carry out Houstoun's wishes by sharing his maps and observations with the learned.[16]

The exchange of letters and plants with Gronovius' English friends was facilitated by his great friend Isaac Lawson. Even after Lawson had received his medical degree in 1737, he was still of service as an intermediary since he became a British army doctor attached to the Flemish forces. In the performance of his duties, he made frequent trips back to England, where he was able to catch up on news of the English botanical world through Mark Catesby, Peter Collinson, and others. He carried letters and plants both ways. Never the author of a learned work, Lawson still made an impressive contribution to botany in helping to keep alive a very fruitful relationship between the botanists of England and the Netherlands—a relationship that gradually withered away after his death. This was due to many causes, but certainly was based, in part, to the loss of his good offices. It may have been Lawson who transported to Holland the first plants sent by Clayton to Catesby for identification, as Catesby and Lawson were close friends. Clayton's plants are first mentioned by Gronovius in a letter written to Linnaeus on November 25, 1735:

Your letters were brought to me Saturday, one with the characters of the Genera which please me; when time permits I shall study it. I would like, if you agree, to add at the end this title:
> To which are added
> by John. Fred. Gronovius
> Explanation on the new genera of plants
> Collected from America and from other places
> Classified in their natural characters

.... As to the fact that the gladiolus has an upper lip observed by the same authority, nevertheless my friend in Virginia comments on this plant, where he writes the lip is distinctly split into two parts, the lower really in two parts, nor does Dr. Boerhaave remark concerning the upper and lower lip but that the two lips are one which he writes presenting this flower: if now Dr. Boerhaave was deceived in this, as to the upper lip being in three parts, the Pontedino differs a great deal from the Gladiolus.[17]

Although this letter does not name Clayton, from this date on most of Gronovius' letters make some mention of the Virginia seeds and plants which Clayton continued to send. Often his enthusiasm was unrestrained as he remarked "Oho! how curious they are." Always he shared these fascinating imports with Linnaeus, and some he sent, through him, to be planted in Clifford's garden.

Clayton sent most, if not all, of his shipments directly to Catesby in England, who usually forwarded them through Gronovius' London agent to Holland. Catesby informed the latter when a shipment was expected, which was perhaps unkind, as the poor Leiden doctor spent the weeks or months until the specimens finally arrived, in an almost choleric state of expectation. Worse still, when the cases were finally opened, he sometimes thought that Catesby had taken more than what he considered a fair share. His indignation was loud when he discovered that Collinson, too, once "confiscated" some.

Encouraged by the enthusiasm of Gronovius and Linnaeus, Clayton not only continued to send plants, but undertook to identify them himself as well. Finally, in appreciation of their interest and assistance he compiled and sent to Gronovius for his library "A Catalogue of Plants, Fruits, and Trees Native to Virginia."[18] Unknown to Clayton, Gronovius decided that he "should publish the Catalogue which you finished with such unbelievable toil," which he did under the title of *Flora Virginica* in 1739. Clayton's first knowledge of this apparently came in the letter to him from Gronovius, which served as the Introduction to the *Flora*. The publishing of the *Flora* by Gronovius, without Clayton's permission, was a bit remarkable. He justified his action in the letter to Clayton on two grounds: the work of earlier investigators, Doody,[19] Vernon, Krieg, and

Banister had been largely lost because it was not published, and he felt that Clayton's "Catalogue" should be printed "lest it likewise be destroyed by envious fate at some time or other." He further said that "I was not able to inform you of this purpose of mine on account of the distance between our lands." In lieu of writing to Clayton, he had written to Mark Catesby in England, "the custodian of the temple of the American Apollo, upon whose friendship we both pride ourselves, and he was my authorization, in order that I might send back 'the child' written in type, and exposed to the public view 'to its father;' and he advised me again and again that you were delighted more by the advantage gained by the public from your *belles lettres* than by the personal enjoyment of your writings." This would all sound very convincing were it not for the fact that we have evidence that he undertook the publication of Clayton's plants as early as 1737. On October 8th of that year, Linnaeus wrote to Albrecht Haller: "Gronovius will, doubtless, soon publish the plants sent by Clayton from Virginia, unless he considers too long about the matter."[20] It is probably unjust to question the motives of Gronovius since he does give a full explanation and full credit to Clayton's "Catalogue" in the Introduction. It is not his fault that many later writers tended to ignore the latter (perhaps because it was written in Latin) and to give much credit to Gronovius and little to Clayton for this work.

Although Gronovius explained at some length to Clayton his reason for having been so presumptuous as to publish his "Catalogue" without asking permission, it is plain that he had no great fear of offending him. He was already planning a second part of the *Flora,* and he was concerned about some plants for which "I by no means trusted to that extent my own observations, for which reason I propose that you must examine them, in order that they can be put in the second part of *Flora Virginica* which I am preparing." Clayton had successfully mastered Ray's method of determining the *genus* to which each of his plants belonged. Gronovius noted that "'The Catalogue of Plants, Fruits, and Trees Native to Virginia' . . . proves this success." In preparing the *Flora* from

Clayton's *Catalogue*, Gronovius added to the genus of individual plants "names of the species which are in *Hortus Cliffortianus* and *Flora Lapponica*; for the rest of the plants, I myself adapted those names which were not clear in that place [in these publications ?] using the method of composing names for species delineated by Linnaeus." Clayton had included in the *Catalogue* a number of plants of which he had never sent specimens to Gronovius. These were marked by Gronovius with an asterisk in the *Flora*. He also "put alongside only one synonym for each plant, the best choice from a writer of the most distinction, from which the rest can easily be derived." These authorities included Linnaeus, Dillenius, Peter Michel, John Ray, Sebastian Vaillant, Leonard Plukenet, and Robert Morison.[21] Part I of the *Flora* consists of 128 pages and approximately six hundred species. The implication has often been made that Clayton merely collected the plants and that Gronovius did the rest. The latter makes it very clear in the Introduction that he has only added to the well prepared "Catalogue" of Clayton. It is also apparent from the discussion of the Gladiolus in the previously quoted letter that Gronovius had a high regard for Clayton's opinions at even this early date.

Not so apparent, perhaps, has been the great part played by Linnaeus, in the preparation of both parts of the first edition of the *Flora*. In an undated letter written before 1738, Gronovius wrote "I have received many seeds from New England with the expectation of many more; and a not unwelcome letter from Catesby, communicating that he had entrusted to my London merchant two chests filled with seeds and plant specimens, sent to me from Virginia by the eminent Clayton, which I do not doubt I shall receive the following week, and consequently a visit from you will be most welcome; we go ahead well with the characters, fifty-two remaining to be printed; which I hope to complete next week."[22] Even after Linnaeus returned to Sweden in 1738, Gronovius continued to seek, even demand, his assistance. In July of 1739, he wrote to Linnaeus: "Before the first of October I shall send, through the same merchant, the rest of the tables which will conclude the first part of the Flora Virginica and thus hasten your comparison of these plants and do hurry your letters and observations on these by ship."[23] Again in November, Linnaeus' expected services are well catalogued, tinged with Gronovius' slight exasperation in regard to Linnaeus' tendency to either overlook, or to ignore, the plant numbers. "I have received letters from Catesby, concerning the new plants received from Virginia, which I expect at any moment. I go forward on the *Flora Virginica*. We have sent the next sheets to be printed. I beseech Linnaeus that he will produce the specific names which he desires for the following plants." Gronovius then proceeded to give examples from the *Hortus Cliffortianus* and the *Flora,* showing how they differed in nomenclature and description. He continued, "I send now the specimens; if they are satisfactory to you I desire the genera, names, and characters of the specimens, but do not forget the numbers. He [Clayton] sends almost no seeds, bewailing the rainy season, which prevented his collection. . . . Now I show my faith in you and send these trifling proofs, viz, the pages of the *Flora Virginica*. From Catesby and others I have received nothing new . . . I send these [Virginia plants] to you that you may not forget again. They are extremely rare, the names of whose species I desire from you and that your observation changes no number."[24] The following year, in an innocent manner, he begins his letter, "Through Mr. Van de Velde I have sent you a parcel which contains specimens of plants sent recently from Virginia, among which you will discover some very curious . . . I also present some Virginia seeds. I learn today that a ship from Virginia again docks in London . . . I send also two copies of the *Flora Virginica* which you will be able to share with your friends . . . Collinson greets you. There is no news from Lawson . . . Lieberkuhn has gone to England." The second page demonstrated that Gronovius was not above a bit of gentlemanly blackmail: "At home I found a large box of seeds and specimens (most elegant) all of which I shall send you a share of, on condition that you send me your observations."[25]

In referring to his generous supply of Virginia plants,

Gronovius knew of its importance to the great botanist, for it was a more than fair exchange for Linnaeus' labours. It has long been known that many of Linnaeus' New World specimens came from Clayton, but the immense number is most impressive in the perusal of Gronovius' letters. One hundred different seeds alone were sent in 1736, for Clifford's garden.[26] Many of these undoubtedly appeared in print for the first time in *Hortus Cliffortianus,* which, in justice to Clayton, should have made their debut in *Flora Virginica.* Clayton's seeds and plants throve in Gronovius' garden and he wrote Linnaeus "a monstrous number of Virginia plants are blooming; how many specimens shall I offer you?"[27] The year after Linnaeus returned home, Gronovius collected seeds from his garden and forwarded them to Sweden with half of a parcel of seeds which Clayton had sent. In 1743 he wrote "I am preparing now a box to send to you in which you will find a very great many [things] which I forsee will not be unwelcome: among them a large supply of American seeds, and all those fish which I have in duplicate. While writing this letter boxes were brought in, sent to me from London, in which are plants and seeds from Virginia and, I am instructed, alive. I shall share a part with you."[28] This worthwhile collaboration seems to have continued throughout the correspondence, which ended (as far as is known) in 1750.

The seeds which Clayton had contributed to Mr. Clifford's garden, involuntarily, did not go unacknowledged. On a November Sunday in 1738, the Amsterdam banker presented Gronovius with several copies of the newly printed *Hortus Cliffortianus.* In addition to his own copy, Gronovius was given copies for Collinson, Catesby, and John Clayton.[29] With such a gift, in which he had played a small part, the Virginian must have begun to appreciate the rewards in this new scientific world he was entering. Gronovius doubtless informed him that such a gift was invaluable, in that Clifford had refused to allow his *Hortus* to be sold, and the only copies distributed were those which he gave to his friends. Clayton's copy was the only one on the North American continent for over twenty years. Clayton was receiving some small recognition in Europe for his collecting even before the first part of the *Flora Virginica* was to appear in print.

Although Gronovius had written Richardson in September of 1738 that it was to go to press as soon as the *Hortus Cliffortianus* was published, which should be any day,[30] the *Flora* was not printed until October, 1739. This delay was not only due to the *Hortus*, but to Gronovius' procrastination to which Linnaeus referred in his letter to Haller: "Gronovius, no doubt, will describe it [the American Polygala] amongst his Virginia plants. I wish he had not so long hesitated to publish his book. He is too timid. You would scarcely believe how many of the vegetable productions of Virginia are the same as our European ones."[31] Gronovius did not hesitate to admit that "time vanishes as I procrastinate from day to day,"[32] but as a busy physician such delay was understandable. Part I was well received both in Europe and in England, and Clayton's name became known in botanical circles. As early as 1740, a small printed brochure publicizing Linnaeus' books listed the *Flora* among various authoritative works employing his system.[33] The following year, Stephen Francis Geoffrey, an outstanding French doctor, had references to it in his *Materia Medica*, published in Paris.[34]

In September of the year in which the first part of the *Flora* was published, Gronovius had practically completed the actual writing of the second part. He was complaining that Catesby had not forwarded some of the Virginia specimens which he needed in order to finish.[35] He need have been in no hurry, as the book did not appear in print until the late fall of 1743. In September of 1740, he wrote to Dr. Richardson "At present they print a new edition of the Fundamenta Botanica of Linnaeus with severall augmentations and corrections Large Octavo. His Characteres Generum will be reprinted too with severall new Genera of plants, which I got lately from Virginy, and shall make the Second part of the Flora Virginica."[36] Each new shipment of Virginia plants may have tempted him to further delay the printing. In the January preceding publication, he wrote Dr. Abraham Bäck in Paris: "For my amusement and refreshment from the laborious public affairs, I have undertaken to print the second part of the *Flora Virginica,* wherein will be found severall new plants not known before."[37] Seventy-seven pages and three hundred species were added to the original first part. Bartram described it thus: "The 2 part of Flora Virginica begins with page 129 & ends with 206 after the same method as [the] first part with the virtues ascribed to some of them according to the practice of the Common people."[38]

Gronovius' pupil had learned his lessons well. By 1740 Clayton was speaking with authority, and Gronovius did not hesitate to quote his observations in correcting Linnaeus' mistakes: "Dr. van Royen has asked in what manner you have observed the stamens of the Chionanthus Fringe-tree to be three. Indeed, Clayton, writing so accurately, had made an investigation on the living plants, discovered four short stamens."[39] Clayton, being able to observe the living material, was of great assistance to Linnaeus, who was so often dependent on dried specimens. The detailed observations written in Virginia were copied by Gronovius and sent to Sweden.[40] It is difficult to assign particular credit to any one of the three men. They were a working team, whose efforts supplemented each other's, resulting in many joint botanical accomplishments. While Linnaeus definitely contributed much to the first edition of the *Flora,* so did Gronovius and Clayton add their share to Linnaeus' publications. Like Mr. Clifford, Linnaeus lost no time in recognizing his debt to Clayton. In 1737, he bestowed upon him the most lasting testimonial which a botanist may hope for, the naming of a genus in his honour. This was the *Claytonia,* whose delicate pink and white blossoms are well-named "Spring Beauties." This genus first appeared in print in Linnaeus' *Critica Botanica* and in his identification of Clayton, he referred to him as an "English Virginia merchant."

VI
THE MIDDLE YEARS

Clayton's hours devoted to science were snatched from a busy, full schedule. In addition to his duties as Clerk of Court, he had family affairs to occupy him. On April 1, 1726, his father presented a petition for a leave of absence "setting forth that he hath been a resident in this Country for above twenty years last past, in which time many great alterations have happened in his affairs in England, which necessarily require his attention."[1] He appointed John Randolph as his substitute for a year.[2] The years which Mr. Clayton had spent in Virginia had indeed seen many changes in the English Clayton family. His cantankerous Aunt Prudence had at last died in 1711, although her estate was not settled for fifteen years;[3] his mother, Dame Alice, had died in 1718. His brother, Jasper, had departed for Gibraltar to take up his new duties as governor shortly before Mr. Clayton arrived. Nevertheless, Mr. Clayton must have had a happy year. His sister Charlotte, Lady Lovelace, and her children, had returned to England in 1709. Thomas, his youngest son, was now a physician. There was an acquaintance to be renewed with the Bowyers, the Symonds, the Pastons, and all the many ramifications of the family connection. There was official business to be done as well. Mr. Clayton presented Virginia's case against the Proprietors of the Northern Neck, who claimed they had a right to the Deodans goods of felons and fugitives, various fines and forfeitures, "treasure trove," and many other perquisites. The Attorney General and Solicitor General of England had ruled in favor of the Proprietors some years previously, but Mr. Clayton was able to persuade them to reverse their decision and to give these rights to Virginia.[4]

On his return home in 1727, Mr. Clayton was probably accompanied by Thomas who established his medical practice in Gloucester. Within a year, the family was reunited for Thomas' marriage to Isabella, one of the nine children of Councillor John Lewis and his wife, Elizabeth Warner.[5] John Lewis was another Virginian of considerable wealth. He owned approximately five thousand acres in the Gloucester area, and a tract of ten thousand acres in a single grant in King and Queen County. Mr. Clayton purchased a tract of land along the Paropotank Swamp from Councillor Lewis for the young couple.[6] This plantation was very close to the land of the John Claytons and the two couples must have seen a great deal of each other. Only one child, a girl, was born to the Thomas Claytons. She was named Juliana, possibly for Thomas' Aunt Juliana, wife of General Jasper Clayton.

The decade 1732-1742 was a tragic one for John Clayton: the family group, completed when Thomas arrived, was almost wiped out during this period. Arthur died December 13, 1733, and Thomas's daughter Juliana, May 12, 1734.[7] Arthur and his wife, Mary, whose maiden name is unknown, apparently had no children. His widow remarried sometime after 1737. Her second husband was the Reverend Patrick Henry, uncle of the better-known holder of that name.[8]

Clayton's father, now in his seventies, was troubled by gout. This was all too obvious to his old friend, Colonel Byrd, who wrote to Sir John Randolph concerning the jungle which Mr. Custis' plantation had become. Remarking that in spite of Randolph's probable use of "Pioneers" to clear the road, "I dare say notwithstanding your fine Horses you were not able to go along faster than Mr. Attorney walks."⁹ In the fall of 1737, Mr. Clayton became very ill, and on November 11, the *Virginia Gazette* noted that "John Clayton, Esq. His Majesty's Attorney-General of this Colony, who has been dangerously ill some Time, still continues weak, but is in a hopeful way of Recovery."¹⁰ This optimism was ill founded for the following week the paper announced: "This morning between 5 and 6, died at his House in the 72ᵈ Year of his Age, John Clayton, Esq. His Majesty's Attorney General, and Judge of the Court of Vice Admiralty of this Colony, the first Justice of the Commission of the Peace of *James* City County, Recorder of this City, etc. Which Offices he executed with Justice and Probity. He bore a good Character among his acquaintance, and his Death is much lamented."¹¹ On "Wednesday Evening the Funeral of John Clayton, Esq. was solemnized, from his late Dwellinghouse to the Church, in this City, in a very decent Manner."¹² It took place at Bruton Parish Church, of which he had been a vestry-man.¹³ His tombstone has not survived, but when the Church was restored in 1907, a bronze tablet was erected:

> To the Glory of God and in Memory of
> the Attorney Generals of Colonial
> Virginia—Worshippers in this Church
>
> | Benjamin Harrison | 1702-1704 |
> | Stephen Thomson | 1704-1714 |
> | John Clayton | 1714-1737 |
> | Edward Barradell | 1737-1743 |
> | William Bowden | 1743-1748 |
> | Peyton Randolph | 1748-1768 |
> | John Randolph | 1768-1776 |

Less than two years after Mr. Clayton's death, the following note appeared in the *Gazette*, October 26, 1739: "Several Persons of Note have died lately in the Colony . . . Thomas Clayton, MD, of Gloucester County, a son of the late Attorney-General, a learned and ingenious Gentleman, etc."¹⁴ Thomas was only thirty-eight, and his wife attributed his death to overwork. She only survived him three years. The Thomas Claytons were buried beside their small daughter in the Lewis' family graveyard at "Warner Hall" in Gloucester County, where their tombstones may still be seen. These are in a good state of preservation and the Clayton arms are clear and distinct on the doctor's stone: "A cross engrailed between four torteaux: crest, a leopard's gamb, erased and erect, grasping a pellet, or tortiau."[15]

John Clayton, as executor, presented his father's will for probate on December 12, 1737. To his daughter-in-law, Arthur's widow, Mr. Clayton left fifty pounds in addition to four slaves, who were to go to the botanist at her death. To Thomas, he gave the plantation on the Paropotank Swamp and eight slaves named Toby, Fuller, Pembroke, Tabby, Osmyn, Daphne, and London. These were already in Thomas' possession and had, no doubt, been purchased at the same time as the land. After the deduction for the legacies and the payment of debts, the ready money was to be divided equally between his two surviving sons. John, as the oldest son, inherited "Morehouse" in England. He also inherited "all the rest and residue of my Estate in England Virginia or elsewhere of what nature or kind soever as well real or Personal." While the bequests to Mary and Thomas are specific, being land, slaves or money, it is difficult to judge the extent of John's inheritance. Mr. Clayton had at various times owned several tracts of land in Virginia and presumably his home in Williamsburg, but just what his estate included at the time of his death is not known. The Prince George County Land Book records a survey run by Robert Bolling for a John Clayton on the south side of Butterwood Swamp on March 23, 1720.[16] In the records of York County there is the following item: "Elizabeth Page of the parish of St. Giles in the fields in the County of Middlesex in the Kingdom of Great Britain Spinster and Mann Page of Rosewell in the County of Gloster in Virginia Esqr (her attorney) by a Letter of Attorney dated 5th December 1727 in consideration of £280 sold unto John Clayton of Williamsburg in Virginia Esqr 200 Acres of Land Scituate in or near Williamsburg in Virginia 12th February 1728."[17] Hanover County Small Book notes: "April 5, 1734—Mark Anthony of St. Paul's Parish & Hester, his wife, to John Clayton of Williamsburg in

James City, 50 a. on Mattadequin Creek."[18] Whether Mr. Clayton still held these various pieces of property at the time of his death is problematical. Likewise, the mortgages which he held on the houses in the Beaufort Building in the Strand in London are not mentioned in the will.[19] In any event, it seems likely that the botanist received a rather substantial inheritance from his father. There is considerable evidence that he and his family lived in comfort and some style, and he left a good-sized estate when he died.

In January 1738, Clayton received the account for the Kentish lands from the steward, Mr. Samuel Durant. In acknowledging Durant's letter, Clayton wrote him of Mr. Clayton's death, saying that he wished him to continue as his agent. "I have so great a value for the memory of my father, and the persons he appointed, that I shall not [stop] the custom of allowing you a box of Tobacco every Christmas, nor giving a ring for w'ch purpose I have wrote to Mr. Perry to deliver the Tobacco as usual, and to pay you for a mourning ring, w'ch you buy as soon as you receive this, not exceeding a guinea or 25 s. in the price. he dyed Nov. 18th, 1737, in the 72nd year of his age. I thank you for the kind offer of Y'r house, but believe my affairs and business here will prevent me the pleasure of seeing my native Country any more."[20]

Micajah Perry's firm had not only been in charge of Mr. Clayton's interests in England, but they, in turn, had been represented in legal matters by Mr. Clayton in Virginia.[21] For some years after his father's death, Perry and Lane continued to represent John Clayton's interests in England, and to act as his tobacco merchants. This company dated back to the last half of the seventeenth century. In 1684, the Reverend John Clayton had written to them from James City, ordering new English books.[22] As mentioned previously, William Byrd had worked for a time in their London offices. They were not only prominent merchants, but their interests went far beyond those of the usual mercantile world. They were the postmasters and, more important, the bankers, not only for individuals, but for the College and for the Colony. They favored customers by using their very considerable influence[23] in government circles to secure appointments. This was such a continual source of irritation to Governor Spotswood that he had written to London in 1714: "Old Perry really talks impertinently of the breach of my Instructions . . . I think it doing little honour to the Government to have its Council appointed in the Virginia Coffee House,"[24] adding that he thought a Virginia governor quite as competent to select a Councillor as a London merchant. Micajah Perry died in 1721, leaving the business to his grandsons, Micajah and Philip. The latter never seemed to show much interest, but the former carried on the traditions of the family, and it was he who acted for the botanist in 1737. It seems likely that Clayton ceased dealing with the firm at Perry's death in January, 1753.[25] Clayton also had an account with a Virginia merchant, William Beverly, a cousin of his wife. In 1743, there was a small entry against his name in Beverly's book.[26]

Clayton's letter to Durant, mentioned previously, contains one of the few contemporary accounts of hunting in Virginia:

To satisfy the gentleman you mention, who is so desirous of Knowing the diversion of hunting and shooting here and the several sorts of game, pray give my service to him and tell him, that we have all the tame domestick beasts and fowls that you have in England, and great variety of wild ones as Deer in great plenty, Bears, Buffaloes, Wolves, Foxes, Panthers, wild Cats, Elks, Hares (smaller than any of y's which run in holes in the earth and hollow trees when pressed by the dogs, and are much like w't you call in England bush Rabbits), Squirrels 3 or 4 Sorts, Racoons, Opposums, Beavers, Otters, musk Rats, Pole cats, minks, and there has been two Porcupines killed here, but they are very scarce.[27] Then for fowls, wild Turkey's very numerous, Partridges (the size and colour like y'r Quails), wild Geese, Swans, Brants,[28] Comorants, Teal, Duck and Mallard, Black ducks, and another sort we call Summer Ducks, plover 2 or 3 sorts,[29] Soris (a delicious eating bird in Shape and way of living like y'r Water Rails),[30] Heath fowls (called here improperly Pheasants) 2 sorts, wild Pidgeons in prodigious great flocks, Field fares,[31] Woodcocks (but what is very strange they come here only in summer),[32] Snipes,[33] Herons, Bitterns, Eagles, Larks 2 sorts one of w'ch are here all the year round, are as big as Quails, the other are seen only in winter and are much like your lark. Now the Gentlemen here that follow the sport place most of their diversion in Shooting

Deer; w'ch they perform in this manner, they go out early in the morning and being pritty certain of the places where the Deer frequent they send their servants w'th dogs to drive'em out and so shoot'em running, the Deer are very swift of foot, larger and longer-legged than the English fallow Deer, and less than the red Deer, the diversion of Shooting Turkies is only to be had in the upper parts of the Country where the woods are of a very large extent, and but few settlements as yet tho' they increase daily. Some hunt the foxes with hounds as you do in England, the shooting of water fowl is performed in the same manner w'th a Water spaniel as w'th you, and of Partridges; and also the hunting our hares w'th small dogs, who drive'em presently into the hollow of a tree, then we either cut'em out with an ax or fill the hole w'th old dead leaves and set fire to'em, the smoke of w'ch suffocates the hare, and she drops down; the bears, Panthers, Buffaloes and Elks, and wild cats are only to be found among the mountains and desert parts of the country where there are as yet but few inhabitants and the hunting there is very toilsome and laborious and sometimes dangerous. Yet the Common Sort of People who live among the Mountains kill great Quantitys of Bears every year; but the greatest destruction of'em is made in the beginning of the Winter when the bears lay themselves to sleep in the caves and holes among rocks of the mountains at w'ch time the people go to the mouth of the Cave w'th their guns loaded and shoot'em as they lye in their dens. We have also great pleanty variety of fish w'ch we take with nets and by Angling as is practiced in England, and now I hope I have satisfied the Gentleman's curiosity, at least I have done my endeavour towards it, as much as the Compass of a letter will allow of and will be very glad in y'r next to know his name.

Clayton having settled his father's affairs, was free once again to indulge himself in the pleasure of plant collecting. He made, at this time, one or more long trips. When John Bartram made his first visit to Virginia in the fall of 1738, Clayton "was gone toward the mountains to seek after some land."[34] Gronovius, in two letters to Linnaeus in 1739, said how impatient he was to learn the results of Clayton's trip.[35] In one letter he gave the length of the journey as four hundred miles, and in the other as five hundred, but he never gave any details concerning it. From the great interest which he expressed it would seem that this was the longest journey made by Clayton up to that time. Betty Clayton's cousin and Clayton's friend, William Beverly, had recently acquired very large grants of land west of the Blue Ridge and settled a large number of Scotch-Irish families there.[36] It may have been this which interested Clayton. The strenuous business of searching for land was leavened by plant collecting. In fact, Clayton's curiosity was so aroused by the many strange things which he observed that Gronovius wrote "he is already wanting for action with plants, now he proceeds to animals." He was not too tempted by zoology for he remained faithful to botany throughout the years. The seeds and plants which he collected on this trip, some of which duly reached Holland, Gronovius found very "curious" and "elegant."[37]

Besides William Byrd II and John Custis, there was only one other Virginian who shared Clayton's botanical interest to any extent at this time. This was Dr. John Mitchell, who lived not too far away at Urbanna. He was Clayton's neighbor, and not too close a one, unfortunately, for only a little over ten years. During that time, Clayton and Mitchell seemed to have enjoyed a congenial friendship, in spite of distance and the fact that both were busy men. Clayton refers to Mitchell in the *Flora* but there are no letters extant between the two.[38] Mitchell, probably born in the British Isles, had not only studied under Dr. Alston at the University of Edinburgh but also under Alston's and Linnaeus' old professor and friend, Dr. Herman Boerhaave, of Leiden. Thus he was well-qualified to be of assistance to the neophyte botanist Clayton. Dr. Mitchell emigrated to Virginia sometime in the early 1720's and was acting as the official physician for the poor of Middlesex County in 1735. He was indeed a "curious" man and his interests ranged from zoology and botany to map making and agricultural practices.

Mitchell's zoological interest, as exemplified in a study of the opossum, was mentioned by Peter Collinson in a letter to Bartram: "Docr Mitchell att Urbanna in Virginia has Imploy'd some of his Leisure time in Examining the Internal Structure of this wonderful Creature & I doubt not but in Time will Clear up the Doubtful points as their Generating is Different from most animals."[39] Mitchell's *Nova Plantarum Genera*[40] was published in 1741, to which he hoped to add a more exhaustive

The Middle Years 79

study. His botanic interests also included dendrology, and he wrote a treatise on the Virginia pines.[41] In recognition of his services to botany, Linnaeus named the "partridge berry" *Mitchella repens* in his honour.

It must have been a great disappointment to Clayton when Mitchell found that Virginia's enervating climate did not agree with him, and he returned to England in 1745, where he became a most active member of the Royal Society. Before sailing, he spent three weeks in Philadelphia, where he saw a great deal of another friend of Clayton, John Bartram. The ship on which he sailed for England, was captured by a St. Malo privateer and all his "learned observations," as well as his instruments, were stolen, although he suffered no harm himself. Mitchell's only possessions which escaped harm were letters to the French botanists, Hamel and Jussieu. Clayton was not only sorry for his friend's misfortune, but he also suffered a personal loss, as he had entrusted many things to Mitchell to be delivered to his friends abroad.

With Mitchell's departure and the deaths of William Byrd II in 1743 and of John Custis not many years later, Clayton's most lasting and intimate botanical friendships were those based on correspondence. Among those friends who shared his keen interest in plants were Peter Collinson in London, and his protégé in Philadelphia, John Bartram, surely two of the most interesting personalities in botanical history. There is no way of knowing when their friendship with Clayton began, but we do know that they knew him as early as 1737. Collinson referred to him in letters to Custis and Bartram in that year.[42] In the case of Collinson, surely he had heard a great deal about Clayton from their common friend, Mark Catesby.

Collinson, while an interesting person in his own right, is particularly remembered as a catalytic agent. His influence over the burgeoning colonial culture can not be over-emphasized. He was a friend and tireless correspondent of many scientifically inclined colonials: William Byrd II, Benjamin Franklin, Cadwallader Colden, John Custis, Alexander Garden, John and William Bartram, Jared Eliot, Mitchell, and others too numerous to catalogue. He taught them, advised them, sent them books, and introduced one to another. Collinson was also the bridge between many of the English and colonial scientists and their colleagues on the Continent, such as Linnaeus, Amman, Gronovius, and George Gmelin.

Peter Collinson (1694-1768) was almost the same age as John Clayton. He was born in London, son of Peter and Elizabeth Hall Collinson. His Quaker father was a mercer and haberdasher, to which business Collinson and his brother, James, eventually succeeded. Their mercantile dealings involved them in a world-wide trade. Collinson knew most of the ship captains of the day, and through their help was able to bring to England many rare plants and seeds from all over the globe.

In such a climate of natural history inquiry as was prevalent in England, Collinson was well qualified to appreciate the excitement of the strange new plants. As such interest became fashionable among the wealthy and noble families of England, he was one of the main intermediaries for plant importation between them and the colonial botanists. In fact, it was with this in mind that he practically educated by correspondence and books that comparatively unlettered Quaker, John Bartram. By 1736, Bartram was supplying the majority of plants and trees for Lord Petre and later for Collinson's other wealthy friends. In writing to William Blackburn in 1742, he summarized these activities:

As you will Observe, there is a great number of Fine Trees, Shrubs & Flowers in North America—There is a very Ingenious Man o'nature of that Country, for whose sake, being a poor man & for the Encouragement of some Curious people Here (in particular our late Dear fr'd) I have taken a pretty deal of Trouble to procure seeds over—and gett them from on board Ship from the Customs House & then Sort & Divide them this takes up more of my Time then I can spare but for the Motives Above Mention'd I did do It. for Except the pleasure of assisting a poor Man, and obliging my Friends, I had my Labour for my pains—& I am inclined yett to continue my good office to a few Deserving Friends. Lord Petre's Subscription is now vacant, w'ch was Ten Guineas a year besides paying Freight & Custom House Charges.[43]

There was even a printed list of plants and exotics available in Bartram's garden at a later date.[44]

Collinson was only thirty-five when he was elected to the Royal Society. He proved to be an invaluable addition, and was indefatigable in promoting interest in all phases of natural history. He worked closely with Sir Hans Sloane in the development of the latter's museum; he encouraged Benjamin Franklin in his electrical experiments, presenting his results before the Royal Society and having them translated into French as well; he persuaded Colden to continue, with a more elaborate account, his *History of the Five Nations*. The manner in which Collinson's philosophy of bread upon the waters rewarded the donor is shown in Dr. John Fothergill's letter to his former teacher, Dr. Alston, in July 1740-1:

Don't know whether I have mentioned in any of my former letters that I am obliged to a particular fr'd for most of these seeds as well as for many other favours, but gratitude I think obliges me to name him, and as I have frequently mentioned to him, for whom I intended the favours he conferred on me in this way, I believe he would be very well pleased with a few lines from Dr Alston. He has this morning sent me a considerable number of seeds of different kinds, which I intend to dispatch as soon as I can. The Gentleman's name is Collinson, very well known among the virtuosos here: he has a good collection of plants in his own garden and has a settled correspondence with the curious in most parts of the world. By his means several things have appeared in the R. Society's collections which would otherwise very probably have been lost. A letter addressed to Peter Collinson Merch't in Grace church Street London will come very safe.[45]

"My Garden is now a Paradise of Delight," Collinson wrote to Linnaeus in September, 1765.[46] He had developed a superb garden at his home "Mill Hill," in Middlesex. Outdoors, the magnificent succession of bloom left the garden seldom without of flower, for he had plants there whose origins were worldwide; indoors, his "stove" was thirty feet high by nine wide, and backed by a trellis covered with clematis and passion flowers. Naturally, his house was filled with flowers at all times. Such perfection in a garden, combined with the rare specimens which it contained, proved too much of a temptation to thieves, and twice they plundered Collinson's garden. The first time, in 1765, they stole two beautiful Loblolly Bays,[47] of which Collinson was very proud, and many other plants. He wrote to Bartram's son John that his countrymen were trying to get an act through Parliament to punish the perpetrators of such depredations, by transporting them to the Colonies "which you will not thank us for."[48] The second time Collinson's garden was plundered, a friend wrote to Professor David van Royen in Leiden:

The gardens of the Curious here are at present infested by *Twyn Dieven*. About 10 days ago they made an uncommon Havock at P. Collinson's. I was there about three weeks ago & saw Several very rare American Plants most of which are now Gone. His Kalmia Angustif. was by far the finest in England. Several such Robberys have been committed this last Summer. Gordon lost 30 *Magnolia accuminatae* and it is said here many of these Plants were carried to Holland and exchanged for Bulbs etc. Should you hear of any thing that might lead to a discovery I beg you make a Memorandum of it untill I have the Honour of Seeing you—These Villains are the common Enemys of the Science and of all the Plants Mr. Collinson has lost I don't believe one will survive being mostly in flower—Some of them were non descripta.[49]

Almost as much of a menace to his stately garden was Mr. Collinson's son-in-law, Mr. Cator. Although uninterested in plants when he married, in ten years' time his father-in-law's passion had also infected him. When he purchased a large estate, whose grounds he was attempting to furnish, Collinson pleaded with Bartram to send Cator plants for it, saying that Cator "is quite cracked after plants, has plundered my garden all he can, and looks with longing on what remains."[50]

Collinson's garden was notable for its many New World plants. A contemporary wrote to van Royen that he "has the greatest collection of American plants of any one person in England, I believe I might venture to say in Europe."[51] Undoubtedly, Clayton was responsible for a large number of these, which arrived in England either as plants or as seeds, successfully nourished by Collinson to maturity. After much experimentation and work with James Gordon, the nurseryman, Collinson found that North American seeds sometimes did not germinate until the third summer in England, particularly the fringe-tree. On the other hand, some, like the cedars, might appear any year from the first to the fourth. He found that the small "soft Herbaceous seeds" were as unpredictable as the hard ones.[52] In his characteristic fashion, he described his garden to Colden in 1764:

As often as I survey my Garden & Plantations it reminds Mee of my Absent Friends by their Living Donations—See there my Hon'ble Fr'd Gover'r Colden how thrifty they look—Sr I see nobody but Two fine Trees a Spruce & a Larch, thats True, but they are his representatives, but See close by how my Lord Northumberland aspires in that Curious Firr from Mount Ida, but look Yonder at the Late Benevolent Duke of Richmond, His Everlasting Cedars of Lebanon, will Endure when you & I & He is forgot . . . regard but ye Variety of Trees & Shrubs in this plantation as Mountain Magnolia, Sarsifax, Rhododendrons Calmias & Azaleas etc etc etc all are the Bounty of my Curious Botanic Friend J: Bartram of Philadelphia and those pretty Fringe Trees, Halesias & Stuartia all Great Beauties I must thank my Fr'd Mr Clayton the Great Botanist of America.[53]

In Collinson's informal catalogue of his garden, which was not printed until long after his death,[54] he specifically mentioned several plants which he received from Clayton: "1748 Two pots filled with Atamasco Lillies, in flower April 18; sent mee from Virginia by Mr. Clayton;" "Chelone, with a red flower. I had the first plant sent me from Virginia; it is very rare in that country;" "Jan 1, 1751, Mr. Clayton, of Virginia, sent me in a box of sand two roots of Virginia Moley, with small white sweet-scented flowers; the Ornithogalum of Flora Virginica; in flower June 10, 1751." Under *Asclepias rubra*, Dillwyn has added: "As Mr. Collinson corresponded with Clayton and Gronovius, there can be little doubt that this was *A. rubra* of the *Species Plantarum*, which appears to have been wholly taken from the *Flora Virginica*; and there is not any specimen in the Linnaean Herbarium. It is said in the *Hortus Britanicus* to have been first introduced to our gardens in 1825." Many plants, such as the "Pig Nut" and the *Elephantopus* are identified with a Latin description marked either "Clayton" or "*Flora Virginica.*" Of the definition of the *Eutoca parviflora* of Bentham, Dillwyn wrote that it "has been obviously abbreviated from Clayton's, who had probably sent the plant to Mr. Collinson, and the specific character which Gronovius framed for the species has been adopted by Linnaeus for his *Polemonium dubium*."

Among the many reasons for Clayton and Collinson to develop a close friendship was the fact that the Englishman had met Linnaeus when he came to London in 1736. Collinson, like Dillenius, was at first not impressed, and wrote to Bartram on December 14, 1737: "The *Systema Naturae* is a curious performance for a young man; but his conning a set of new names for plants, tends but to embarrass and perplex the study of Botany. As to his System, on which they are founded, botanists are not agreed about it."[55] However, it was not long before Collinson was a great admirer of the new system. By 1743 he was writing Linnaeus "Your system, I can tell you obtains much in America. Mr. Clayton and Dr. Colden att Albany on Hudson's River in New York, are compleat Professors as Is Doc^r Mitchell att Urbanna on Rapahanock River in Virginia."[56] Even Dr. Colden's daughter was an enthusiast and had the distinction of being the "only lady that makes profession of the Linnean system."[57] Collinson may have been mollified by the naming of *Collinsonia* in his honour in 1737 by Linnaeus, for he wrote him: "I am glad of this conveyance to Express my Gratitude for the perticular regard shown mee in that Curious Elaborate Work the Hort's Cliffort'o—Something I think was Due Mee from the Common Wealth of Botany: for the Great number of plants & seeds I have annually procured from Abroad and you have been so good to pay It by Giving Mee a Species of Eternity (Botanically Speaking). That is a name as long as Men and Books Endure —this layes Mee under Great Obligations, which I shall never Forgett."[58]

One of Collinson's first returns for the gift of plants by Clayton must have been his encouragement to the Virginian in searching for the non-flowering plants. Collinson often sent puzzling New World plants to Dillenius at Oxford for identification and in 1740 he wrote Bartram: "Pray see what further mosses thee canst collect for Doctor Dillenius. He defers completing his work, till he sees what comes from thee, Clayton, and Dr. Mitchell."[59] Dillenius was busy completing his *Historia Muscorum,* which was published the following year. From Collinson's vivid description, it is easy to picture the Oxford professor studying these unknown species of cryptogams forwarded from London: "To See a great tall Unwieldy man adopt the Minutiae of Vegetables for his favorite pursuit, study & amusement, better adapted to a light nimble man of low stature . . . Happy for future Botanists that he cou'd so curiously and Exactly Draw and Engrave. Else it wou'd have been almost impossible for an ingenious Engraver to Distinguish so minutely their Botanic Characters & their delicate fine branches and leaves and the seed vessels of these least of Vegetables."[60] Clayton sent more than twenty mosses which were included in Dillenius' book. There these appeared in print for the first time; others, Linnaeus had introduced as new species—but they were all Clayton discoveries. The same was true of the fourteen species of algae which Clayton sent to Oxford. Some of the specimens are still preserved in the Sherardian Museum there.

The correspondence of Clayton and Collinson must have been voluminous, from various oblique references, but none of it survives today insofar as we know. From the four excerpts which we have from Clayton letters, the contrast between the Clayton-Collinson correspondence and that of the Clayton-Bartram letters is apparent: the former deals much more with scientific theory and discussion, while the latter is more concerned with botanical observation. Collinson often acted as a clearinghouse of botanical information gathered from his English friends and his own large correspondence, carried on as he sat before his cheerful fire at "Mill Hill" chatting with his friends. He wrote to the Virginian, John Custis, February 20, 1737/8: "Pray have you never Observed a sumach that produced Tuffts of a Very Bright scarlet most Lovely to Look on, I se this year seeds or Tufts of such an One, sent Here by Mr. John Clayton of Glocester County."[61] And again to Mr. Custis on April 2nd, 1744: "It is a Thousand pities but that such Curious Gentlemen as you, Colonel Byrd, Mr. Clayton & Dr. Mitchell should annually sow seeds of the Umbrella Tree to preserve it from being Intirely Lost."[62]

Perhaps the greatest contribution of Collinson's friendship was the bringing together of John Clayton and John Bartram. The following is from the letter of introduction written by Collinson to John Custis, and no doubt one like it was written to Clayton, when Bartram was preparing for his first trip to Virginia:

Dont be surprised if a down right plain Country Man—perhaps he may be a Quaker too Into the Bargain & you know they are said to be an odd sort of a People but this makes mee call to mind an old proverbe the Devil is not so Black as painted. Now if such a Medly Composition should come alltogether, Dont be startled. That you may not Mistake the Man He will bring a Credential from Mee, I so much persuaded my self of such an interest in your Friendship you'l not Look att the Man but his Mind for my sake. His conversation I dare say you'l find compensate for his appearance—He is well Versed in Nature and Can give a good Account of Her Works. He Comes to Visit your parts in serch of Curiosities. In the Vegetible kingdom perhaps you'l find him more knowing in that Science than any you Have Mett With. He is Imployed by a Sett of Noble Men (by my Recommendation) to Collect seeds & specimens of Rare plants, and he has been very successful in this affair which proceds from His thorough knowledge in these Matters. Be so kind to give him a Little Entertainm't & Recommend Him to a Friend or Two of yours in the Country, for He does not Value rideing 50 or 100 Miles to see a New plant. Pray Direct Him to the Umbrella Tree, this plant or Tree will make Him think his Journey worth Comeing. I have a further Desire in his waeting on you, the Gardens of pensilvania are Well furnish'd with European Rarities possibly He may assist you with some plants that you Want & you may assist Them for I presume you have Vessills passing too & fro Often from one province to the Other. His name is John Bartram.[63]

John Bartram's (1699-1777) grand-parents came to Pennsylvania in 1682, the year in which Philadelphia was founded. They settled to the west of the city. Bartram, a stonemason, inherited land from an uncle and later bought more on the Schuylkill River where the Bartram Gardens are now, and where still stands his hewn stone house built in 1731. J. W. Campbell described Bartram as follows: "Mr. Bartram was an ingenious mechanic. The house in which he lived he built himself, he was often his own mason, carpenter, blacksmith, etc. and generally made his own farming utensils. His stature was rather above the middle size; his body erect and slender; his complexion was sandy; his countenance cheerful, though there was a solemnity in his air. His gentle manners corresponded with his amiable disposition."[64] Bartram fathered eleven children. He said of his wife that she "brought me nothing in money, all her riches consisted in the good temper and great knowledge of housewifery."[65] It was just as well that she was endowed with such virtues, for she was often left to carry on the business of the farm as well as of the household for months at a time, while her husband was collecting.

Bartram's correspondence with Collinson dates from 1730 to the latter's death. Not long after the publication of the first part of the *Flora Virginica* Bartram received a copy, either from the co-authors or from Collinson. He had sent Collinson a large number of plants for identification, and in December of 1740, the latter enclosed a list of these with numbered references to the particular book in which they appeared, saying "As thee has the Flora Virginica thee will find most if not all the plants mentioned there."[66] The accompanying letter attempted to assuage Bartram's annoyance with the baffling multitude of botanical names.

Lond December 20, 1740

Fr John

It is to be hoped that thy patience will be rewarded with some knowledge as the other part of the Sheet will inform thee. There is many names to be met with In old Botanists, the Discoveries of such numbers of plants in your World has oblyged has oblyged [sic] our Moderns, being New Genus's to give them New Names. if thee hath any Complaints Doc Gronovius is answerable

I am

My Good Friend
Much . . . .
P. Collinson

Collinson, as one of two agents for the Library Company of Philadelphia, established in 1742, recommended that Bartram be given a free share in the Company, and Bartram was eventually made a life member.[67] Collinson often sent goods to Bartram in care of the Library Company in order to save freightage.

In England, Collinson had arranged the patrons for Bartram. The income which they allowed him, in addition to the goods which Collinson sent in exchange for the plants which Bartram was sending him, was sufficient to finance his trips and adequate for a fairly comfortable existence. Bartram's household consisted of servants and some slaves, who were able to farm in his absence. Nevertheless, Bartram never felt that he was overpaid for the strenuous and dangerous collecting trips, but he seemed to enjoy every minute of them. That he would feel even more rewarded, Collinson wrote to Linnaeus in 1743, "I hope John Bartram our collector will send more this year—for his Great Pains & Industrie pray find out a New Genus and name it *Bartramia*."[68]

Collinson acted as Bartram's agent, choosing dresses and calico and Russian linen for Mrs. Bartram and clothes for John. Mrs. Bartram was so well pleased with his choices that her husband wrote his friend that she said she would have chosen the same things herself had she been in London. Collinson sent Bartram books of all sorts, and interested his friends in the Pennsylvanian. As mentioned before, he often acted as an intermediary for his friends, writing Bartram, "Doc Dillenius gives his service & has sent 3 or 4 Reams of the largest size paper being sheets of his Hortus Elthamensis which will make noble Books for Specimens."[69] In 1740, Mark Catesby wrote to Bartram suggesting that the two of them might do a little horsetrading: he would send twenty plates (with their corresponding descriptions) from his book, which was worth twenty guineas, to Bartram each year in exchange for plants.[70] The arrangement seems to have been quite satisfactory to both parties, and in 1744 Catesby wrote to Bartram, "The hope of getting some good seeds of it delights me more than the possession of that last Cargo you were so kind to send me. Mr Clayton six years past sent me ample specimens of this same tree by name of Magnolia Maxima precox, and this year Dr. Mitchel did the same by Mr Collinson and added some of its cones tho' the buds were not good, and with all sent this account of it."[71] Collinson even supplied Bartram with a microscope for which he had paid a guinea.[72] When Bartram built a greenhouse, Collinson promised him some geraniums for it as soon as he installed a stove.[73]

When Bartram's son Moses was stranded in London after his American ship did not return to the Colonies, Collinson looked after him. Moses wished to return home on an English ship, but Collinson who considered British sailors the scum of the earth and a bad influence on youth, would not allow it. Moses finally found an American ship and spent many years as a sailor, often writing his father's old friend, whose interest in him never abated. As late as 1756, Bartram wrote that "poor Moses has been tumbling and tossing about the world."[74] Collinson was equally interested in William Bartram, who at fifteen and sixteen was sending to England exquisite drawings of plants, which Collinson considered the equal of any of those of Ehret or Edwards. He sent some of the drawings to Gronovius to have engraved in Holland and had Billy's drawing of a tortoise printed in the *Gentleman's Magazine*.[75]

When Bartram was preparing for his first trip to Virginia in 1738, Collinson wrote to him, "One thing I must desire of thee and do insist that thee oblige me therein: that thou make up thy drugget clothes, to go to Virginia in, and not appear to disgrace thyself or me; for though I should not esteem thee the less, to come to me in what dress thou will,—yet these Virginians are a very gentle, well-dressed people—and look, perhaps, more at a man's outside than his inside. For these and other reasons pray go very clean, neat, and handsomely dressed, to Virginia."[76] Bartram may have previously protested such extravagant attitudes, for Collinson wrote grandly, "Never mind thy clothes; I will send more another year."[77] This was a mistake, for Bartram followed his friend's advice all too readily, and the following year Collinson wrote to him in tones of mock horror: "One thing I forgot to mention before, and what very much surprises me, to find thee, who art a philosopher, prouder than I am. My cap, it is true, had a small hole or two in the border; but the lining was new. Instead of giving it away, I wish thee had sent it me back again. It would have served me two or three years, to have worn in the country in rainy weather."[78] In the meantime, Collinson was preparing Colonel William Byrd II and Isham Randolph,[79] as well as John Custis and other Virginia friends, for Bartram's advent.

Bartram's description of his eleven hundred mile Virginia trip, completed in four weeks, was in so brief a letter that Collinson protested. He was exceedingly curious about the country through which Bartram had travelled, and even more interested in hearing details concerning his old friends and his correspondents, their homes and gardens. In reply, Bartram wrote him a more detailed account, the first draft of which is among the Bartram Papers in the Historical Society of Pennsylvania. He crossed the Potomac River, "then traveled down the river about a hundred miles crossing Pianketank rode to John Clatons where the river was prety wide here I had the misfortune of a grievous disapointment for Claton was gone toward the mountains to seek after some land." After a general description of the country, he continued: "but there gardens is poorly furnished with Curiosities John Clatons & Col. Birds is best furnished with variety of plants but falls short of ours in pensilvania which is supplied from england france holland & germany."[80] His actual letter to Collinson (rather than the draft) must have substituted Custis' garden for that of Byrd's, as the latter wrote to John Custis: "It on the one hand gives Mee pleasure to heare of the kind Reception J. Bartram rece'd under thy Roof. He was much Delighted with thy Garden which is the best Furnish'd & next John Claytons of any He Mett With—in all that Journey."[81] John Custis was perfectly charmed by the Quaker, and Clayton evidently tremendously disappointed to have missed him, as was Bartram. Collinson wrote to Bartram: "I am sorry that our Brother Clayton was not at home. It was, no doubt, a great disappointment, that you could not open your budgets[82] and compare notes."[83] Colonel Byrd, also, was most enthusiastic about Bartram, writing him on November 30, 1738, that his letter had taken twice as long coming from Philadelphia as the author had. Collinson must have been particularly interested to hear of the Colonel's garden for he had known him well when Byrd was in England. He regarded him as "a very polite, ingenious man."[84]

Bartram had made this trip in the fall of the year, that he might collect seeds. These, and plants, wrapped in paper, he packed in his two saddlebags, where the long, rough trip mixed them altogether. Eventually they arrived in England, unnamed and a perfect potpourri, along with turtle eggs and insects. Collinson, being very busy at the time, sent the plants to Gronovius, who mounted them "neatly on fine white paper, that they look as beautiful as so many pictures, and names them into the bargain."[85]

Perhaps it was this year that the Bartram-Clayton correspondence began. Writing to Collinson in 1743, Bartram refers to the *Aralia spinosa* (Hercules' club) and also to the *Arbor vitae*, probably from Isham Randolph's plantation on the James River, both of which he had brought from Virginia.[86] Whether he was referring to his 1738 trip or a later one we do not know. He is not known to have made a second trip at this time. In any event, Bartram and Clayton are not known to have actually met until 1760, although they had corresponded for approximately twenty years.

Bartram, in his letter to Clayton on September 1, 1744, refers to one of the Virginian's in August of that year, He addresses him as "Dear friend John Claton," which rather implies that their friendship was of several years' standing. The whole tone of this letter indicates a fair amount of intimacy. It would be interesting to know if the *Flora Virginica* which Collinson tells Bartram to consult in 1740 and again about the sweet and sour gums in May, 1742,[87] was a copy which he had sent, or one which Clayton had presented. In any event, by December, 1744, Bartram wrote to Collinson that he was corresponding "very freely" with Dr. Mitchell and John Clayton.[88] The following copy of a letter is the only survivor of this early correspondence and the only known one from Bartram *to* Clayton:

Dear friend John Claton   Septem the first 1744

A few days ago I received thy obliging letter of August 13 which I have read with great satisfaction & am very thankful for thy information about Stewartia and Smith's Magnolia which agrees with the description I have had of it from P. Collinson. The Staggerweed seed I gathered in October,[89] behind your ble mountains where some plants had been cropt & produced new shoots was in flower. it flowers early with me at the same time that the true Napaea[90] double & is very like it. in this vail I found a curious peranial Seneca[91] growing high & leaves very sweet & a strange species of the mallow or alcea & other peranial the male & female growing & several other plants—the leaves near 18 inches diameter & the diminutive species of the zanthocelum.[92] With other odd plants of two diaternus I can't remember particularly where I found them Down thicket on cold clay, moist ground, not near any house [torn and obscure] & near 10 Feet high. We have the same sort of sene & a peranial. I sent it to Dillenius & he called it sene ———.[93] I climbed on the Cattskill mountains first to discover a Balm of Gilead Fir[94] in May, next to gather seeds thereof in August. I hired a Guide to go up with me who was no man of curiosity & so consequently was soon weary of staying there so that I had no opertunity of making the ful discovery of near all the great variety of curious plants there on produced but if ever I go up them again I design to be guide my self & stay on them as long as I please but as far as I went I found a surprising variety of trees of several sorts of the new found land spruice, firrs-pines, birches various species, Quicken trees 12 foot high,[95] chery trees the cluster kinds. A curious species of viburnum with a rough great kind of leaf shaped like a heart, some male & female distinct & some dwarf yew. of plants several species of Cristophoriana,[96] Aralia,[97] & Araliastrums,[98] Lady's bower, very beautiful herb paris[99] with many other odd kinds. As for animals I saw but few uncommon ones only a fine kind of Lizard[100] an ash color with 4 Golden spots on each side & about 5 inches long they lay on the top of the water of a great Lake near the top of the mountain & when I drew near to observe them they would dive down to the bottom & creep under the stones, but neighboring inhabitants tells strange stories of a little creature about the bigness of a middling dog nearly the shape of a Lion & another creature they call a tiger but I don't give a Bandana of credit to & as the Indians hath been settled for ages around there the game is much destroyed yet as they appear next to the North River which river flows to the southwards of a hammock of springs ——— very difficult of access by reason of Lakes, swamps, thickets & prodigious ledges of rocks & cragy caverns. in which some of the native inhabitants escape the vigilence of the cuning hunter. indeed the west to northwest sides (where the sources is of the great-river Susequehana & the head springs of your bay & our river Delaware rises gradually & uncommon animals resides. In the northern part is a porcupin fisher, an amphibious like creature about the bigness of a racoon & a little creature about the bigness of a squirrel of yellowish colour & excellent furr & such multitude of pidgeons that the ground is covered a foot thick with their dung some say much more. The Larch sheds its leaves in autumn pray doth that tree the mentions on the south branch of James River. Thee may easily know the paper-birch. do but Lance the bark perpindicular on one side & the may easily pil 10 pieces of paper as fine as parchment around the tree. I have put in this letter a specimen of birch paper & the bark of a twig of another species of birch which may be the same with what the observed near the Fals of Potomac & one quill of a porcupin which killed by the indians up Susequehana where I gathered a handfull of quils & brought home to oblige the Curious. Now dear friend I think I have answered thy letter in ever perticular & if I have not enlarged so much as thee expected pray let me know & I shall endeavour to mend it & in the mean time thee may be assured I am thy real friend.[101]

VII
RECOGNITION BY THE NATURAL HISTORY CIRCLE

After publication of the second part of the *Flora Virginica* in 1743, Clayton was recognized by other botanists as an important contributing member of the international natural history circle. This group, which maintained almost constant correspondence, was represented in a number of national scientific societies.

Thus it was that John Bartram made certain that Clayton, his Virginia friend, became a member of the new society which was being formed in Philadelphia. In England, the need for a clearing-house for scientific observations and experiments had been met by the Royal Society of London, and other such organizations. It was rapidly becoming apparent that such a medium for exchange of information would be a welcome addition to intellectual life in the New World. In 1743, Franklin and nine other Philadelphians founded the American Philosophical Society to fill this need. The members represented professions or subjects—a doctor, a mathematician, a chemist, a mechanic, a geographer, a botanist, and one who represented a general category loosely termed "Natural Philosophy." A president, a secretary, and a treasurer comprised the executive. Franklin directed, as Postmaster of Pennsylvania, that all Society communications were to be post-free.

The Society was not long limited to ten members. On April 4, Franklin wrote to Cadwallader Colden concerning corresponding members.[1] On April 29, Bartram wrote to Colden: "Our Philosophical Society increaseth finely. I think we have 7 members initiated last meeting of which thee was one by unanimous consent."[2] Colden was very flattered and lost no time in communicating his pleasure to Collinson: "No doubt you will hear of a Philosophical Society now forming at Philadelphia. They have given an invitation to several in the neighboring Colonies to join with them & have done me the honour to take me into their Society, tho I be not in any manner acquainted with any of them except Mr. Bartram who has undertaken the Botanical part."[3] Men from New York and New Jersey were not the only corresponding members asked to join. Franklin wrote to Colden, upon his election to membership, "And there are a number of others in Virginia, Maryland, Carolina, and the New England Colonies who we expect to join us as soon as they are acquainted that the Society has begun to form itself."[4] Clayton knew of the Society as early as 1744, for Bartram wrote to Colden "I find by my correspondents in Europe that they have been informed of our Phylosophycal Society & have great expectation of fine accounts therefrom tho I durst not so much as mention it to my correspondents for fear it should turn out but poorly; but I find the mentioned to Collinson, hee to Catesby, & hee to Gronovius[5] which was to him from Claton[6] these accounts I showed to franklin & he layeth ye blame on us."[7] Actually, it was most unfair of Franklin to blame them, for he had written to Collinson himself about the Society as early as 1743.[8] As soon as Gronovius learned the news, he lost no time in continuing the chain-letter process, by communicating to Linnaeus: "In Philadelphia, they have established a Literary Society, and the most worthy members adorn it, such as Clayton,

Colden, Mitchell, Bartram, and all who are eager to promote natural history."[9] Although the names of two other Virginians, Dr. Arthur Lee and Colonel Francis Lee, appear on the Philosophical Society's membership rolls, neither Clayton's name nor Mitchell's are there. The early records are missing and it is only by chance that we know of either's membership. It was through a letter of Bartram to Colden that it was first known that Mitchell belonged to the Philosophical Society,[10] and only through Gronovius' letter that it has been established that Clayton was also an early member.

Collinson was delighted and wrote to Colden, "I can't enough commend the Authors & promoters of a Society for Improvem't of Natural Knowledge Because it will be a Means of uniteing Ingenious Men of all Societies together."[11] This was certainly the case, for Franklin forwarded to Colden the treatise on yellow fever which Dr. Mitchell had sent him, resulting in a correspondence between the two doctors. The Virginian, in answer to Colden's letter, wrote that this paper was just a very rough draft, not ready for publication, but that he had sent it to Franklin to be kept in the Philosophical Society's records.[12] There it was found by Dr. Rush half a century later. Perhaps this inspired Franklin to write to Collinson "I am now determin'd to publish an American Philosophical Miscellany, Monthly or Quarterly. I shall begin with next January."[13] Unfortunately, it was many years before such a journal became a reality. In fact, the Society itself lost much of its primary enthusiasm. Franklin complained to Collinson that "The Members of our Society here are very idle Gentlemen; they will take no Pains."[14] Colden summed up the situation in words which would apply to many a society: "As to your Philosophical Society, I can say nothing but that as it is certain that some have been too lazy, so others may have been too officious; which makes the more prudent afraid of them."[15] But there was more to it than just inertia. Peter Kalm, who had come to this country in 1748, armed with introductions to Colden, Franklin, and others of Collinson's friends, wrote "In 1743, a society for the advancement of the sciences was erected here. Its objects would have been the curiosities of the three Kingdoms of nature, mathematics, physik, chemistry, œconomy and manufactures. But the war, which ensued immediately, stopped all designs of this nature, and since that time nothing has been done towards establishing anything of this kind."[16] In 1768, the newly reconstituted American Philosophical Society, and a similar group, The American Society for Promoting Useful Knowledge, united after much diplomatic bickering, and held their first joint meeting in January of 1769.[17]

It seems unlikely that John Clayton ever attended a meeting of the Society, but it alerted him to some of the scientific accomplishments being achieved in the Middle and Northern Colonies. Collinson, Bartram, and Mitchell had certainly informed him of much that was going on to the north of Virginia, yet it must have been a great satisfaction to Clayton to know that he belonged to an organization which had national ambitions for the dissemination of knowledge. Because of his remote situation, he could only play a small part, yet it gave him a status for introduction to other members. When he finally met Benjamin Franklin in Williamsburg, it was as a fellow member rather than as a complete stranger. Whether he met or corresponded with any other members of the Philosophical Society not known to him before has not been recorded. There is one, however, who is well worth mentioning in some detail. This was Cadwallader Colden (1688-1776). Collinson had suggested that Colden write to Clayton, but no Clayton letters survive in Colden's voluminous correspondence. Nevertheless, the two men moved in the same scientific circles both at home and abroad, and their common friends were legion.

Colden might well have made a greater contribution to botanical science had he not been a man of many and diverse interests. He seems to have devoted himself seriously to botany for only a brief period of his career. He studied it under Dr. Alston at the University of Edinburgh, receiving his A.B. degree in 1705, and, proceeding to London, he studied medicine. In 1710 he emigrated to Philadelphia, where he remained until 1718, practicing medicine and carrying on a business. He then moved to New York where, in 1720, he became surveyor-general of the colony, and the following year a member of the Governor's Council, a position which he held until his death.

At first glance, Colden's life appears that of a genius at finding sinecures, but actually his interests were so varied and time-consuming that he resented spending even a modicum of time on the dull business of earning a living. As he used deputies for the performance of his duties as surveyor, by 1727 he was able to complete the first part of his *History of the Five Nations*. Still, he found even such responsibilities distracting so, in 1739, he retired to farm at his home, "Coldengham." There his wife, like the long-suffering Mrs. Bartram, supervised farming operations, in order to free her husband for more important things. The Colden children viewed the move to the country with great distaste.[18] Colden thought botany might be a most suitable occupation to divert his daughter Jane, since young ladies, with their interest in clothes, expressed a definite fascination with colour and beauty. Therefore he had translated Linnaeus' *Tables* into English for her use,[19] and Jane Colden became the first lady in America to "profess" Linnaeus' method.[20] "Miss Jenny," as the learned John Ellis called her, also learned to make "impressions"[21] of leaves on paper, using printer's ink. This proved so intriguing that Jane made three hundred of them, one of which Colden sent to Dr. Gronovius, saying that he considered them much more accurate than any description. In this technique, no filament, however delicate, is omitted in the silhouette of the skeletal leaf.

For a time, Dr. Colden was an enthusiastic botanist himself. When Peter Collinson wrote to him in March of 1740, urging him to extend his *History of the Five Nations* to the year 1697, he asked him if he had ever been interested in natural history, and suggested that he take up its study.[22] Then, in 1742, a student from Leiden presented Colden with a copy of Linnaeus' *Tables*.[23] The challenge of the new system was so great that Colden immediately started collecting and classifying the plants growing at "Coldengham." In

1743, Gronovius wrote him "The second part of the Flora virg. is printed; of which I take the liberty to send you a copy, besides a copy of the First part."[24] Colden was already familiar with this book since he had written Collinson in November of 1742: "I have inquired of Mr. Bartram & others to discover this Maryland Ipecocuana but can discover no roots under that name but two both of them taken notice of by Mr. Clayton in Gron—Flora—Virgin."[25] At the end of his letter Gronovius had added that he would appreciate some American plants from Colden, and must have been slightly astonished to receive shortly, not only an impressive collection of plants, but a lengthy manuscript describing them. Gronovius was so impressed that he immediately forwarded both to Dr. Linnaeus for comment. In April, Gronovius wrote to Colden requesting that he send all his "Characters" and quoting from a letter he had just received from Linnaeus: "I have received the letters dated Sept 17th: from these I have learned you had been pleased to produce in America a new Botanist with great judgment if he will be so very outstanding as you and Clayton the American plants will be more fixed than the European."[26] Linnaeus had Colden's manuscript published in the *Transactions of the Royal Society of Uppsala* under the title "Plantarum in Coldinghamia Americae Provincia" in the volumes for the years 1743 and 1744.[27]

In order to show his appreciation of Gronovius' and Linnaeus' interest, Colden lost no time in forwarding plans of Mr. Franklin's new stove to the two men, saying that it might "preserve your health while it keeps you warm at your studies."[28] In thanking his friend, Gronovius told him not to be too surprised to see a description of the stove in Dutch shortly, and in 1746 he wrote to Linnaeus "From Philadelphia, that most elegant city, I have brought together to be printed a little book concerning the new furnace machine."[29] Gronovius and Colden corresponded for many years, but by 1755 Colden was complaining that he had heard little from the Dutchman. By that year, too, Colden had gradually persuaded Jane to take over the botanical interests as well as much of the accompanying correspondence for the family, as he had journeyed into other fields. Unfortunately, nowhere in this correspondence is Clayton mentioned.

Thinking that Colden and John Bartram would be very congenial, Collinson had suggested that the latter call at "Coldengham" when next his travels took him to that area. This Bartram did in the late summer of 1742. He found Colden "facetious, agreeable"[30] and the two became firm friends, each helpful to the other. Bartram was grateful to Colden for sharing his academic skills. When Gronovius wrote to him, Bartram often asked Colden for assistance in deciphering the Dutchman's mixture of English, Latin and Dutch. On sending some of Gronovius' observations, Bartram wrote Colden that he was welcome to keep the original but "I wish thee would be so kind as to coppy it over in English which I can better understand."[31] In one letter, thanking his friend, Bartram wrote: "I have received thy kind letter of december 31st with thy translation of Gronovius' observations on the fossils & shells that I sent him. I am much obliged to thee for doing it. now I can understand ye doctors meaning: before I was doubtfull; ye Lattin pusels me."[32] Bartram's insatiable hunger for understanding of the mystifying world of erudition was personified by a note written on the back of one of Gronovius' letters which he was forwarding to Colden:

Dear Friend
this day I received this open but sealled within A packet of mine so I tooke ye freedom to read it As well as to scribble on it—I wish I could have understood ye books but as little as I can understand lattin I perceive it is a curious performance"[33]

As Bartram valued Colden's erudition, Colden was equally impressed by the Quaker's vast knowledge of nature, garnered over the years of his travels. He urged Bartram to write a book on American plants, and elaborated further: "This I believe may be done with the most advantage to your self by publishing it by subscription in monthly papers of about one shilling Value & to take Gronovius's Flora Virginica for the Foundation of your work & method."[34] Generously, he added that he would assist Bartram with the Latin. Bartram thanked his friend for his suggestion, admitting that he had long con-

Recognition by the Natural History Circle 101

sidered such a project. However, he was reluctant to be hasty, and wished to thoroughly study a book given him by Dr. Douglas,[35] who had described eleven hundred plants growing near Boston. A Virginia doctor had recently visited him and he wrote, "ye Ingenious Doctor Mitchel hath discribed curiously many of ye plants in virginia & hath promised me A book as soon as possible he hath sent it to london to be printed."[36] When he had received this and studied it as well as that of Dr. Douglas, then he might consider starting upon his own book. Unfortunately for eighteenth century botany, this was never done.

A discussion of rhubarb culture is the only instance of a direct reference to Clayton in Colden's correspondence, and it occurs in a letter of Collinson to Colden in 1756. Although the squire of "Coldengham" had done little with botany since the late 1740's, this did not preclude an interest in certain aspects of agricultural experimentation. Collinson was convinced that Dr. Garden was mistaken about certain of his rhubarb seeds being from the East,[37] and he wrote to Colden:

for I have had Seed through their Means[38] and the Jesuits in China. I have raised plants from all these & have had them many years in my Garden they thrive well but never produced ripe Seed— & the Roots have been tryed by our Doct'rs but want the Efficacy of the Eastern—well that was Imputed to our want of Heat—then to remedy that defect it was Sent to Mr Clayton in Gloucester County in Virginia. He expected to do Great Matters with It—but still it does not come up to the Virtues of the Eastern—this makes us Suspect that Wee have not Yett the Right Sort but some Bastard Species—I wish you would write to Mr. Clayton who is a very Learned Friendly Obligeing Gentleman. . . . He will I doubt not send you his observations on the Rhubarb & I dare Saye it bears Seed with Him So he can furnish you.[39]

As with so many of the Clayton research trails, where the path becomes obscure and the end is never found, it is not known if Clayton and Colden developed the friendship which Collinson suggested.

One of the projects which had distracted Colden from botany was the completion of the second part of his history, which he sent to Peter Collinson in order that he might arrange for its printing by Osbourn. Clayton's fellow Virginian, Dr. Mitchell, was then living in England and he helped Collinson to design and draw the title page for Colden's book.[40] Collinson also arranged for the printing of Colden's volume on *The Principles of Action in Matter* in 1751.[41] In his mercantile capacity, he attended to the ordering of a coach for Colden but, as a friend, he directed that all the details be meticulously completed. It was painted a "Glaizd Crimson," the door panels being decorated with lighter red flowers on a silver background; there were glass windows as well as mahogany shutters; the doors were lined with leather, and the carriage itself with a light-coloured cloth trimmed with "Coffy" lace and rows of fringes; even the floor had a carpet.

Collinson was useful to Colden in other respects: he not only selected books suitable for Colden's son, but later used his influence at court to help young Alexander become Postmaster of New York. It must be admitted that his advocacy was not completely disinterested, as he admonished John Bartram: "When thou writes by the packet, always inclose it to my friend Alexander Colden, Esq. Postmaster at New York; and then it costs me nothing."[42] Collinson's recommendations certainly were of value when Alexander's father had his eye on the deputy-governorship of New York, to which position he succeeded in 1761. When Benjamin Franklin was visiting Collinson in England, the Quaker wrote to Colden: "In our Temperate Cupps Wee pour a Libation to the Memory of our Worthy Frd the Govr of N. York wishing Him Health & prosperity."[43]

Occasionally a particular plant seemed to involve a large number of the botanical circle. Such a plant was *Stewartia Malachodendron* L., or "Silky camellia,"[44] sent to Gronovius by Clayton. Linnaeus was impressed with the beauty of this shrub and his description of it was published in *Acta Regia Upsalenti* in 1741. In 1745, at Lawson's request, Gronovius asked Linnaeus to forward this article with any later additions to it that he might send it on to the "kind" Catesby who wished to use it in the Appendix to his *Natural History*. Gronovius added that in asking this favor he was helping two friends, and if Linnaeus complied he would be doing likewise.[45] Linnaeus must have disregarded the suggestion for the plant description for *Stewartia*, used by Catesby, was written by Mitchell, who had called the plant *Malachodendron*.[46] In the *Species Plantarum*, Linnaeus compromised on nomenclature by using Mitchell's as the specific name. Clayton had written a detailed description of *Stewartia* which he sent to Collinson in 1753.[47] It may have been intended for Linnaeus' use in preparing the *Species*, but Collinson never forwarded it until 1757. *Stewartia*, like *Gardenia*, was a minor sensation. The day after Christmas in 1743, Ehret wrote Bäck from Chelsea Garden: "I must let you know that Professor Linnaeus has described that plant which Mr. Catesby has given you, if you can remember a specimen under the name of Anonimos Magnolia affinis p. p. Clayt. it has flower't at Mr Gray's last year, by wich opportunity I have made a good Drawing, and sent a copy through Dr. Lawson to Dr Linnaeus, the name he has given't (by the desire of Dr Lawson and Catesby) was STEWARTIA a Lord of Iland Bute in Scotland a ingenious Gentleman who knows Dr Linnaeus's Methods extremely well."[48] As late as 1768 it was still "scarce and high-priced." In 1777, William Gordon of London sent plants for the Leiden garden. These included a *Stewartia* and a *Ginkgo*.[49] These have not survived, but one of the *Ginkgo* trees which Van Royen planted in 1785 is a treasured exhibit in the garden today.

Linnaeus was not as generous as Gronovius. Collinson, in thanking Bäck for sending him a packet of "Rare Tracts" and some seeds, remarked that "Doc'r Linnaeus never sent me a grain in so many years."[50] He did not hesitate to voice his complaints directly to the culprit himself, and in language not nearly so restrained: "My good friend, I must tell you freely, though my love is universal in Natural History, you have been in my museum and yet you have not sent me the least specimen of either fossil, animal or vegetable. Seeds and specimens I have sent you from year to year, but not the least returns. It is a general complaint that Dr. Linnaeus receives all, and returns nothing. This I tell you as a friend, and as such I hope you will receive it in friendship."[51] In spite of such impertinence, and as was often the case where Collinson was concerned, Linnaeus did not appear to be insulted. Whether Collinson's remarks promoted a more generous spirit on the part of the Scandinavian is not noted.

Clayton was satisfied that Linnaeus was willing to study and name the plants which he sent—so many of which were new species and even new genera. There is no indication that he was disturbed by the fact that credit for the discoveries enhanced Linnaeus' reputation rather than his own. He was content with his friendship. The good fortune which led to the study of Clayton's plants by Linnaeus, at Leiden, also led to an association between the two men which seems to have endured for many years, and to have been mutually beneficial. The extent of their correspondence is difficult to judge, but there are indications that they exchanged seeds, plants, and ideas over a long period of time.

In 1739, Linnaeus left Holland and returned to Sweden to practice medicine. He complained at first that his countrymen "even hesitated to trust him with their dogs,"[52] but his flair for the dramatic and his unquestionable genius insured his recognition before too many years had passed. In 1740, he became a professor at the University of Uppsala. A great advocate of field trips and a superb lecturer, his classes soon became immensely popular.[53] Within a few years he was appointed Dean of the College of Physicians, later becoming Rector of the University until his resignation in 1772. He became physician to the Royal family. When a patent of nobility was granted to him, with typical Linnaean flourish, he adorned the helmet of his crest with a sprig of *Linnaea borealis,* a small creeping, American evergreen plant, named by Gronovius in his honour. In addition to his many duties, Linnaeus still found time to publish the large number of biological treatises which made him famous throughout the world and brought him membership in various foreign academies. He was the only Swedish member of the Berlin Academy of Science. He was very active in his own Swedish

Recognition by the Natural History Circle 105

Royal Academy of Science, founded in 1739, and of which he was the first president.

On May third, 1747, Linnaeus proposed the name of his friend, John Clayton, for membership in the Society. At this same meeting Bäck proposed Bernard de Jussieu and Peter Collinson, and the three nominees were all duly elected to membership along with several others.[54] Clayton's only surviving letter to Linnaeus is the one in which he expressed his appreciation of this great honour.

To an eminent, great and learned man, Master Charles Linnaeus, frequent visitor at the court of his Royal Majesty, professor of Medicine and Botany at the Royal Academy of Upsala, member of the Guard and of the Senate; member [of the Academies] of Montpelier, Stockholm, Berlin; his friend: John Clayton sends his best regards.

I have received your letter, famous one, and I have read it through with the greatest pleasure and I wish it as much as you yourself do that it were in your power to visit this country for here there is no Botanist and no Philosopher whom I am at liberty to consult under present circumstances, and your works, especially *Hort. Clif., Gen. Plan.*, and *Fl. Lapp.*, are beside me night and day. To hear that so many Virginia plants have appeared in your garden at Upsala from seeds sent across the ocean gives me great pleasure. The seeds of Collinsonian and Claytonian Polygala[55] with the spear-like leaves which you desire are not at hand at the moment, but they will be collected during the coming summer and sent to you. The seeds of Claytonia[56] sent through your kindness in August I planted as soon as I received them in a suitable place in my garden in hope of results. I have received the fourth dissertation which you sent and I am deriving great pleasure from it along with grateful thoughts. I am sending a few seeds enclosed to your friend, D. J. Sandin,[57] in order that he may forward them to you. Recently, from notes written in English, I learned that D. Gmelin,[58] professor of Chemistry and Natural History in Petersburg, Russia, had made a classification of the Flora of Siberia which I gladly examined thoroughly to see whether he has proved himself in Siberia such as you have already shown yourself before this in Lapland. Pardon my inexperience in the use of the Latin language since I have lived so long in these rich regions without practice and without conversing with learned men that I have almost forgotten the learning of my youth, such learning as you believe spontaneous. I promise that I shall try to the utmost to deserve this honour which you recently conferred on me in order

that I may prove to be a worthy member of so great a Society, for I shall have seemed to have acquired renown when such a learned and illustrious society deemed me worthy of being selected a member. May you live long and happily, brilliant man that you are, ornament of the Academy of Upsala, and may God preserve and keep the patron of the greatest and best men in the whole of botany, medicine, and literature.
I wrote this in Gloucester, Virginia, October tenth, 1748 A.D.

Devotedly,
John Clayton[59]

Clayton's reference to Gmelin's work on Siberian plants demonstrates the manner in which amateurs and professionals cooperated in the dissemination of botanical news. George Gmelin was one of five German brothers, all of whom were botanists. In a large quarto, illustrated with fifty engravings and entitled *Flora Siberica,* he had published the results of an expedition to Siberia which began in 1733 and lasted almost ten years. Peter Collinson received a gift of this book and in 1748 wrote, "In perusing the preface I observed many wonderful Phenomena which might well deserve the knowledge of the curious. As I believe the book is in few hands & in Lattin, I prevailed with my Learned & Ingenious Fr'd Doc'r Fothergill to give an Extract of It which I hope will be an acceptable Entertainment to the Royal Society."[60] Accordingly, Collinson gave Fothergill's short account of the book before the Society, which was duly recorded in an epitome of the proceedings of the meeting published in the *Gentleman's Magazine,*[61] which John Clayton read in Virginia.

The *Claytonia* seed sent by Linnaeus to Clayton was undoubtedly the species which had been called *Limnia*. In addition to the two North American species of *Claytonia,* there are those which grow in Asia, Australia, and New Zealand, but there is no European species. This seed, therefore, must have been sent to Linnaeus by Gmelin who had procured it in Siberia. In a summary of the *Proceedings* of the Royal Academy of Science in Sweden, the following note appeared: "Mr. *Linnaeus* has given the description and figure of a species of the plant known by the name of Limnia, which, in his opinion, is the same with the *Claytonia* of M. *Gronovius*. It much resembles the *bear's-ear*, but its calyx is of two separate pieces, and its fruit yields but three grains."[62] On hearing Linnaeus' view, Gmelin was convinced that the former was correct.[63]

Another member elected to the Swedish Academy at the May third meeting was the botanist Johann Gottlieb Gleditsch (1714-1786). It is interesting to note on page 161 of the second edition of the *Flora Virginica*, "*Gleditsia Claytoni* apud Linn. char." [the second edition of *Genera Plantarum*, 1742]. This is the "honey locust," now *Gleditsia* (L.). Their common friend, Collinson, was not impressed with Gleditsch, for he wrote that he had been disappointed by his work, finding it "Trifling & inconsistent."[64]

Clayton wrote to Gronovius in November, 1748, that he had received Linnaeus' letters and had written to him. He mentioned that he had sent a great many seeds to Mr. Sandin,[65] a minister living near Philadelphia. It had evidently taken eighteen months for Linnaeus' notification of Clayton's election to the Academy to reach Clayton. There often seemed to be such a delay in transmission as evidenced in one of Bartram's letters to Linnaeus in 1753: "I received about two months past thy letter dated August the 10th, 1750. I was exceedingly pleased to receive so kind a letter from one who so deservedly bears such a superior character for botanical Learning, but was very much concerned that I could not have had it sooner than above two years after it was written, & much the same misfortune happened to those pamphlets thee sent to Dr. Colden & Mr. Clayton which our worthy friend Benjamin Franklin shewed me last week having just received them, which he intended to send according to direction by the next post."[66]

Some of the seeds which Clayton sent to Linnaeus were forwarded through the good offices of Peter Collinson. One of the shortest letters ever written by this Englishman, not noted for his brevity, was in this regard:

Dear Doc. Linnaeus

The Inclosed Seeds By the hand writing came from Mr. Clayton by way of Philadelphia cost mee *postage one shilling & six pence—*

I have not yett received the 6:8:0 for Mr. Catesby 3 books sent September the 3d:1748

     I am much yrs 6:8:0
     P. Collinson 1:6 postage
           6:9:6 of inclosed
              paquet

Lond'n June 14
 1749[67]

It was only after many dunning letters and five years of impatient waiting that Collinson finally collected part of the debt. There is a receipt signed by Peter Borgstron in the Linnean Society: "Received of Mr Carl Linnaeus for account of Mr Peter Collinson in London 2 Guineas which I promise to pay to said Mr Collinson first opportunity by Post. Stockholm the 8th Sept'r 1753."[68]

In 1748, Linnaeus' student, Peter Kalm, visited the Middle Colonies and New England.[69] The son of a Finnish clergyman, born in Sweden in 1716, he matriculated at Abo Academy with the intention of becoming a minister but his bishop persuaded him to change his field to natural history. With this in mind, he transferred to the University of Uppsala, where he became a student of Linnaeus, accompanying him to Russia and the Ukraine in 1744. Three years later he became professor of "œconomie" at Abo, but was given leave almost immediately to accept the offer of a trip to America under the auspices of the Swedish Academy, who wanted a man to search for plants of economic value to Sweden. They were especially interested in a mulberry which could withstand the Swedish climate, in order to develop a silk industry. On his way to America, Kalm stopped in England where he made the acquaintance of Catesby, Collinson, Mitchell, and others of Linnaeus' friends. Gronovius was distressed that he, too, could not meet Kalm, but hoped that Kalm would start a "friendship with Clayton, Colden and Bartram."[70] It was not long after his arrival that Kalm met the latter two, and Benjamin Franklin as well. He made his home in New Jersey, where he married a pastor's widow and from where he took long trips to the northern provinces. Sometimes Bartram accompanied him, and they became firm friends. There is a delightful account of their trip to Niagara Falls, complete with an eighteenth-century engraving which shows how the Falls have changed over the years. Clayton must have read the article avidly, as it appeared in the January issue of the *Gentleman's Magazine* in 1751. Bartram's knowledge of plants was invaluable to Kalm, and he told him much of the flora of the southern colonies, but unfortunately Kalm was unable to visit them. Kalm refers to Clayton in his book, *Travels in North America*, published upon his return to Sweden. He noted that Clayton and Mitchell had made "accurate observations in Virginia and part of Maryland."[71] Towards the end of his stay, Kalm conceived the idea of writing a history of contemporary botanists. On January fourth, 1751, he wrote to Colden, asking him to please send details of his life for this contemplated volume: "of Clayton I hope D. Gronovius will give out his vitae historiam."[72] Apparently Kalm never completed this book. He returned to Sweden in 1751.

VIII
CLAYTON'S TRAVELS

Clayton always found a great deal to interest him in the *Gentleman's Magazine* when it finally reached him. He must have been a bit surprised to find himself mentioned in an article entitled an "Essay on the History of Botany," signed B. Cl——t [perhaps Benjamin Clement, a member of the Royal Society]. One paragraph read:

And here all lovers of this science must acknowledge the obligations they lie under to those eminent botanists Gmelin, Catesby, Kalm, Osbeck, Hasslequist, Clayton, and other curious gentlemen, who have been, or are now carried forward by an ardent desire of promoting their favorite study, and exposing themselves to innumerable dangers, and painful travels, in vicissitudes of climates, rigours of seasons, and abandoning themselves to the inhospitable regions and inhumanity of savages . . . to furnish us with plants hitherto entirely unknown. . . .[1]

It must have been very gratifying to Clayton to know that at least one of the English botanists had some appreciation of the problems of plant explorers. John Bartram certainly would have been pleased, since he frequently commented on their lack of understanding of the difficulties involved. Clayton's travels were not as extensive as Bartram's, but were more extensive than has generally been realized.

Although Clayton may have met few of the scientifically inclined north of Virginia, he did travel briefly in that area in 1746. Isaac Lawson brought the news from England to Gronovius.[2] Presumably, it was from Catesby or Collinson that he had heard of the Virginian's trip. Gronovius immediately wrote to Linnaeus that: "Mr. Clayton had made a vast journey into Canada, and collected a great many unknown plants. I hope he will be safe." This is the only reference to the trip which has been found, so no details are known. It seems most unlikely that Clayton undertook any such expedition on his own. It is far more likely that he took part in some official one. He was often referred to as "Cap. Clayton," and certainly would have been a member of the militia. It is possible that he was a member of Captain Beverly Robinson's company of one hundred and thirty-six officers and men, which sailed in June of 1746 on the H. M. S. Fowey. Robinson's company joined the British and other colonial forces at Albany, from which place an unsuccessful attack was launched on Canada. There was apparently no great enthusiasm for taking part in this action, and Robinson's company was all that Virginia could muster.[3] It is possible that Clayton's botanic interests may have made it more attractive to him than to some others. He would seem to have been a bit old for this sort of thing at fifty-two, but perhaps he was able to go along more as an observer than a combatant. In any event, no other official expedition at this time seems to be known.

The journey to Canada was not Clayton's only long trip, despite statements that he collected only in Virginia, east of the Blue Ridge Mountains. Barton recorded that:

Mr. Jefferson has informed me, that Clayton never crossed the Blue-Ridge. This appears very probable, for had he crossed this great mountainous tract, he could not but have observed (ardent and active as he was, in the pursuit of his favorite study) many of the fine vegetables which are common in this part of Virginia, but which are unknown to the east of the Ridge. After all, however, it is difficult to conceive, that the vigorous botanist, should have consented to leave altogether unexplored, the vegetable treasures of the western parts of Virginia, especially toward the latter period of his life, when, by reason of the removal of the Indian tribes, it was much more safe to visit, and travel through those parts. Several years before the death of Clayton, Mr. John Bartram (of whom we have given some account in the first part of this Journal) repeatedly visited the western, or transmontane parts of Virginia, and was the first botanist to discover a considerable number of plants, of which no mention is made in the *Flora Virginica*.[4]

Bartram, however, writing to Collinson, September 30, 1763, implied that Clayton *had* travelled west of the mountains:

The first time I crossed the Shenandoah, I saw one or two plants, or rather stalk and seed, of the *Meadia,* on its bank. I jumped off, got the seed and brought it home, sent part to thee, and part I saved myself; both [of] which succeeded, and if I had not gone to that spot, perhaps it had been wholly lost to the world. John Clayton asked me where I found it. I described the very spot to him, but neither he nor any person from him could find it after.[5]

And Clayton himself makes it quite definite in a statement in the *Flora Virginica,* evidently overlooked by Barton and Jefferson. In reference to *Napaea,* the glade-mallow, he said: "I brought it back only from the calcareous rocks in the great western valley between the dark blue mountains and it appears in the woods of Augusta County."[6]

Bartram's description of the Valley will explain why he and Clayton could not resist it. He had been travelling in the south, and coming north, crossed the New River and the Alleghanies:

traveling along new Virginia between the North & So Mountains to Potomock river: this great vale of rich limestone land of 300 mile long is A fine part of Virginia watered by the many large branches of three great rivers Potomock, Staunton, A great branch of Roan oak: & two large branch of James river all of which heads in the several ridges of the North mountain: the largest branch of James River is caled Jacksons river on which is 5 wonders or great curiosities first A natural bridge or arch 200 foot high 39 broad & 68 long that unites two mountains 2 A vast cave in A mountain seven mile long 3 A stream on A mountain where water plunges down 200 foot perpendicular 4 A great spring flowing out of the mountain runing and stoping periodicaly 5 A great warm spring 30 foot diameter & those people that sitts in it A little time will be all in A sweat & another about seven mile farther is so hot as to harden egges as is affirmed by those that have been there.[7]

Not only had Clayton collected in the Valley of Virginia, but at least once he seems to have journeyed far to the west of it. On August 27, 1748, Gronovius wrote to Linnaeus: "Clayton's last letters had a presentiment of Bartram's death, which I should grieve over; he relates his own journey into Pennsylvania all the way to the Mississippi, on which he calls to mind a great many curious things."[8] Clayton was very premature, if he was serious in his presentiments concerning Bartram. He probably was merely indignant, as he often was, that he had not heard from Bartram recently. One's first thought is that Gronovius was probably confused. Surely Clayton did not go all the way to the Mississippi, and certainly not by way of Pennsylvania. Further consideration suggests that it is quite possible that he did go to the Mississippi. It is true that the geographic limits of Pennsylvania were not well defined at that time, and it is also true that tributaries of the Mississippi, such as the New River, the Kanawha, and the Ohio, were sometimes called the Mississippi. Little was known of the geography of the western territory. Clayton, however, was one of the few Virginians who had reason to know something about it. He was acquainted with John Peter Saling (Salling, Salley) and very probably knew him well, and Saling had been to the Mississippi.

In 1742, Saling, John Howard, a Shenandoah Valley settler, and four others explored west as far as the Mississippi. They were captured by the French, but after many adventures, reached home. Their information was of assistance in the drawing of both Joshua Fry's and John Mitchell's maps. Their exploration was used, in conjunction with that of Colonel Wood, and Batts and Fallam, to bolster England's claim to the Mississippi Valley.[9]

It is certainly significant, that on June 17, 1748, two months before Gronovius wrote to Linnaeus concerning this trip, a land grant was made:

To Nicholas Davies, John Clayton, Jr., Kemp Whiting, William Bernard, John Peter Saling, and Charles Sinclair, 30,000 acres beyond the North Mountain, beginning near the Saling River extending on both sides of the said River & Thence Westward and southerly in three surveys so as not to interfere with any Lands already Granted and on Condition they do within four Years settle on some part of the Land one family for each Thousand acres & to pay Rights for such Lands only as shall be unsettled at the Expiration of the said four Years.[10]

Not only was Clayton's son associated with Saling in this grant, but also his cousin, Kemp Whiting. This was some six years after Saling and Howard had explored the Mississippi.

The botanic fraternity suffered a great loss by the death of two valued members in the later 1740's. Isaac Lawson, who had so often acted as intermediary between English and Continental scientists, died at the end of May, 1746, at Breda in Holland.[11] He had contracted a malignant fever while attending his sick soldiers. He had remained a close friend of Linnaeus after the latter's return to Sweden, lending him money and doing him many favors. In appreciation, the botanist named the genus *Lawsonia* in his honour. Gronovius noted that "The death of the great Lawson shatters me completely . . . in whom a true friend and a great loss by death."[12] With his death, much of the informal camaraderie between English and Continental botanists was lost. He had been eminently responsible for the fellowship which existed and his frequent trips between England and Holland promoted a feeling of intimacy between them that no correspondence could replace.

Mark Catesby died on December 23, 1749.[13] When he had returned to England in 1726 after his second trip to America, he had worked for Fairchild, the nursery-gardener in Hoxton.[14] Later, he moved to Fulham where he had a large garden and house behind St. Luke's Church. During these years when he was intensely occupied with writing and illustrating his books, loans from Collinson enabled him to continue.[15] Not until 1747 did he complete his *Natural History*. There was material for a third volume, but his death prevented its completion.[16]

Both Lawson's and Catesby's deaths had a definite impact

on John Clayton. In the case of Lawson, and the consequent loosening of ties between Gronovius, Collinson, and Catesby, communication of Clayton's affairs, and the transmission of his plants and letters were not so regular as they had been. As a result, Gronovius, without this stimulus, became more involved in other activities, and his interest in botany waned. In the case of Catesby's death, it was a very personal loss which Clayton felt. He must have been bereft without his friend's many letters, his kindly advice and his constant assistance in forwarding seeds and specimens to Holland. As a consequence, he turned to his more recent friend, Peter Collinson, for advice and discussion, and an intellectual intimacy developed.

Clayton found Collinson as congenial a correspondent as Catesby. In many ways, their relationship was even more stimulating since the Englishman's main interest was botany. In this, his knowledge surpassed that of Catesby. In addition to being fascinated by all phases of horticulture, he had more than a surface acquaintance with the most recent discoveries and theories in the many branches of botanical study. His garden was equalled by few in England and not many private ones in Europe excelled it. His correspondents were numbered in the hundreds and were scattered all over the world. His position as a most active member of the Royal Society was well-established and seldom was a meeting held at which he did not present a paper. As Collinson's interests included all the areas of natural history, the subjects ranged from Dr. Douglas' article on the New England white pine to proposals for establishing peace with the North American Indians; from Collinson's own observations on Cancer-Major, made on the Isle of Wight where he had spent a summer, to Benjamin Franklin's electrical experiments which Collinson had had translated into French and published; from the natural history of the Alpine mouse to the life cycle of the North American cicada; from Dr. Bradley's observations on a comet to his own dissertation on "mule plants," from experiments with Sweet Williams and carnations.[17] Thus, it is not surprising to find Collinson reading one of Clayton's letters at the meeting of the Royal Society on the thirteenth of February, 1752.[18] John Clayton had sent him an extract from a friend's manuscript on the subject of an unusual type of weather, and "some uncommon phenomena relating to it, not before, as I know of, taken notice of by any writer." Clayton continued:

The author says, he can't omit taking notice of a very particular sort of weather, which frequently happens here, tho' for the most part in the spring, latter part of the summer, and sometimes in the winter (if mild). It is generally called here *smoaky* weather, and it is looked upon as a certain presage of drought, it never raining during its continuance, which perhaps is sometimes a fortnight or more. All objects upon the earth, at the distance of 150 yards, and the trees in the horizon appear as if enveloped with smoak. The sun and the moon, when approaching the horizon, appear red, and the first may be long looked upon without the least dazzling or uneasiness to the eye. Now it is the received opinion among the common people, and even some others too of a more improved understanding that this proceeds either from the smoak of the tar-kilns in the south parts of *Virginia,* and in *North Carolina,* or else from that of large fires made by the Indians, when they use that sort of hunting called *fire-hunting,* in which they set fire to the woods in a vast large circle, managing it so as to make the circle still less and less as it burns, and when they have brought it to a convenient size some of them jump in, others stay without, and they generally kill a great quantity of deer, bears, elks, etc. all which, through a natural timidity, will not venture to break through the burning. But I cannot possibly think that it is occasioned by either or both of these imaginary causes, though they should act Conjunctly, they not being by any means adequate to the effect. . . .[19]

Clayton's correspondent continued further with his own elaborate explanation, to which Collinson added his observations that:

it arises merely from a great calm, suddenly succeeding moist and somewhat warm seasons. For the earth being heated more or less by the sun, sends up large quantities of vapours; these, condensed by the tranquil atmosphere unite into particles too large to render vision clear, and too light to fall down in mist or rain. The moment the wind shifts to a cooler quarter, the particles coalesce, as the writer observes, and rain ensues. . . . A woody country, with vales of rich black mould, will be always, *caeteris paribus,* most liable to such phenomena, on the borders of swamps, and near the sea, in profound calm weather; and such seasons must be extremely dispiriting to the inhabitants, rendering them indolent, lifeless, and subject to putrid fevers, during its continuance.

The manuscript also dealt with whirlwinds, horizontal lightning, and other diverse subjects, but Collinson did not enlarge on these topics. He did read Clayton's own postscript, which he had added to the letter:

P. S. In the *Gent. Mag.* for April, 1750, p. 176, after describing the humming-bird, with its nest, etc. it is said "this is the only species of the humming-bird that visits the *English* Colonies in *North America.*" And it is indeed the only sort that I ever saw; but a Gentleman,[20] who lives upon *Pamplico* river, in *North Carolina,* who is a kind of virtuoso, and, I think, seemingly a man of veracity, was here with me last summer, and discoursing the various sorts of humming-birds, he assured me that he had frequently seen a sort of that bird flying from flower to flower in his garden, which was different from ours described in the *Mag.* aforesaid, and whose colour all over he compared to that of the hilt of a mourning sword, or steel mourning buckle.

The Society ordered thanks to Mr. Collinson for "this curious communication." It was then that he sent it to the *Gentleman's Magazine* where it was printed in the June issue under the title "Letter from a Gentleman in Virginia."

Botany's practical applications interested Peter Collinson very much. He wanted to know the feasibility of introducing various foreign crops into England. His curiosity did not end there, as he enlisted men in the Colonies to carry on similar experiments. One of these was John Clayton, who had early been indoctrinated with such ideas by Byrd, who was continually looking for grape vines which would flourish in Virginia. Another of Collinson's recruits in this field was Jared Eliot, a minister and doctor of New Haven, Connecticut. Although his father was a Harvard graduate in the class of 1658, he graduated in one of the earliest classes of the newly-founded Yale University in 1706. His ministerial duties did not preclude an intense interest in agriculture. The results of his studies and experiments he published in a series of six essays on husbandry from 1748 to 1759. These were printed by Benjamin Franklin and the two men became firm friends.

Here again we have an instance of the "botanical fraternity" working its magic. Agriculture was one of the very few fields in which Franklin could claim little knowledge so, in a letter to Eliot the end of the year 1751, he did what he could for his friend that he might remedy this lack.[21] He enclosed part of a letter from Collinson to him, saying that the Englishman had read Eliot's essay and was a great admirer of his. He added a letter of Bartram's, remarking that he was a "plain illiterate man" but yet corresponded with some of Europe's greatest naturalists. Franklin explained that since he was unable to "converse" with Eliot intelligently on agriculture, he was providing him with two correspondents who could. International cooperation in eighteenth century agricultural research is well defined in Collinson's letter to Jared Eliot on March 1, 1754:

I can tell you good News of the Thessaly Wheat. I Sent Some to John Clayton Esqr in Glocester County in Virginia who has had Success & is Delighted with It as you will See by the paragraph from his Letter. in a Little While He will be able to Supply you Wth Seed—So you See my Dear Friend it is not good to have but one String to ones Bow—and He had as bad Success with the Barley So you may make an Exchange.[22]

The paragraph to which Collinson referred was one which he had copied from Clayton's on the back of his letter:

I sowed the Wheat in September now June 1:1753. It agrees well with our Climate being now 6 foot high with Large Bearded Ears & almost Ripe—it agrees with Sicilian Wheat that I have formerly grown here. but the other Sort is quite new to Mee the Ears are now very large & bearded (has Long Grains and from the first formation of the Ears they reclined or hung Downwards Makeing an acute angle with the Stock.
    fr. Jno Clayton Esq in Gloucester County, Virginia

The previous spring, March 1753, Collinson's wife, Mary, had died.[23] By May, he was again writing to his friends, among them Linnaeus. He told him that Parliament had decided to buy Sloane's collection. He hoped soon to welcome him as a member of the Royal Society of London and enclosed some corrections made by Clayton on Catesby's plate of the "Prickly Ash," or "Tooth-ache tree."

To Doc'r Linnaeus
Observations on the Xanthoxylum communicated to mee by Mr Clayton of Virginia

Yrs.
P. Collinson

In the first volume of Mr. Catesby's work I think he has made a mistake in the figure of the Xanthoxylum, and the Flowers are by no means like his draught, in the first Place they have not the least Tincture of red, neither are the Staminas any thing like his. at first Sight it appears to have no Stamina.—and I suspected they were Male & Female in different Trees, and that what I saw were the Female, but as I have 4 or 5 of the Trees in my Garden I examined 'em all and found their fructifications to be exactly the same upon each Tree. I then apply'd my Microscope, and saw clearly that what Seemed to be the Petals are really the Stamina (and It has absolutely no others) having at each Point or Summit some very minute Particles adhering w'ch I take to be the Farina, and also at each Point of these Mock Petulas, there is a small succulent Protuberance of a whitish Colour something transparent to which the Farina adheres, and which I conjecture answers the Purpose of the Antherae in other Plants, under these Stamina is a very Small quinquifid green Calyx or Perianthium. The Seed is covered by a round Green Skin or Capsula, no more than one Seed in each Capsula, and they grow generally two (tho' sometimes three). Sticking so closely together, as to make as it were but one Body upon a little Footstalk about the 10th Part of an Inch long. I forgot to mention that the whole Flower is Green, not the least appearance of white except by the help of the Microscope at the end of the Chives.[24]

Collinson was of assistance in procuring scientific books for Clayton from the Continent. There were other favours which he did for his friend, not the least of which was the introduction of Clayton to James Gordon, the nurseryman at Mile-End, London. Gordon was instrumental in introducing a great number of new plants into England, and his business must have been very lucrative as he made five hundred pounds over a four-year period from the sale of the *Gardenia* alone.[25] Collinson could recommend him most highly:

The Skill & Ingenuity of some Men is surprizing—I was at James Gordon's Gardener at Mile end:—There he showed me a Pot of seedlings of the Cactus or Great Melon Thistle—possibly the first ever raised from Seed. But what displays his great knowledge &

experience in vegetation is his way of raising the finest Dusty seeds; I never saw or hear of any man before himself, that could raise the Dusty seeds of the Kalmia's, Rhododendron's & Azaleas—These charming Shrubs that excel all others, by his care—he furnished every Curious Garden and this Year after 20 years Trial—he showed me the Loblolly Bay of Caroline, coming up from Seed in a way not to be expected—And his sagacity in raising Plants of every description from Cuttings & Roots surpasses all others by which our Gardens are enriched with an infinite variety—And for many years I have not been of a little assistance to him in procuring seeds and Plants from all Countries.[26]

In bringing Gordon and Clayton together, Collinson was furthering this objective. Clayton ordered his seeds from Gordon and the two men found their association mutually beneficial, since the Virginian sometimes supplied the nurseryman with North American seeds.[27]

Collinson's continual interest and vigorous personality must have been a comfort and an inspiration to the Virginian isolated on his plantation in the faraway province. On the other hand, the Quaker had great respect for the opinions of the colonial botanist and wrote Bartram on February 10, 1756, "I thought thine and our friend Clayton's observations so material on Dr. Alston's System, that I put them in the Gentleman's Magazine."[28] In the October, 1754, issue of this same publication, there had appeared an article on the sexes of plants by Charles Alston, M.D., Regius Professor of Botany at the University of Edinburgh.[29] He had been a student of the great Boerhaave, and taught Colden, Garden and Mitchell. Alston had reviewed the theories of Grew, Ray and Linnaeus on the subject and to confute these he had cited several experiments which he had made with spinach, mercury, hemp, and violets. He concluded that plants were not bisexual and that both male and female parts were unnecessary for their reproduction. Alston was considered one of the outstanding botanical authorities, and the University's garden was justly famous. In spite of Alston's reputation, the two colonials, Bartram and Clayton, lost little time in voicing their dissent with this opinion to Collinson. These appeared in the *Gentleman's Magazine* in 1755, under the title "Some Remarks Made on Dr. Alston's Dissertation on the Sexes of Plants by Two Celebrated Botanists of North America, both dated June 10, 1755." Clayton's views were clearly stated:

I was surprised to see in the *Gent. Mag.*, for *Oct.*, last, a little essay by Dr. *Alston*, botanic professor at *Edinb.* endeavouring to overthrow the long established doctrine of the different sexes in plants, and of the necessity of the embrio's being impregnated in some manner by the male dust, or farina of the antherae, in order to the seeds being perfect, and prolific, capable of producing a plant again of the same species.

I wonder that some of your botanists in *England*, or other parts of *Europe*, have not yet answered it, for I have not yet heard that they have.

My opinion on the other side of the question is too well grounded and confirmed, by considering what has been wrote by *Grew*, *Bradley*, *Logan*, *Linnaeus*, Dr. *Parsons*, and some others,[30] to be even staggered by these few experiments, which may possibly be accounted for, as the axiom of the generation of plants (being analogous to that of animals) stands still unimpeached.

At first, some species of violet are known to be what *Linnaeus* calls *monoecia*, or to have male and female fruitful flowers in the same plant.

Then as to the experiments on the spinach, hemp, mercury, etc. who will venture to affirm, that the farina of flowers cannot be carried a great distance by the wind, and when it comes near enough to the stigmas, be strongly attracted by them, and brought into contact. I know that our female fruit-bearing mulberry and persimmons, frequently grow above a mile distant from the male; and I have two female rhamnus's[31] in my garden, which blossom every year, but as there are none of the male species of that shrub in the country, at least near where I live, my female shrubs never yet have perfected their berries.

Then as to the specimens I sent you of the bastard Quarnoclif[32] and other bastard or mule plants, is there not all the reason in the world from thence, and a multitude of other irregular vegetable impregnations, well known to all botanists, and some gardeners, to conclude, that the same law is established in the main, tho' with some little variety of circumstances, but the great author of Nature, for the continuance of the species of plants as for that of animals.

J. C.[33]

In reference to the modifying phrase "bastard or mule plants" Dr. Conway Zirkle, says that "thus far, 'J. C.' (John Clayton?) is the only eighteenth-century botanist yet found who used the word 'bastard' unambiguously in an English sentence so that we know that it meant 'hybrid.' "[34] This, Dr. Zirkle considers important historically as an English botanist hitherto referred to a plant which he disliked as a bastard, rather than giving the word its present connotation.[35]

Specific records of Clayton's activities during the 1750's are practically non-existent. One, which concerned him directly, was a lawsuit in 1754 which he instituted against a neighbor, Thomas Boswell, from whom he had originally acquired some of his land. The botanist contended that one of Boswell's cornfields was partially planted on his land. From the plat,[36] which was ordered to be made by the county surveyor, John Throckmorton, it seems apparent that Clayton should have won his suit but, because no Gloucester County court records of this period survive, we shall probably never know the outcome. This same year a survey was run of the prison grounds, showing the old courthouse, which later burned, two prison buildings, the ordinary, and William Kemp's house.[37]

In addition to Clayton's correspondents, there were new and old friends at home. Among the oldest, was the Reverend John Fox, rector of Ware Church, whom he knew intimately over a period of thirty years. It may have been due to the scholarly attainment required for ministerial appointment that two of Ware's incumbents were very close and congenial friends of Clayton. Ten years younger than the botanist, Fox had been educated at The College of William and Mary, becoming Master of the Indian School there in 1729. His interest in the college lasted many years: he served as a "Visitor" in 1742, and again on the Board of Visitors in 1761.[38] In the spring of 1731, Fox visited England briefly in order to be ordained.[39] He continued teaching until January 21, 1737, when "the Reverend Mr. John Fox was unanimously elected Minister of Ware Parish, in Gloucester County, in the room of the Reverend Mr. Richards, sometime since deceased."[40] And in February of 1738, "the Rev. Mr. John Fox, Minister of Ware Parish, in Glocester County, was marry'd to Mrs. Richards, Relict of the Rev. Mr. Richards, late Minister of the Same Parish."[41] This marriage was tragic and brief. Of their three children, the two daughters died when small: Susannah at three, and Mary at four, leaving only John as the surviving child. Mrs. Fox died in 1742 at the age of thirty-eight. A stone to her memory and that of her two little girls, was erected in the church.[42] John was sent to the school of the Reverend William Gates, held in the glebe house. There were, at one time, twelve scholars, among whom was John Page, a little fellow of nine, who later became a young friend of the older Clayton. The Claytons' cousins, the Whitings, attended the school and so did Edward Carter and Robert Tucker of Norfolk.[43] From this school, young John Fox went to William and Mary for three years from 1754-1757. Not long after this, when he made several trips to Philadelphia on business, he acted as courier for his father's friend, when he carried Clayton's letters to Bartram. With his son away at school, and no other family left, the minister must have been very grateful for "the particular intimate friendship" that he enjoyed with Clayton, a friendship that lasted until Mr. Fox's death in 1764.[44]

Another friend was Benjamin Franklin. When Franklin and Colonel William Hunter of Hampton, Virginia, had been appointed joint deputy postmaster-generals in 1753, they were allowed to receive payment of six hundred pounds for their efforts, provided they could obtain it from the net profits of the operation. Unfortunately, they managed to lose nine hundred pounds during the ensuing four years. The postal service was not only expensive, but extremely inefficient, and its use seems to have been a matter of last resort! In 1739, the *Virginia Gazette* had proudly announced a great improvement: northern mail, which arrived once a month, could now immediately proceed south as far as Edenton, North Carolina. Parks, the printer, was in charge of this southern route. There was now postal service of sorts from as far north as Boston to Charleston, South Carolina, and from there "frequent opportunities to Georgia." It took one week for mail from Philadelphia to reach Williamsburg.

Despite the expense the postal office was a welcome one to Franklin. It permitted him to send both his personal correspondence and that of his friends free of charge. Even more important, his newspaper, *The Pennsylvania Gazette*, was not charged postage, giving it a distinct competitive advantage over its rivals.

Postal business brought Franklin to Virginia in the early spring of 1756. He wrote his wife from Williamsburg that he had had a fine trip requiring but four days to arrive at Colonel Hunter's. On the way they had met Colonel Washington. He was now recovered from his dizziness and felt "gay as a bird." Virginia was a delightful country and the inhabitants "extremely obliging & Polite." He was even more pleased to find that after the short journey he was "in the midst of Spring: Peaches on the Trees as big as Kidney Beans, and Asparagus on the Tables they say they have had these three weeks."[45]

Clayton and Franklin saw each other during the Philadelphian's stay in Williamsburg. It was then that Franklin suggested to the botanist that he direct his mail under a cover addressed to him. In this fashion, postage charges could be avoided. Clayton not only sent mail to Bartram and Garden and Collinson through Franklin, but he also received it from them and from Linnaeus. Thus we find Franklin writing to Dr. Alexander Garden at Charleston, April 14, 1757: "I forwarded your Pacquet & Letter to Mr. Clayton as desired, & free of Charge to Him."[46] It can readily be seen that this was a great boon to Clayton and Franklin's other friends, and encouraged their frequent and lengthy correspondence. Since Clayton sent his letters in covers addressed to Franklin, it might be expected that he would occasionally enclose a letter to Franklin himself. If he did, none have survived, and there is no record of any correspondence between the two men, in spite of the fact that Clayton always referred to him as his friend.[47]

Clayton and Franklin had many friends in common, and their meeting must have been pleasant. Franklin could give Clayton first-hand accounts of many whom he had personally met like Sir Hans Sloane, and others to whom he was very close, like John Bartram, Jared Eliot, and Cadwallader Colden. He could report on the three weeks which Dr. Mitchell had spent in Philadelphia before he sailed—the man whom Franklin identified as "our Dr. Mitchell" when queried by Eliot concerning the cartographer Mitchell whose map appeared at this time. He could describe Linnaeus' friend, Dr. Kalm, and Logan, the man who had done such fine work on the sexes of plants. Clayton must have questioned Franklin as to why the American Philosophical Society was no longer active.

Franklin not only transacted postal business with Colonel Hunter when he visited Virginia, but he received an honorary degree in recognition of his scientific contributions. He had previously been so honored by both Harvard and Yale. On April 2, 1756, The College of William and Mary bestowed upon him an A.M., the first honorary degree awarded by the college.[48]

The letters between Clayton and Alexander Garden, which Franklin so obligingly forwarded for them, do not appear to have survived. We have only the references to their correspondence. Garden, born in Scotland in 1728, was a much younger man. He came to Charleston in the spring of 1752, after a brief period of teaching at King's College, now Columbia University. As a recent graduate in medicine, his immediate reactions to the botanical ignorance of most Charleston doctors, as well as the reason for his interest in Clayton, are expressed in the following excerpts from a letter written January 21, 1753, to his former botany professor at the University of Edinburgh, Dr. Alston:

Upon the Whole I find most of Practitioners here totally ignorant of Botany, that if it was not from what they Learn from the Negroes Strollers & Old Women, I doubt much if they would know a Common Dock from a Cabbage Stock & this is the plain reason why I'm not able to give you a fuller & more satisfactory account of this matter, as I've had but little practice myself yet, since ever I came into the province which is not a year ago.—All the help I have on Botany are very few, being only Physikists. By your Catalogue of the Edinburgh Garden, which I had from you 1751 when I had the honour to attend your Lectures & Demonstrations in the Gardens. Since the Botanicall season was over I've got Clayton's description of the Virginia Plants revised by Gronovius. I've this year collected a good many Plants & made out Descriptions of all that I could not find in any of the Books, which I had on that subject. I'm pretty sure that there are some of them entirely new, and many, far from being ascertained as to yr Class. Gen. or Species such as the lallays: about which plant I've had a Dious [?] Dispute with one of Bernard Jussieu's[49] Disciples here, who is the only one, that understands any thing of Botany in the Province.[50]

Garden's annoyance at the colonial indifference to botany was somewhat assuaged by a northern trip when he met Bartram at Dr. Colden's. The intense excitement engendered in those hours of congenial company, which was undoubtedly augmented by young Jane Colden, is vividly portrayed in Garden's letter to Linnaeus the following year.[51] Colden brought out his treasured botanical works of reference, among which were Linnaeus' *Fundamenta Botanica* and *Classes Plantarum,* with neither of which Garden was familiar. Upon seeing the tremendous impression which these books made on their new friend, Colden and Bartram showed Garden their letters from the great Dr. Linnaeus.

Garden's return journey was broken by a stay in Philadelphia. He described for Colden a visit he had with Bartram while there:

One Day he Dragged me out of town & Entertained me so agreeably with some Elevated Botanicall thoughts on oaks, Firs, Rocks etc. that I forgot I was hungry till we Landed in his house about four Miles from Town. There was no parting with him for two Days . . . His garden is a perfect portraiture of himself, here you meet with a row of rare plants almost covered with weeds, here with a Beautifull Shrub, even Luxuriant Amongst Briars, and in another corner an Elegant & Lofty tree lost in common thicket . . . He had many plants whose names he did not know, most or all of which I had seen & Knew them.[52]

Emboldened by his friends' success, Garden decided to start his own correspondence with Linnaeus the spring following his return from the north. In his second letter to the Swedish botanist he deplored the paucity of Americans who had studied plant life, saying that "Mr. Colden, Mr. Bartram, and Mr. Clayton are the only botanists whom I know of on the continent."[53] We can gather that he lost no time in cultivating at least a correspondence with the co-author of *Flora Virginica* from a letter Peter Collinson wrote to Colden May 19, 1756: "I have had a Letter from Doc'r Garden, he Seems an Ingenious Man—I recommended Mr. Clayton to him. I find they correspond together."⁵⁴ Perhaps Garden stopped by Clayton's home for a visit on his way south, but we have no evidence of anything other than references to their enthusiastic correspondence. Garden named the yellow jessamine *Ellisia* in honour of John Ellis. He had a drawing of it made by Mr. Roupel of Charleston, and sent it to England to be engraved. He wrote to Ellis that he wanted a half dozen copies as "I must send one to Mr. Colden, one to Bartram, and one to Clayton. Please to roll them around such a stick as silks are rolled on, for when they are folded they spoil greatly."⁵⁵

In 1763, Linnaeus proposed Garden for membership in the Royal Society of Arts and Sciences of Uppsala and he was duly elected. It was a just compensation for the innumerable plants and zoological specimens which Garden had sent to Sweden. Through the years, Garden toyed with the idea of joining the Royal Society of London, but the twenty-one pounds' initiation fee required of foreign members for the honour dismayed him.⁵⁶ Even Ehret, the famous botanical illustrator who had made his home in England, was required to pay this sum. Benjamin Franklin seems to have been the only North American whose fees were waived.⁵⁷ It was not until 1773 that Garden finally joined the Society. Perhaps this monetary consideration was the reason why Clayton never became a member, although he has frequently been credited with being one. His accomplishments should easily have merited his election. Not only had his grandfather been a member, but such a large number of his friends were, that it seems unlikely that Collinson or some other one of them did not inquire of Clayton if he were interested in joining.

During the Revolution, Garden's sympathies lay with the Loyalists, and at the close of the war he returned to England. There he died from tuberculosis in 1791. Since his publications were meager, he is perhaps best remembered as the man for whom Linnaeus named the *Gardenia*. This was at the suggestion of their common friend, John Ellis, who wrote to Daniel Solander, a student of Linnaeus, in 1760, "I rec'd your kind letter and only answer to that part of it where Doctor Linnaeus says he can't call Warner's Jasmine Gardenia. I am sorry for it as it will be an absolute affront to Dr. Garden."⁵⁸

IX

"FLORA VIRGINIANA CLAYTON II"

It is unfortunate that little of Clayton's correspondence has been found for the late 1740's and 1750's, as several interesting questions are raised by various letters of his friends at this time. Some degree of strain developed between Gronovius and Clayton. The details are not clear but, on February 13, 1753, Collinson, writing to Bartram, said:

I can't imagine at the long silence of Doctor Gronovius;—whether it is his employ in the government, or whether his taste for Natural History abates, I can't say; but this our friend Clayton tells me,—that he writ him a letter complaining of the expense that attended the conveyance of his specimens to Holland and as good as forbid him sending more; so that it seems to me the last vice that attacks human nature has laid hold on him—that is, coveteousness. I wish it may not be so; but it is more than probable. Postage becomes chargeable, and so he is silent. He is two letters in my debt, and used to be the most punctual correspondent.[1]

Perhaps Collinson was being rather uncharitable toward his old and faithful correspondent. There was an extenuating circumstance. Gronovius was in very poor health. As early as 1750 he wrote to Linnaeus that he had been ill, and in 1754 he wrote to Bartram:

> My own and public affairs, and an indifferent health, have hindered me to show my thankfulness to all my friends and benefactors, being in great fear to become totally paralytic; but since I turn myself to a way of living, as our old patriarchs did, I am quite recovered, for I drink no wine, coffee or thé, but only small beer, and milk mixed with water. My dinner consisted in gruttos and greens boiled in water, without butter, * * avoiding all the delicate aromata which the East and West Indies send to us. What a change it must make in my body, that was from his youth customed at dinner and supper, to a bottle and a half wine, besides the rest when I get a friend! However, I can tell to you, that I left it all at once; in three days the swelling of my feets and cruel pains went off, and I my selv became not at all week, but contrary I get a great strength, and sleep exceeding wel.[2]

Collinson eventually received a letter, for on March 14, 1755, he wrote to Gronovius: "It was with great concern that I heard of your late severe illness. . . . I hope it will please God to prolong a Life so very usefully spent for the sake of your Family & Friends and give you a share of Health to Finish your Flora Virginica so curious a Work & so much wanted as will Ever Doe Honour to your Memory."[3] Collinson was using his old technique of combining flattery with needling to stimulate his friends to greater activity. He added the needling in a later paragraph: "J. Bartram writes mee he has put in a Box a Choice Collection of Okes—& some Drawings of his sons—which you may *Expect Soon*—with Many Curious Remarks—this will Enrich your Flora Virginica the last Edition was Deficient in this article—the acorns are on the Specimens which will be great assistance for the Species."

Clearly Collinson had taken it upon himself to see that Gronovius completed a new edition of the *Flora Virginica* before anything happened to him, for on June fifth of the same year he wrote again saying that the package from Bartram had, at last, been forwarded. "His Son's Drawings are very fine. I wish they could be published—if that could be Done there is some Natural History belonging to each species, which you shall Have besides very fine Specimens of the Oakes &

acorns and another Quire of all the Evergreens of North America but it is to be hoped *your new Edition of the Flo. Virg. will take in all.*"[4] Again on October 14, 1755, he wrote: "We have long Lived in hopes of Seeing a New Edition of the flora Virginica—which would be a work of deal use—I look upon Rauwolph as done for your amusement."[5] There was evidently other correspondence during this period, but we have only one other bit of needling to complete the picture. On October 18, 1756, Collinson wrote: "I had Long before this Time Thanked my Dear Friend Doc'r Gronovius for his Favour, if I could have communicated anything worth the *Postage.*"[6] He added that he was delighted to know that young Laurens Gronovius was learning English, and then continued, "At the same Time Wee commend the Son, Wee Lament his Good Fathers detaining from the Press his New Edition of the Flora Virginica a Work *so much Wanted & so much Desired—& no one* is so well Qualified *as Himself* for so useful a Work—Therefore Wee all flatter our Selves, with Hopes, it will be no longer Detain'd from the Publick."

Gronovius had originally planned to follow Part Two of the *Flora Virginica* with a third part. As early as March 31, 1744, he wrote to Bäck: "Stewartia is a new genus of plant, whose specimen was sent to me by my friend John Clayton from Virginia. . . . I shall make mention of it in the 3th part of the flora virginica, for which I have a good fournishment, and it will comprehend some new Genera, viz Proserpinaca, Polypremum, Menandria, Callicarpa."[7] Part Three did not appear, and by 1747 Gronovius was talking of a new edition instead. On January 6 of that year he wrote to Linnaeus: "No news from America because the French and Spanish intercept all ships. Mitchell, the famous doctor from Virginia, where he wrote a natural history covering all regions, on returning, lost all, except his own body, together with a great many things sent to me by Clayton, Colden and Bartram. This is the fortune of war. . . . Now I have completed into readiness the second edition of Flora Virginica. It is running short so much and a bookseller is undertaking the expense of it."[8] Evidently he exaggerated when he said that it was "completed into readiness" for on May 12 of the same year he wrote to Linnaeus: "It is not permitted to consider the Flora Virginica unless time allows; account books keep me from these occupations."[9] A year later, on May 5, he wrote: "I have received a great number of exciting plants sent by Clayton from Virginia, as well as very rare seeds, all of which I shall share with you at the first opportunity."[10] He made no mention of the *Flora* in this letter, but he wrote again on August 27, 1748: "I shall send you the Arum maximum triphyllum #811 and a similar one, #809, and I wish your opinion concerning these, with those already received, I shall add to the new edition of the Flora Virginica."[11] In this same letter he mentions Clayton's trip to the Mississippi and adds that he will soon "send proofs which I shall prepare for the new Flora Virginica." Five years later, on June 2, 1753, he wrote to Dr. Charles Alston, at the University of Edinburgh, asking him to bring a manuscript of Mitchell's with him when he came to Leiden, because he needed it to finish the *Flora Virginica*.[12] It is not difficult to see why Collinson was tearing his hair. He would not have been any happier if he had been able to read Laurens Gronovius' letter of 25 February 1757, to Linnaeus in which he said: "My father is describing Biblical flowers and is thinking about a second edition of the Flora Virginica."[13]

Thus it is plain that Clayton continued to send Gronovius many plants for years after the second part of the *Flora* was published. Not all of them reached him, but many did. Since Gronovius was assuring other people that he was about ready to publish a new edition, he presumably wrote the same thing to Clayton. It is not surprising that Collinson and others with an interest in it became exasperated with the procrastination of Gronovius. We do not have Clayton's comments, but one can imagine his disgust. Against this background we must evaluate the following development. On Christmas Day, 1757, Collinson wrote to Linnaeus: "Virginia Sep'r 7: 1757 Mr. Clayton writes to Mee—That at Last, I have compleated a New Edition of the Flora Virginica but *when* or *where or how it is to be* printed He says not a Word."[14] Linnaeus might well have been a bit puzzled, unless he had received a previous word about this, since on September 19, 1757, Laurens Gronovius had written to him: "My father is preparing a new enlarged edition of the Virginia plants."[15]

Collinson was not long left in doubt concerning Clayton's publication plans, for on April 25, 1758, John Ellis wrote to Linnaeus:

Mr. Clayton of Virginia has lately sent Mr. Collinson his Flora Virginica greatly enlarged and improved. Mr. Collinson has put it into my hands to look it over. It is intended to be published immediately, as soon as the plates can be got ready which Mr. Ehret has undertaken, and to dissect each New Genus, to shew your system the better. I am now writing Mr. Clayton to dispatch as soon as he can all the specimens of the rarer plants to New York to come by the Packet, that we may not delay the work.[16]

The "copy" of this letter which Ellis retained differs in wording from that quoted by Smith and is of interest,

Mr. Collinson has put into my hands Mr. Clayton's new Edition of his Flora Virginica in Manuscript with very great additions. We propose to have it printed in England and to add some new genera rec'd from other Friends in N. America. It is to be illustrated with Elegant Figures of plants by Mr. Ehret which will be properly depicted. It will be [a] curious work.—We shall have all the specimens from Virginia from whence he takes his descriptions.[17]

There is no way of knowing whether Collinson asked Clayton to let him publish the book, or whether Clayton sought his help. The time which elapsed between Christmas and late April would hardly have been sufficient to support the former idea, but it is quite probable that Collinson knew of Clayton's undertaking at an earlier date. He may even have suggested it. Since he had already published the writings of Colden, Franklin and Logan, it is not surprising that he would be eager to add Clayton's. We have abundant evidence of his concern at Gronovius' delay in publishing.

John Ellis (1710?-1776), the man who was asked by Collinson to look over Clayton's manuscript, was a very active member of the biology group in the Royal Society at this time. He was a merchant, importing such things as Japanese Varnish from Egypt. Later (1764) he became an agent for West

Florida and for Dominica (1770). He gave frequent papers before the Royal Society on a variety of subjects and had worked with Collinson in cataloguing Sloane's collections for the new museum which had just been established. His most important biological contributions were his studies of corals. Among his correspondents in America, in addition to Clayton, were his cousin, Robert Ellis, the governor of Georgia, and Alexander Garden. In May, he wrote to the latter:

Mr. Collinson often desires me write to you to know what kinds of Palms & Palmettos you have among you. I believe the one you sent as a Species of Palm is no more than the tree yucca but beg you please (when ever you send a new genus described according to method) to send the specimen with it. Mr. Collinson has lately rec'd and put into my hands Mr. Clayton's New FLORA VIRGINIANA which he has sent him to be printed here. We shall have an opportunity of printing by way of Appendix your new genera that are ready when you please to send them. Some you have sent which I shall mention to you. Mr. Clayton mentions a palmetto which I suppose grows with you in large size. We want the specimen of the blossoms to describe it.[18]

The Mr. Ehret who had undertaken to do the plates for Clayton's book was Georg Dionysius Ehret (1708-1770). Like Ellis, he was a member of the Royal Society, and he had done the illustrations for Ellis' *Natural History of the Corrallines*, published in 1755. He was born near Heidelberg, the son of a poor farmer, and had been apprenticed as a boy to a German gardener. His drawings of flowers came to the attention of the Margrave of Baden, who encouraged him to undertake a career in botanical illustration. Thus began his travels which took him to many parts of Europe, and brought him many patrons, one of the first and most helpful being Dr. Trew of Nuremberg. In Paris, Bernard de Jussieu suggested that he visit England, where he met Sir Hans Sloane and Philip Miller, whose sister-in-law he later married. He returned to the Continent as he was determined to visit Holland, perhaps to study the fine collections of tulips and hyacinths in a country whose economy was strongly dependent on their culture, and whose blossoms he had painted for the Margrave of Baden as a youngster. Impressed with what he had heard of Linnaeus, he walked from Leiden to Clifford's home in Haarlem, in order to meet him. The two men became close friends, and Clifford engaged Ehret to illustrate Linnaeus' book on his garden, the *Hortus Cliffortianus.* This association of the Swedish botanist and the young German artist resulted in the latter's learning a scientific approach to his study of his models. His drawings combined not only the beauty and grace of the true artist, but the scientific accuracy which made them valuable to the practising botanist. Linnaeus considered him so outstanding that, in 1743 when Ehret had already become established in England, he inquired if he was interested in coming to Uppsala. If he was, he said that he would "procure" him a salary.[19] Ehret was sorely tempted by the offer, which would have meant being with the man whom he considered his friend above all others. By then he was married to Miller's sister-in-law, who was understandably reluctant to leave her native land.[20]

In 1736, Ehret returned to England where he remained permanently. He was the most eminent English botanical illustrator of the eighteenth century. His patrons included the Royal Physician, Dr. Mead, the Duchess of Portland, and Sloane, then president of the Royal Society, for whose *Transactions* Ehret executed many drawings. Of Ehret's plates, Garden wrote: "They are indeed inimitable, and far exceed anything which I could have imagined within the power of human art."[21] This is the same reaction which one feels today in viewing his exquisite drawings, perfect in line and colour and composition from the artistic standpoint, satisfying to the exacting scientist. He became quite the rage as the fashionable instructor of noble young ladies with artistic inclinations. In addition to the many drawings done for his various patrons, Ehret's serious accomplishments included illustrations for many of the finest botanical works of that period, including Brown's *Natural History of Jamaica,* and his own book on the *Exotics.* He had just completed the drawings for Ellis' book when he was engaged to do the illustrations for John Clayton's "Flora."

Clayton's new edition of the *Flora* was to be illustrated by the most celebrated botanical artist of the day. Collinson was sparing no pains in his capacity as publisher to be sure that the book would be a credit to its author and to his friends in the Royal Society. The sort of perfection which he was seeking took time. Clayton had to collect and ship certain rare plants to be drawn by Ehret. The plants took time to reach England and Ehret was a very busy man. It is very natural then to learn that a year after its arrival in England the book had still not been printed. Alexander Garden, at Charleston, wrote Cadwallader Colden in New York, the latest news from London, March 31, 1759: "neither have I learned that there is any thing new in the Literary way appeared lately in any part of Europe. Dr. Linnaeus's new Gen. Plant. & Syst. Naturae were not come over to England in Sept last, neither was your new Edition with the Appendix on Electricity published as I was informed, nor Clayton's Flor. Virgin. published tho I was told that Mr Collinson intended to give it to Miller to put in the press soon."[22] This could have either been Philip Miller at Chelsea Garden or Millar, the well-known printer of the more serious books. His shop was situated "over against St. Clement's Church in the Strand."[23]

Only one letter of Ehret has been found which refers to the new edition. On December 30, 1759, writing to a friend, he refers to an anonymous plant on page 26 of the *Flora* and adds that in a manuscript sent by Clayton to Collinson two years ago this plant has been given the name of *Amsonia*, perhaps for a doctor in Carolina.[24]

Still another member of the fraternity commented on Clayton's new edition, and this was also in connection with *Amsonia*. Daniel C. Solander wrote to Linnaeus on 16 November, 1761: "All the information I could give relating to Amsonia will be seen from the annexed description made from the living plant which flowered this year with Mr. Gordon & Mr. Collinson—the other particulars I gained from a M.S. of Mr. Clayton's Flora Virginica, prepared for a new edition, but whence the name was taken I know not, nor can I learn from any botanist in London, they believe that Clayton named it after someone in North America."[25] In Linnaeus' copy[26] of the *Flora Virginica* (Part One), the name *Amsonia* is written in the margin beside the description on page 26. Thus Clayton's manuscript, completed in the fall of 1757, and received by Collinson in the spring of 1758, was still not printed in November, 1761. His English friends seem to have been no more efficient than Gronovius.

Unfortunately none of those who mentioned Clayton's manuscript made any comment on the rather peculiar situation involved. Gronovius had not only published the first edition, but supposedly had been working for years on a new one. Yet five different members of the fraternity mention the Clayton manuscript without reference to Gronovius. It is not difficult to understand why Clayton, Collinson and others were disgusted with Gronovius, but it *is* surprising that they could write to his old friend and collaborator, Linnaeus, about publishing the new Clayton edition in England, without comment on the one Gronovius was presumably doing. One feels forced to believe that they really thought Gronovius had given it up. Correspondence with him seems to have broken down at this time. Although Laurens Gronovius was writing to Linnaeus, his father's letters to the Swedish botanist ceased after 1750. But Gronovius had found time to edit Rauwolf's *Flora Orientalis*, even if Collinson did regard it as something done for his amusement.

Several weeks before Solander wrote to Linnaeus about *Amsonia*, and referred to Clayton's manuscript, Laurens Gronovius wrote to Linnaeus (October 24, 1761) and mentioned some plants "which are added in the same manner as in the older quarto published by my father, to another and enlarged edition of the *Flora* Virginica."[27] Thus, in the late fall of 1761, two new editions of the *Flora* were apparently nearly ready to go to press.

On January 1, 1762, Laurens Theodore Gronovius wrote the Introduction to the second edition of the *Flora Virginica*. As his father had done with the first edition, Laurens made his introduction a letter to Clayton, explaining the circumstances of its publication. This edition evidently came off the press promptly, because by February first Laurens was sending copies to Linnaeus.[28] In the Introduction he says that after the publication of the second part of the first edition, his father had waited almost sixteen years for plants from Clayton. At last "a small bundle arrived," but that most of those sent afterwards, when war was raging, had been destroyed by "the cruel hands of pirates which spare not even our pursuits." This would sound rather convincing, if one did not remember that eighteen years earlier his father had said that he had "a good fournishment" for the third part of the *Flora*. The "small bundle," somehow does not quite agree with his father's statement fourteen years previously that "I have received a great number of exciting plants from Virginia."

Laurens said that his father had completed the third part of the *Flora*, four years previously, but when it "was ready for the press he was urged by every lover of botany to publish a completely new edition."[29] Laurens continued that his father had been "rather advanced in years and occupied with other affairs" and did not feel up to undertaking a new edition, "but kindly consented to my request that I might undertake the publication of this edition." None of Laurens' explanations would suggest that as early as 1752, according to Collinson, the elder Gronovius had complained of the cost of postage and "as good as forbid his [Clayton] sending more" plants to Holland. Nor would we have any idea that Collinson had been trying for years to persuade him to get on with publishing the new edition. The second edition of the *Flora* was not then the product of years of concentrated work on the part of J. F. Gronovius, but rather something which he apparently toyed with for many years and finally turned over to his son to finish.

There is absolutely no suggestion in Laurens' letter that he knew anything whatever concerning the fact that Clayton had completed an edition of his own four years previously. Is it possible, in view of all the known international correspondence on the subject, that he was entirely ignorant of the other edition?

Despite the many references to Clayton's new edition prior to 1762, not one of later date has been found. It presumably was never printed, since it is entirely unknown. Were Clayton's English friends taken by surprise when the new Leiden edition appeared? Did they then feel that they could not publish Clayton's? What became of Ehret's drawings and Clayton's manuscript? Why had it taken so long to prepare the manuscript for the press? These are but a few of the questions which present themselves. Only speculative answers are possible to any of them. The most reasonable explanation of the whole business would seem to be that Collinson and his group were too ambitious when they planned an elaborately illustrated edition of the *Flora*. Ehret was busy with much other work, and plants from Clayton for him to draw were doubtless slow in coming. Everyone connected with the undertaking was well occupied with other matters. One suspects that they felt sure that Gronovius had given up and that they had plenty of time. It seems truly ironic that they apparently were guilty of the sin of procrastination which beset Gronovius. The manuscript perhaps was returned to Clayton and lost in the previously mentioned fire. Many of Ehret's drawings of Virginia plants are still in existence. Which, if any, of them were drawn for the Clayton edition, there is no way of knowing. It may be significant that Ellis, only three months after the appearance of the new Gronovian edition was referring to Ehert as "a haughty, insolent German blown up with conceit of his superior perfection."[30]

Only one further trace of Clayton's edition has been found. Fortunately it gives some information concerning its content. The Linnean Society of London has in its collections a letter book of John Ellis. This is a somewhat worn, lined notebook, not unlike many inexpensive ones sold today. In it are found sixteen pages of notes, the first of which is headed "*Flora Virginiana Claytonii.*" These pages give the classes which Clayton used and the subclasses and genera which he had assigned to each class, frequently with a synonym for the genus. There are, as might be expected, many similarities between Clayton's and Gronovius' versions, but there are also notable differences. For example, Clayton has added a twenty-fifth class to the twenty-four used by Gronovius,

Palmae—to take care of the palmetto which would not fit anywhere else. Gronovius did not seem to include it. Clayton's Class I, Monandria, has two subclasses, Monogynia and Dygynia. Gronovius has only Monogynia. Clayton has placed the genus *Corispermum* (*Stellaria*) under the Dygynia. In the Gronovian version this genus has been placed in Class XXI, Monoecia Monandria. The genus *Marrubium* is placed in Class II by Gronovius, but appears in Class XIV of Clayton. The genus *Amsonia*, which the fraternity had been discussing for several years, does not appear in the Gronovian edition. Clayton had placed it in Class V, Pentandria Monogynia. *Meadia*, which Bartram felt he had saved for posterity, and which Linnaeus named *Dodecatheon*, appeared in Clayton's edition. Neither *Meadia* nor *Dodecatheon* are in the Gronovian edition. Some twenty-five or more genera appear in Clayton's manuscript which are not in Gronovius' *Flora*. Ellis' notes seem to suggest that Clayton frequently took issue with Linnaeus and other authors, as when he used the genus *Penstemon* and gives *Chelone* Lin. as a synonym, although Linnaeus used *Chelone* as early as in the *Hortus Cliffortianus*; or again, when he called the fringe tree *Oleaster* and gives *Chionanthus* Lin. as a synonym. Linnaeus had called the plant *Chionanthus* in both the *Hortus Cliffortianus* and the *Species Plantarum* (1753). Clayton's description of the plant as given by Gronovius, notes the resemblance of the fruit to the "Oleae Hispanicae." We have no way of knowing either how complete or how accurate Ellis' outline may be. Thus comparison of the organization of the two editions is best left to the interested specialist. (See Appendix for text of Ellis' outline.)

It is, of course, the edition of Laurens Gronovius which is usually intended when reference is made to the *Flora Virginica*. This has been the widely used edition on which its reputation has been based. It was not illustrated, as Clayton's proposed to be, or as his friends proposed for him. In fact, the only illustration in the book is a map of eastern Virginia, which Gronovius credited to Clayton, showing Clayton's collecting trips as dotted lines. This map is, in part, responsible for the erroneous belief that Clayton collected only east of the Blue Ridge Mountains. The fact that the map was either made by Clayton in the 1740's, or copied by him from one of that period, seems to have been generally overlooked. If one checks the dates of formation of the counties shown, the most recently formed was Amelia County in 1735. None of the seven counties formed during the 1750's appear: Dinwiddie and Halifax in 1752; Prince Edward, Sussex, Bedford and Hampshire in 1754; and Loudoun in 1757.

Laurens Gronovius certainly deserves great credit for undertaking to complete the *Flora* after his father had clearly bogged down at the task. To what extent he is responsible for its content is very difficult to say, but one suspects that it was very largely dictated by his father. In spite of the fact that the elder Gronovius did not feel up to doing the work himself, it would be difficult to believe that he did not tell his son how to do it, especially since Laurens was more of a zoologist than a botanist. Its completion was one of the father's last satisfactions, for he died a few months after the new edition appeared.

Fortunate as Clayton was in his long association with Gronovius, it is difficult not to wonder what might have happened had someone like Isaac Lawson been able to keep up an active liaison between Leiden and London. If the publication of the new edition had been one in which they had all collaborated it might have been a much more impressive work. It did not include many things which might have been in it. On May 22, 1762, Collinson wrote to Bartram: "Doctor Gronovius has sent thee a present of a new edition of his *Flora Virginica*, which I have got bound, and given to our friend Franklin to convey to thy hands with two other tracts."[31] On December 3, Bartram replied with scanty enthusiasm: "My thanks to Gronovius for his new edition of the *Flora Virginica*. It's pity the plants beyond the South Mountain, and the draft of that fine country, had not been in it."[32] Bartram in another letter refers to the "South or Allegheny Mountains." Evidently he was disappointed that collecting which he and Clayton had done west of the Alleghenies was not included. Both Collinson and Bartram seem to imply that this is the publication of the elder Gronovius, rather than Laurens.

The plants west of the Allegheny Mountains are not the only things lacking from the new *Flora* which one might have expected to find there. Despite the fact that Linnaeus had adopted the binominal system of nomenclature in the *Species Plantarum* in 1753, the *Flora* retains polynomials throughout. By July, 1740, and perhaps earlier, Clayton was sending Gronovius detailed descriptions, or "Characters" of plants, using the headings Calyx, Corolla, Stamens, Pistil, etc. or abbreviations thereof.[33] Gronovius sent many such descriptions to Linnaeus as those of *Calla virginiculis* and *Acacia triacanthos*, which he sent on September 9, 1741. The *Calla* description appears unchanged, with the headings, as *Calla aquatilis*, or Pole-Cat-weed, on page 141. The *Acacia triacanthos* appears as one of the synonyms of *Gleditsia Claytoni*, the honey-locust, with a very brief description, not at all like that of his letter, on page 161. The same letter contained a full page description of *Liquidambar*, the Sweet gum. The *Flora* has only a brief sketch. Many other examples of such descriptions contained in Gronovius' letters to Linnaeus, but not used in the new edition of the *Flora* could be cited. In fact, less than a dozen descriptions using the headings mentioned, are to be found in the *Flora*. Why some were used and others were not, is not apparent.

Stewartia, which had been something of a sensation, had flowered in various gardens abroad, and had been described by Linnaeus as early as 1741, is given almost no description at all.

Another plant which might have been expected to have been given quite a bit of space was Alexander Garden's Indian Pink Root [*Spigelia?*]. He had corresponded at some length about it to various members of the fraternity since he first wrote to Dr. Alston on the subject in 1753. On Thursday, February 27, 1755, an extract from a letter from Alexander Garden to Dr. John Watson was read before the Royal Society.[34] It contained a description of the Indian Pink Root and proposed a new name for it. Catesby had placed it in the genus *Solanum* and Gronovius, in his *Flora Virginica,* had called it a *Lonicera,* but Garden considered both to be "erroneous." He had created a new genus for it—*Huxhamia,* in honour of Dr. Huxham. Garden definitely expected it to be given special attention in Clayton's edition, for he wrote to John Ellis on February 17, 1759, "I hope Mr. Clayton's book will soon be published; it must be very useful. He will have an account of our Pink root in it."[35] The plant certainly did not appear in the new Gronovian edition as *Huxhamia,* nor is there any Lonicera for which a synonym of *Solanum* is credited to Catesby.

Strangely enough, Garden, who carried on an extensive correspondence with Ellis, was slow in hearing about the Gronovian edition. Writing to Ellis on July 15, 1765, he said "*Apropos*: mentioning Gronovius puts me in mind of enquiring after the new edition of his *Flora Virginica,* which I understand from John Bartram, has been published some years, and that he has a copy sent him, either by Gronovius the father, or the son, with many emendations and additions. Pray let me beg you would be kind enough to desire Mr. Wilson to send me a copy of it."[36]

It will be recalled that Collinson on March 14, 1755, had sent Gronovius a "Choice Collection of Okes" from John Bartram to enrich his *Flora,* and that he noted that the first edition was "Deficient in this article." It is interesting that the new edition contains just seven species of oak. On June 5, 1755, when Collinson actually sent the oaks he had promised, he also sent "another Quire of all the Evergreens of North America." This was presumably "A description of the Evergreens of New England by Paul Dudley. Mss munere Petri Collinson" that appears among the authors cited in the new edition.[37] Yet there are very few evergreens included, and only one, the white pine, actually cites Dudley.

All of the foregoing analysis suggests strongly that Laurens Gronovius pulled together as best he could what his father had started, but that neither he nor his father had included all of the material available to them which might well have been included. In spite of this, the new edition was much enlarged and improved as compared to the first edition. It was reasonably well indexed, and the bibliography cited some one hundred and forty-seven books, manuscripts and articles. Most of the mosses, algae and fungi were new, as were many of the ferns. It was a book "of deal use" as Collinson had known it would be.

The *Flora Virginica* has a certain fascination for the reader of Latin today in the comments which Clayton makes about many of the plants. These may concern the habitat in which he found them, the uses which the Indians or the Colonists had made of them, or some oddity about a plant which aroused his interest. Thus, of *Asclepias* he says "The mountain people dye draperies and hair with the root." *Orchis* root "stimulates beauty." *Marchantia* "mixed with black pepper is praised for the bite of a mad dog." *Cupressus* furnishes the wood for "the roofs with which all the buildings here are covered." *Rudbeckia* "bears a sharp-tasting root and is very valuable in treating the saddle-sores of horses." The less affluent colonials regarded the *Typha* or cat-tails in high esteem. Clayton wrote, "Because it is sweet, the poor regard this plant as a delicacy, in spite of being crammed full of woolly seeds." He discovered *Orobanche* "near the boggy Poropotank-swamp in September. It flowers in sterile places at the roots of trees." *Betula* "bark is pleasing to the taste and is called by the Seneca Rattle-Snake-root. It appears very hard by the Falls of the Potomac River towards the West."

Of the many plants whose medical uses Clayton gave, a number are still used by commercial drug firms, although their specifics may be different. Clayton wrote that *Aletris*, or "Stargrass," was used for insect stings and as a gentle cathartic.[38] The seeds and roots of *Angelica* or "Belly-Ache Root" were used for colic, gas, flatulence, dyspepsia, anorexia—today's uses are not too dissimilar.[39] Clayton said of *Cassia* "The leaves, as a purgative, are similar to the leaves of the Alexandrine Senna."[40] He remarked of the Jimson Weed (*Datura Stramonium* L.): "The whole plant is narcotic; it cools off the outside and is valuable in frost-bite." Today doctors prescribe it to relax asthmatic spasms and as an anodyne similar to belladonna.[41] The ground-up root of "Indian Physik," as the common name implies, was useful as an emetic. Another emetic was the "May apple" (*Podophyllum* L.) which Clayton collected on the mountain slopes. Today the rhizomes are still collected from the wild plants, and the resin obtained from them is useful as a cathartic.[42] The *Helleborus* was considered by Clayton to be employed unwisely by some who "used it foolishly to expel worms in very young children. The Indians kill boys' lice with a powder of the leaves."[43]

It should be noted that Clayton gives considerable evidence of interest in ecology. His comments often include not only the character of habitat in which the plant thrives, but also the time of its flowering, other plants associated with it, methods of propagation, other than flowering, effects of weather, and relations with animals. *Kalmia* was "regarded as being very poisonous for cattle." *Neottia* "flowers in the shade in the autumn." *Mimulus* "rejoices in moist places." *Senecio* "likes shady moist places. It blooms in May." *Quercus* (Willow oak) "sometimes in a mild winter is not deciduous." *Lythrum* "flowers early and droops very quickly and thus is only seen early in the morning." Of *Eupatorium* he says "I have found it by itself and in shady places among Verbenas and Serratulas: it flowers at the beginning of August." *Mentha* "flourishes on shady, moist ground around springs." *Acrostichum* "appears on the roots and trunks of trees and, in the mountains, on the rocks." *Conserva* "is eaten avidly by deer in the summer." He even did some experimental work along these lines. When puzzled by the fact that *Convolvulus* never seemed to bloom, but kept propagating vegetatively, he "collected this root in my garden, continuously cutting off the ends, by this practise it produced one flower in the year 1741. On the 30th day of July the corolla was plainly snow-white and embellished on the edge with a pale red."

One new genus named by Clayton, which still retains its name, appeared in the Flora. This was *Agastache,* of which he said, "I have entitled it Agastache, as they are plants bearing many and large spikes. An inhabitant of the mountains, flowering in August."

The *Flora* continued to be useful for many years. Strange as this may seem, it is the only Flora of Virginia which has been published in the last two hundred years. As early as 1767 there was thought of adding to it. On June 10 of that year, James Manson wrote from England to Van Royen at Rotterdam, about a young Virginia doctor: "Sir, I took care of your letter for Doctor Arthur Lee with great pleasure and I hope he will send you so many plants, well dryed, as may induce you to write a supplement to the Flora Virginica."[44] In 1792, James Greenway, of Dinwiddie County, Virginia, had undertaken a new Flora. This was never published. In 1812, Benjamin Smith Barton published the first 74 pages of what was to be a new *Flora Virginica*. This was to incorporate all of the 1762 Gronovian edition with Barton's additions. Unfortunately it was never completed.[45] Eventually, Asa Gray's *Manual of Botany* supplied the need for a Flora of this region.

The scientific value of the second edition will be discussed in a later chapter. Its charm for a modern reader has been well expressed by Dr. John Dunn (1862-1934) in a letter to a friend:

"A most delightful book!" I exclaimed to myself as I unwillingly laid aside Gronovius *Flora Virginica* of John Clayton, and I began to wonder why this thin old volume I had found so charming, why it was so warming, why its pages so fragrantly aglow. And then I recalled that Quintus Horatius Flaccus, whom I knew intimately enough to call "Horace," still condescends to walk with me, and that from his many talks I had learned enough Latin to appreciate how much *dog* Clayton and Mitchell and Banister put on their writings. I recalled, too, the pictures of the gropings of Linnaeus and his followers as they endeavoured to found securely their "artificial system" and I could understand why *Digitalis* and *Chelone* and *Gerardia* were, in *Flora Virginica* all brothers under their skin and are at the same table and why the "ranunculus hortensis . . . floribus luteis" and the "ranunculus aquaticus . . . floribus albis" sat for Linnaeus both at the same committee meeting.[46]

X
YEARS OF HARVEST

Summer's heat of 1760 was barely noticed by John Clayton for it had at last brought a longed-for visitor to his home—the man with whom he had corresponded so long, John Bartram. As the visit was fleetingly brief, the botanists wasted no time in attempting to compensate for the twenty years in which they apparently had never actually met. In the heat of the Virginia sun, they strolled through Clayton's garden and rode about the plantation. There was much to talk about: Clayton's new edition of the *Flora*; friends Franklin, Garden, Eliot, Collinson, Gronovius, Linnaeus, and others; the latest reports from the botanical world; but, above all else, there was Clayton's garden to be shown his old friend. In fact, there were so many things to do that Clayton completely forgot to show Bartram his prized herbarium and other "natural curiosities."[1] He neglected to question him in regard to several puzzling plants in the garden. They did remember to discuss at length what seeds and plants they might exchange and how they would be sent. Bartram was unwell, but in spite of a troublesome cough and fever, insisted that he had to leave regardless of his friend's concern. It was with relief that Clayton heard seven months later that Bartram had suffered no ill effects.[2] The Virginian was desolate after his visitor left and wrote him, "as we were just beginning an acquaintance, the parting with you so soon, made me very melancholy for some time and I have since frequently wished that I could have prevailed with you by some means or other to have stayed with me much longer." Clayton's enthusiasm over their meeting can be judged by the fact that he sent three letters to Philadelphia before he received one. The first he wrote in July. To his delight he had found that his neighbor, Captain Bentley, was going directly to Bartram's city in September where he would stay for a month, which time would be perfect for removing any rooted plants. Captain Bentley volunteered to transport any which Bartram might care to send to Clayton. As Bentley was coming by ship, this guaranteed a safe conveyance to within three miles of Clayton's home. It was far better than the original plan of sending their plant exchanges to Colonel Hunter's at Hampton. Clayton wrote a short note the next day, in addition to the one he wrote August 30, saying, "I have sent you, inclosed, some seed of a new plant, which I presume is a stranger in your northern part of the world. Indeed it grows here only in the southern parts of the colony. I have it in my garden, but have quite forgot whether I showed it to you when I had the great favour of your company. If I did, I believe I told you that it was to be called Amsonia after a doctor here; but I think the name inscribed upon the inclosed more proper, as it answers to the particular form of its seed." With the *Amsonia* seed, he included some of *Pyrethrum,* but he was doubtful of its value. In all three letters he reminded Bartram of plants which he had promised to send, among which were Arbor Vitae, Loblolly Bays, Lupines, and "Northern Spruce Firr."

Bartram's letter was written in mid-November, but Clayton did not receive it until the end of January, 1761. By that time, it was considerably battered from handling and, in the process, had lost the "Striped stock Gilly flower seed" which Clayton had particularly wanted. Bartram suggested several future meeting-places, but Clayton felt that it would be impossible for him to join Bartram at any of them. He confessed that he was in a quandary as to how to send future communications: "When Mr. Franklin was at W'msburg, he desired me, if I had occasion to write to you, or Dr Garden, by the way of Philadelphia, to send the letters, under a cover directed for him, in order to save paying postage, but now as he is not in America, I don't know very well how to act, if I should have no other way of writing to you than by the Post."[3] His concern was, of course, for Bartram who must pay the postage on the mail received.

His difficulties were partially solved by an event in the previous month which may have caused the delay in replying to Bartram's letter. This was the wedding of his close friend, William Byrd, III, whose first wife had died leaving him with four small children. The bride was Mary Willing, daughter of Charles and Anne Shippen Willing of Philadelphia.[4] She was Franklin's god-daughter, which made her doubly welcome to the community. In directing her reading, Franklin had cultivated a knowledgeable woman, a rather unusual type for the eighteenth century when women's minds were considered negligible. Packages of books still came to her from her godfather, sent all the way from Europe. The new Mrs. Byrd had several brothers. Since they were frequent visitors at "Westover," they were of assistance to Clayton in transporting his letters to Philadelphia.

His first experience in employing these services was disappointing.[5] He had entrusted his letter to someone who had directions to leave it at Colonel Byrd's. Instead, the rascal had committed the unpardonable sin of depositing it in the post office in Williamsburg. As a result, it was a long time before Bartram received it. This delay was not the only cause of the paucity of Bartram's letters. As a correspondent, the busy, itinerant Quaker was far from satisfactory. After a long silence on his part, Clayton complained on March 16, 1763: "I have been in great expectation a long tedious time of having the satisfaction of receiving a letter from you, but alas! my wishes and expectation have hitherto been quite disappointed, and if it were not for my correspondence with Mr Collinson, and now and then meeting with persons from Philadelphia, I should be totally in the dark as to your being still in the land of the living . . . I hear by common fame that you have made some excursions in quest of vegetables, as far as the Lakes Michigan and Superior, and should be highly[6] delighted with some few sketches and epitome of your travels and discoveries in the vegetable kingdom. I had much rather have it from you, than at second-hand from our friend Collinson, who is generally, upon such a topick too concise. I should in particular be very glad to know if you saw anything of the Canadian Bonduc, or Nickar-tree,[7] and if you brought any of the seed home with you, should esteem it a great favour to be admitted to participate with you, in that, or any other curious seed where your stock is sufficient."[8] Clayton's exasperation produced two long and welcome letters from his friend, in which Bartram described his expedition at length.[9] He included such glowing accounts of unusual plants that Clayton again begged him to send him some seeds and roots, wishing that he could view them all and converse with his "worthy friend" in his garden. Clayton promised to forward some of the red-flowered "turtle-head" shortly. In return, he would appreciate some seed of the "Carolina Tippity Twitchet" (Venus fly-trap), with directions as to its culture. He was certain, now that their common friend, Mr. Franklin, was again in the country, that he would be good enough "to frank a small parcel of seeds from you to him who is your sincere and affectionate friend."

Some years previously both Clayton and Bartram had hoped to share in some seeds which would have travelled a long distance to reach them. John Ellis, on December 12, 1760, at the request of the Society for the Encouragement of Art, Science and Commerce had sent tea seeds imbedded in balls of wax "to all our Govern'rs & Chief Botanists in N. America." Ellis wrote Linnaeus that "as these seeds were brought from Ningpo near the Lat. of 20 N. in China where the weather is attended with snow & frost from this time of the year to the middle of February I do not doubt but they will succeed."[10] The list of men to whom the balls were sent included Franklin, Garden, Clayton, Bartram, Colden, Linnaeus, Arthur Dobbs of North Carolina, James Wright, and Pickering Robinson of Georgia. In April, Ellis wrote to Garden: "I must now tell you of a great misfortune you have had. The New York packet, with Tea-seeds in wax, sent by me to you and all the Governors on the continent of North America, was taken by the French Dec. 27th last. They were all packed in sundry letters, by Mr. Hampden our Post-master-general."[11] The tea seeds planted by Ellis himself failed to germinate.

The late spring of 1764 was saddened for Clayton by the death of his very close friend and neighbor, the Reverend John Fox. In order to settle his father's affairs, the son made several trips to Philadelphia, on which he carried Clayton's letters and parcels to Bartram, including the following one:

June 30, 1764

Dear worthy friend

Having so good an opportunity I could not forbear laying hold of it to acknowledge myself highly obliged to you for your agreeable letter of the first of last month, the seeds of the Meadia & specimen of one of its flowers inclosed. Since I wrote to you in February last, I find I have several of that plant come up in my garden, the largest pushed out 4 or 5 leaves, but gave not the least sign of blossoming. I placed 'em in a cool, shady situation, yet, though we have had hitherto the coolest summer I ever knew in Virginia, their leaves are all mouldered away and gone. I think they appeared to be eaten by some imperceptible insects. It pleases me to hear of your fine collection of vegetables, although I am debarred from gratifying my eyes with the sight of 'em, or my heart with the company and conversation of the esteemed collector. The young gentleman who brings this, is the only son of a very worthy clergyman, very lately deceased, who was minister of the parish where I live, now thirty years, during all which time there was a particular intimate friendship between us. He comes to seek an estate in your Province, which was purchased, as I am informed, by his grandfather and consists of a tract of land lying near a place called the Walch Tract and when his grandfather dyed, there were some slaves upon it. He has got a considerable estate in this County and is a very honest, well disposed, good-natured young man. The Stavesacre seed is not near ripe, but you may depend upon my saving a sufficient quantity of it for you and of any other plant in my garden that you'l let me know will be acceptable. If you have any of the seed of the Carolina Sensitive leaf to spare, or any other curious plant or shrub, I shall be very much obliged to you for a small quantity by the return of Mr. John Fox, who will wait upon you and take great care [?] of anything you will be so kind as to send to Dear Sir

Your most sincere and affectionate friend
John Clayton

I fancy he would take the trouble of bringing me a small box with some roots of that sensitive leaf planted in earth as he goes up our Bay of Delaware in a very good vessel.[12]

Clayton is still referring to *Meadia* in 1764. Ten years earlier a critical review of Linnaeus' *Species Plantarum* had appeared in the *Gentleman's Magazine* with the following comment on the name of this plant: "But of all others, why should the name Meadia be altered for that of Dodecatheon? The former appellation was given by *Catesby* to a very beautiful *American* plant, not reduced to any genus, in honour of his patron Dr. *Mead,* and it is well described and figured in his *Natural History of Carolina.*"[13] Ellis had expressed his disapproval directly to Linnaeus in a letter May 31, 1757: "I am sorry you changed the name of Meadia of Catesby, it gave great offense to the lovers of Botany, particularly as you changed it to an obsolete one."[14]

Clayton was taken ill with intermittent fever the end of October, 1764, and remained unwell for months, chafing at being confined to the house.[15] His morale was not improved by a severe winter, with below-freezing weather for weeks at a time and many snows. In March, he was cheered by the good news from Collinson that Bartram had been appointed King's Botanist. With his letter of congratulation, the Bartram-Clayton correspondence comes to a close, but later letters were probably lost or destroyed.[16] It is possible that they may lie in some obscure autograph collection, or in private hands.

Clayton was now seventy-one years old. His children were grown and he had quite a number of grandchildren to interest him. His oldest son, John, and his wife, Elizabeth Willis, had settled at Richmond, the new city which had been laid out by William Byrd II. They had six children: John, William,

Henry, Jasper, Mildred and Anne. The large land grant which John, Peter Saling, and others had received in 1748, was probably in the nature of a speculation. For serious farming operations he needed land closer home. How much of this he may have had we do not know, but in 1759 he made a verbal agreement with his younger brother, William, to relinquish all rights as the oldest son to their father's English property of "Morehouse." In return, William deeded him a "valuable tract of land lying in the County of Hanover in the state of Virginia and sundry slaves together with the stocks of cattle, horses and hogs, Indian corn and sundry articles such as plantation utensils and also one hundred pounds in money."[17] Possibly this was the land described in the *Virginia Gazette*, July 11, 1766, in an advertisement of one hundred acres of land for sale in Hanover County, called "Horseshoe," which, with another tract in New Kent County, was "to be sold (during the life of John Clayton of Henrico County, who is very healthy and about 40 years of age)."[18] In any event, it was this agreement between John Clayton, Jr., and his brother William, which lead to the preservation of copies of their father's and grandfather's wills. In 1790, John or his son, John III, seems to have regretted the bargain, and brought suit against William for the recovery of "Morehouse." Copies of the wills were produced as evidence for the defense. They found their way to England, and eventually returned to this country in the 1940's with the Jennings' papers. This was fortunate, since the original wills had been lost along with other Gloucester records stored in Richmond for safe-keeping, when the city was burned during the Civil War.[19]

Clayton's son, William, and his wife, Elvira, lived a little closer to Gloucester than did John and his family. William, following in his father's and uncle's footsteps, was Clerk of Court, for New Kent County. He was a member of the House of Burgesses 1769-1774,[20] a colonel in the militia,[21] and a delegate to the 1788 Convention. The William Claytons' plantation was known as "East Greenwich"[22] and there they lived with their three children, William Beverly, Elvira, and Mary Anne.

The other four surviving Clayton children lived in Gloucester, two married and two single. Jasper was deputy clerk to his father in 1762.[23] In 1763, he became Deputy Sheriff of the County. He had a three-hundred acre plantation and two carriages on which his tax was one pound, two shillings, seven pence.[24] He had three sons and one daughter, the eldest son being named John and the second, Jasper, to insure confusion of names! The third son was Thomas Whiting Clayton. Hargreaves gives an amusing, if perhaps prejudiced, account of this youngest son and his father a few years after the botanist's death: "I was well acquainted with Jasper, for he being a widower, paid his addresses to Col. Churchill's eldest Daughter, and his hopefull son Tom courted the next at the same time.... Therefore were I to tell my story right, I should trace the Family of Clayton's as far back as possible but the present Branch in Virginia is not worth the Enquiry, for Jasper is an Ignorant fellow, and so great a lyar, that he is become a Proverb, and his son Tom is a vain Cock's-comb-ical puppy." Hargreaves continued, saying that the botanist had left an herbarium "which Jasper learnedly call'd 'Petrifactions,' not withstanding I did all in my power to persuade him, that they were not yet turn'd into Stone, but he would not be convinc'd. At another time, talking to him about certain Plants, he seriously told me that he verily believed they were Poison, for he had heard his father say, they were Antidotes!! Now, the best of all is, Jasper pretends to be a Botanist—and sets an high value upon his Petrifactions, Books of Natural History, etc. of which his father left him a great number."[25]

Clayton's daughter, Lucy, married John Hughes. They had two sons, Jasper, born in 1757, and Thomas. The other daughter, Catherine, was still unmarried at the time of her father's death and her brother, Thomas, also seems to have remained single. Apparently he was the only one of Clayton's sons to study abroad, although it will be remembered that Clayton had planned to send John to Cambridge. Thomas studied medicine at the University of Edinburgh. Nothing is known of his earlier education. An unidentified Clayton at Eton in 1753 could have been he. Seemingly the botanist was impressed by the reputation of the University of Edinburgh, even if he did disagree with Dr. Alston on some botanical matters, since he broke the family tradition of Cambridge. Edinburgh was popular with Virginians at this time. At fifteen minutes past noon on May 19, 1758, young Thomas Clayton was examined by three members of the faculty: professors Hamilton, Balfour, and Neill. Having satisfactorily defended his thesis, *De Parca et Simplice Medicina*, and passed the examination of his knowledge, he was awarded his degree. One can imagine his father's pride in this event, and his pleasure in the following dedication of Thomas' thesis: "These first studies, by right, are owed to John Clayton, armiger, the very best father who spared no costs in introducing [me] to learning."[26]

Clayton had made certain that his son Thomas met Peter Collinson while he was abroad. They evidently became good friends, as they continued to correspond after Thomas returned to Virginia to practice. The cool climate of Scotland seems to have spoiled him for the heat of eastern Virginia, for he wrote to Collinson a year later, "The greatest inconveniency that attends this climate of Virginia is the intense heat—insomuch that I have been obliged to lay down in the coolest room in the house from Tenn in the Morning to six o'clock in the Evening—and all the Time in a perfect sweat—."[27] Perhaps it was the heat which discouraged him from answering letters, for one C. Bentinck wrote to Van Royen in 1762: "It disappoints me that I am unable to have any American seeds. A year and a half ago I wrote young Clayton, whom I had learned had returned to Virginia, but I do not know if he received my letter for I have had no news."[28] Perhaps the Virginia weather was too much for Thomas, or possibly the life seemed dull after Edinburgh and London. In any event, he returned to London to practice. The degree of his success there may be judged from the following letter of Peter Collinson, who was as usual being the good Samaritan:

London March 25, 1768

Copy to Dr. Tho. Clayton
My Dear Doc'r

It is ungenerous to confess Faults but its better to mend them— it is our duty both in a Moral and Religious Sence.

Never think of the gratifications of London as Innocent, these are Transient if Illicit. is the pain & suffering of Body & Mind a compensation for such momentary Joys. the gay scenes of Youth quickly fade away. Happy are they that can reflect on them with that peace and serenity of mind, which is the result of Temperance & Moderation in all occasions.

But what do I hear wisper'd about that Doc'r Clayton is a gentle Clever Fellow & knows his business, but gives way to such indolent, Lazy Habits, Lays a Bed & Loiters about, is very indifferent of going any where when sent for, a Poor recompense for so Liberal an Education are these things so you know well—if not, they do you an injustice.

Consider how well Qualified you [from] the first scene of Life. Now is the Time to Lay the foundations of future busyness & prosperity. Then Exert your Genius, be indefatigable in your application—Give proof of your abilities & Lett the Least acts of your Life meet with a General Applause—it gives me a Peculiar satisfaction to know you have met with success—to some advantage —my dear Doc'r it is all in your own power. You cannot accuse your Father he has done his part. If you, that are so well accomplished [do] but yours all will be well. it will be a disgrace to Human Nature, ingratitude in the highest Degree to the great author of your being, for those fine endowments, if you suffer yourself to sink into supineness and Stupidity in the Prime of Life, in the Vigor of Youth, when Reason, when Interest, when Duty calls on you to Quit the Couch of Ease & fly on the wings of morning, to assist & Relieve your fellow Creatures in Distress.

To one of your Good Understanding much less might be said— but it proceeds from the Respect I have for you and an anxiousness for your welfare. Accept of these overflowings of good will, with that candor with which they was Dictated, & believe me to be what I really am

Your Sincere Friend
P. Collinson[29]

This letter had the desired effect, as Tom returned to Virginia shortly afterwards. In October of 1769, he was inserting an advertisement in the *Gazette*: "To be sold, at Gloucester court-house, for ready money, on Thursday the 4th of November next, being court day, A valuable Negro man named Toney, in the possession of Dr. Thomas Clayton, and taken by execution. He was formerly the property of Mr. William Kennon, and sold by him to the said Clayton. Therefore if any person has a right of claim to the said slave, they are desired to make it known, at or before the day of sale, to the sheriff."[30] Tom's Virginia practice seems to have been more successful than his English one for the 1770 Tax List described him as owning four hundred and fifty acres, three negroes, four horses, and a carriage.[31] Clayton must have considered Tom already well-provided for, as he only left him the sum of one hundred pounds.

Clayton was delighted to welcome home the prodigal. Though he might be indolent and lacking in ambition, young Tom was a gay and amusing companion for his father. He could tell him of the many changes in his native land and of Collinson, and perhaps other friends, whom Clayton only knew by correspondence. Since the study of botany was an important aspect of medical curriculum of the period, the two men had much in common. Governor Page later wrote that the botanist had a "high relish for witty conversation, and classical allusions, which his son, the doctor, and Mr. Fontaine, the minister of his parish, often highly gratified."[32]

Like Tom, the Reverend James Maury Fontaine was a comparatively young man. A nephew of John Fontaine, he had succeeded Mr. Fox, and in addition to his ministerial duties, he ran a small school in Ware Parish. Like his predecessor, he served on the Board of Visitors of The College of William and Mary. With this connection, both in his and Fox's time, Clayton was in a position to realize the improvements which had been made in the college. This, and the superficial approach to life acquired by Tom abroad, may have influenced Clayton in seemingly being content to see his grandsons attend the Virginia college, rather than an English or Scotch one. As early as 1763, Lucy's son, Thomas Hughes, was a student at the grammar school run by William and Mary. In 1770 he entered the college, where he was joined two years later by Jasper Clayton's son, John.[33]

Another controversy between Clayton and his neighbor, Thomas Boswell, with whom he had a property line dispute in 1754, occurred in the summer of 1768. In order to satisfy his creditors, Boswell had advertised a lottery, assuring the public that all his misfortunes were not due to lack of industry, but rather to accident and to a proclivity on his part for a too "hospitable, friendly, & generous temper" in acting as security for his friends. Each of the three hundred and five tickets was to be sold for five pounds in order that a sum of 1525 pounds might be realized. The drawing would take place at Gloucester Court House the last Thursday in August. Prizes included land and slaves, among whom were "Sam," 26; "Ned," 19; a "little Negro woman named Rachel about 18"; and another, whose name was "Beck." The lottery was under the management of several gentlemen including Clayton's son, Jasper, and his in-laws, James and Francis Whiting.[34] Lotteries were considered eminently respectable, and many were held. A list of the managers of one read like an historical "hall of fame": John Randolph, Fielding Lewis, George Washington, Richard Henry Lee, and Edmund Pendleton.

When Mr. Boswell turned to the back page of the next week's *Gazette,* he realized that interest had been aroused in his lottery, but unfortunately just the type which he was attempting to avoid:

Upon the appearance of a Scheme in the Virginia Gazette, for disposing of sundry Slaves, etc. by lottery lately published by Capt. Thomas Boswell, of the county of Gloucester, I think it highly necessary to inform the publick in time, in order to prevent, as far as is in my power, the trouble and expense of future law suits, that the following Negro slaves, designed as prizes in the said lottery; viz Sam, Rachel, Beck, and Ned, with all the present and future increase of the said two female slaves, were mortgaged to the subscriber on the 13th of May, 1762, by the said Thomas Boswell, for the sum of 250L. current money, which sum, with interest thereon from the 13th of May, 1762, is at this time due to
JOHN CLAYTON[35]

In view of Boswell's effrontery in offering as prizes slaves mortgaged to Clayton on the Clerk of Court's own door-step, the botanist's announcement appears most restrained. Nevertheless, Boswell must have convinced Clayton of the economic soundness of the whole proceeding, for on June 16 the public read: "Since my advertising in last week's Gazette that four of the Negroes mentioned in Capt. Thomas Boswell's lottery to be disposed of were mortgaged to me, I think it necessary to acquaint the publick that I have received sufficient security for the payment of the money due from him, and that I have no objection to his lottery going forward,"[36] signed by John Clayton. The lottery did not take place in August as planned, but was postponed until November. Like so many events of that period, which titillate one's interest and suspense only to find no one has recorded the outcome, the prize-winners were never announced in the *Gazette*.

"Morehouse," his English property at Hawkhurst, had become a source of concern to Clayton. The management of any estate three thousand miles away was difficult under the best of circumstances and an owner was utterly dependent on his agents. Samuel Durant, his father's steward, had given up his stewardship, refusing to collect the rents from the various tenants.[37] Clayton was forced to appoint a new man, Thomas Redford. He was extremely fortunate in his choice. Redford was a man of undistinguished origins, but he was most responsible, very intelligent, and one who shared Clayton's interests. From a contemporary's account, it is quite obvious that Clayton could not have found one more suitable:

> It were unjust to quit the account of this parish without a tribute to the memory of Mr. Thomas Redford, a respectable inhabitant. He was a man of strong natural understanding, and had by constant application acquired much knowledge; as the information he possessed, however, was all his own attainment, he had often formed sentiments that were peculiar, and which increased acquaintance with science, and commerce with the world, sometimes compelled him to alter.
>
> He was for many years assistant to the Receiver-General of the County; and his unceasing punctuality and strict integrity recommended him to be agent for several noblemen and gentlemen who had estates in the neighbourhood, and who did not reside; in this capacity his letters were always well written, and a proof how much superior native good sense is to unmeaning civility and parade.
>
> He was occasionally an anonymous writer in the Gentleman's Magazine, and his style and character are sufficiently marked to those who were acquainted with him. A Disquisition on Spiders darting their Webs was one of his subjects of controversy, in which like many theorists, he maintained the impossibility of the fact till experience had convinced him of the fallacy of his principle.

He died, after a long and painful illness, October 1774, at the age of 67.

Such a man was truly the ornament of his native village.[38]

These essays on the spiders may have brought Redford to Clayton's attention. Collinson evidently had started the controversy, which Redford answered, stating his observations in a series which started in 1767, and which were signed "Mary Street, The Weald, Kent."[39]

With the appointment of Redford, Clayton's troubles were not yet at an end. Durant wrote him a disagreeable letter, demanding his salary, although he had refused to receive rents for Clayton. Moreover, he still had in his possession maps of the estate and some "muskets with their bayonets," which Clayton directed the Nortons to have him turn over to Redford. It was a comfort that they, at least, were handling his affairs so well, and Clayton wrote to John Norton in August, 1768: "I am vastly pleased with the account of your proceedings at Hawkhurst and approve of every step you have taken being perfectly well satisfied with the raise of rent & that which will be raised at the expiration of my Steward's lease, and greatly obliged to you for espousing my interests so acutely."[40]

Not only did Redford act as a steward for Clayton, but he also leased a part of the property from him. Yearly, he forwarded his accounts to Virginia through the offices of the Nortons. Clayton was well satisfied with his stewardship and, in 1771, their lease was renewed for twenty years. A beautiful parchment attesting to this, is preserved in the archives of Colonial Williamsburg, Inc. It sets forth in great detail duties of the tenant, and reserves the right to the sale of timber to Clayton, as well as "the privilege of Hunting, Fishing and Fowling on the said premises and the Game, Fish and Fowl thereon produced to take away and dispose of." With the renewal of the lease, the increase of rent which Clayton had wanted had not been arranged by Norton as had been done in the cases of the other tenants. For some reason it had been overlooked, and Clayton reminded him of this omission several times.

At Clayton's death, and Redford's shortly thereafter,

another man of the same name, presumably his son, assumed the stewardship for William Clayton. During the Revolution, he paid the taxes and collected the rents which he forwarded to George Flowerdewe Norton in London. From time to time, William drew on the Nortons for the amount due to him on the Kentish lands.[41] The taxes were recorded as paid by this younger Redford until 1790, when it must be assumed that "Morehouse" was finally sold, and the Clayton family broke the last ties with their homeland.[42]

In his reply to John Norton, September 1, 1768, Clayton enclosed a letter to be delivered to Peter Collinson.[43] Ironically, his old friend had been dead almost three weeks. He had been taken ill the beginning of August and had died within a few days. Thomas Collinson's account of his death is peculiarly touching as it expressed so clearly his uncle's gentle character and happy philosophy:

Thro' the whole of his Disorder he express'd the most chearful Patience and humble Fortitude—He told me at first that let the Event be what it might, he was content. That it was totally indifferent to him whether he was to go then, or to continue 4 or 5 years longer—Few men he added have enjoy'd Life more—been more exempt from Pain & Disease; and now (he subjoin'd) it is come so late in Life I am thankful to Providence he has preserv'd me so long—I chearfully resign—And am not afraid to dye—no Complaints—No Murmurs were heard. He accepted with the kindest Notice all the Assistance administer'd. Told us he submitted to the various Medical & Chirugical Operations, both as being his Duty, and to give Satisfaction to his Family . . . If Success attended, it was well; if the contrary: it was also well. Then the good Man took leave of all Visibles—He had used them, without abusing them. He had lived pleasantly, usefully and honourably—might be justly called a Friend to Mankind—and an unwearied promoter of Knowledge in general & of Natural History in particular.[44]

Collinson's death was a bitter blow to Clayton. Now he and Bartram were the elder statesmen in the botanical fraternity, and both were increasingly conscious of their age.

Clayton was seventy-three. His sturdy physique was still capable of strenuous field trips, but his sight was not so acute. The increasing business and the enlarged operations of the courthouse had required that he seek some assistance. Accordingly, he had requested the Nortons to find a young scribe for him.

This was not as simple as it had been a few years previously, when apprentices could be readily obtained through the Blue Coat School in London, which had been established in 1688 for the education of poor children. There being no boys available at this institution, John Norton finally found the answer to the problem in the nephew of one of his employees, James Withers.[45] This man's exact status is unknown. His connection with the firm dated at least as far back as 1750, and by 1769 he was certainly one of their most trusted chief clerks, if not a junior partner. His importance to the business was acknowledged when he was left to represent the Nortons in England when they emigrated to the States after the American Revolution. Withers' sister, Elizabeth, had married a man named Beckley. Presumably the family was not prosperous since they agreed to send their eleven year old son, John James Beckley, to be apprenticed to the Nortons' friend, the well-known man-of-letters, John Clayton. As reluctant as they may have been to send such a youngster so far away, they must have recognized this as a unique opportunity for their child. It was reassuring to worried parents that John's Uncle James would hear news of him through the Nortons, the Virginia member of the firm being within a few miles of Gloucester. So well pleased were they with John's situation, it was not long before they sent a second son, Nathaniel, to be employed by Messrs. Burnley & Braikenridge. Nathaniel did not prove as adaptable as John, and returned to London after three years, and again John was the only member of his family in Virginia until his sister accompanied Frances Norton to Caroline County from London.

In July, 1769, George P. Goosley rode out from Yorktown to call on John Clayton.[46] His father was the manager of the Virginia Fleet, and the young man had just arrived in the Colonies with the hope of "a position of privilege & profit." This involved traveling from plantation to plantation, securing promises of tobacco shipments for the ships which Norton and

Company had leased. A commission was paid on any business which was thus acquired. When Goosley informed Clayton that he was managing the tobacco cargo for the "Liberty," Clayton readily agreed to send his hogsheads aboard as soon as possible. He knew that it mattered little to the Nortons which ships conveyed his tobacco to London. On another humid July day, Goosley came again. This time he was accompanied by a lively little boy, John James Beckley. They were already well acquainted, having sailed on the same ship, and Clayton was grateful to the younger man for his kindness in delivering the child safely.

John Beckley was a fine tonic for the aging Clayton, still saddened by Collinson's death. It was a very hot and sultry summer, climaxed by storms of hurricane strength in the early fall. Neither homesickness nor the violence of the New World's weather could depress young Beckley's spirits and he continued in "perfect health & sprightliness." He was even more welcome, because he was such a well-behaved child. He ate at the table with the family and was treated quite like a son. On the orders to Norton were many items of clothing for the boy, particularly shoes which he outgrew and outwore quickly. Clayton ordered him a small saddle that they might ride together to the courthouse and about the plantation.[47]

Beckley's companionship was welcome, and his assistance in the office even more so. Clayton set young John to work immediately. He found that the boy's skill with numbers was quite remarkable, although his penmanship could still be improved. When one compares the exquisitely written communications to the Nortons composed by Beckley with those scrawls of Clayton, one marvels at the high standards which the botanist was requiring of his apprentice. Several weeks later, when he sent Beckley's indentures to the Nortons for conveyance to Withers, he was able to report "from several tryals I have made of him already in some of the difficult branches of our business, I have the pleasing hope we shall be able to carry on the business of my place with more satisfaction & safety (to myself at least) than for many years heretofore."[48]

Beckley remained with Clayton until the botanist's death. Those five years were of tremendous value to him, and much of his later success could be attributed to the careful training which he received in Clayton's office as a boy. Governor Page summed it up in a letter in which he said, "Mr. Beckley was whilst very young trained up in the Clerk's office of a Gentleman of Learning & of rigid Attention to Method & Accuracy."[49] While he received this technical training, Beckley was exposed to Clayton's character as a man: his uncompromising standards, which would not allow a false statement to go unchallenged, no matter on whose authority; his penchant for hard work; his willingness to forego recognition provided the job itself was completed; his lack of snobbery; his gift for friendship, and his rather quaint, undeviating formality.

After Clayton's death, John Beckley became prominent in many fields. A lawyer, he was eventually elected first Clerk of the United States House of Representatives. Thomas Jefferson appointed him the first librarian of the Library of Congress. He was not only a protégé of Jefferson's, but an intimate friend of both James Madison and James Monroe and a host of other well-known men of the period in the north and in the south. His political ideas had some influence in the shaping of the United States Constitution, and his political efforts with Madison were tremendously effective in founding the Democratic Party, then called the Republican. Throughout his life, much of his success could be directly traced to his incomparable abilities as a clerk, abilities deriving from habits which Clayton had inculcated.

The botanist only made one hogshead of tobacco in 1769. It is to be hoped that this arrived safely in England. There were many hazards involved even after a crop was harvested. Thus Clayton lost some, if not all, of his 1751 crop as set forth in his petition to the House of Burgesses March 3, 1752: "A Petition of *John Clayton* and *Charles Blackwell* was presented to the House, and read, setting forth, that they had each of them, *to wit*, the said *John* 9935 *Lb.* and the said *Charles* 5275 *lb.* of Tobacco drowned in the Warehouse on *Eastermost River*, in the County of *Gloucester*, and praying the Relief of this House in the Premises. *Ordered,* That the said Petition be referred to the Committee of Claims, that they examine into the Matter thereof, and report the same, with their Opinion thereupon, to the House."[50] The weather may have been unfavourable for tobacco, but it did not discourage Clayton's plans for the garden. The following spring, he asked Norton to have two orders for seeds and roots filled at James Gordon's at Mile End, whom he had "formerly dealt with for this sort of thing & always received'em in good order."[51] Clayton stipulated that Gordon pack the roots in small earthern pots, and put his order aboard the "Hanbury," Captain Esten's ship, since she was due in Virginia just before Christmas. He had found by bitter experience that summer shipments seldom survived.[52] On August 24, Clayton rode over to Yorktown, where he spent some time visiting aboard the "Golden Fleece." While on the ship he scribbled another note to John Norton, saying that Captain Robertson had brought last year's order, though there had been a long delay before Clayton had received it. His order for the next year's supply, he enclosed with the letter and instructions that the goods be sent on a ship coming up the York River, with the master directed to forward Clayton's order as soon as possible.[53] In March, he sent a duplicate of the order, fearing that the ship had been lost. He also informed Norton of his disappointment in regard to Gordon's order. Mr. Archer's brig had brought him the bill of lading for a box and a basket, "the former I have got in good order but the latter is entirely lost. I have sent twice to Mr. Archer at York for it, but all to no purpose, he says he believes it was sent to Col. Ryland Randolph who lives up James River near four score miles from me. It was contrary to my directions that there were any roots put in a basket, for I mentioned seed not rooted plants. The seed would have come Safe in the box with the rest. at the bot of the invoice Mr. Gordon acquaints me, that if I disapprove of his fashion of sending plants instead of seed, he will *not* insist upon being paid for them, provided I will send him some plants (mentioned in his postscript) wch grow wild here, which at the proper season for their removal I certainly will do. I hope to receive all the seed which could not be procured in September last by Capt. Esten on the first Ship afterwards and should be very glad of a little of the Palmatoo Rhubarb seed fresh & good from Mr. Gordon by the first opportunity."[54] The plants which Gordon desired, were duly collected by Clayton that fall, and sent to the London nurseryman in the care of Captain Robertson, who sailed from Virginia in October.[55]

As Clayton grew older and found it necessary to limit the extent of his botany field work, he must have derived increased pleasure from his garden. He had devoted a great many years of his life to its development, and he seems to have been justly proud of it. Here, presumably, he grew all of the more attractive or more interesting plants which he had found in many years of collecting. Here, too, were many obtained from friends at home and abroad. Undoubtedly, many of the English plants which he had known as a boy mingled with those of his own collecting and those sent by friends. He might well have said, as Collinson did, "it reminds Mee of my Absent Friends by their living Donations." There is no description of the garden in any writing of Clayton or his contemporaries that has been found, but many references to it are of interest. The impression seems to prevail in Gloucester, as indicated by Dr. Dunn, that the garden was brick-walled.[56] It may very well have been, but no evidence has been found that it was. Remains of old brick walls have been considered to be evidence of the location of the garden.

When Bartram first saw Clayton's garden in 1739, he was impressed by the variety of plants, but felt that it and the other gardens of Virginia lacked some of the European plants to be found in Philadelphia gardens. This deficiency was probably remedied later, for we know that Clayton ordered both seeds and roots from Gordon, and that he exchanged many plants with Bartram himself. A fair number of plants are definitely mentioned by Clayton as being in his garden, others he speaks of planting and still others he hoped would be sent him. One can only speculate as to their survival. In the latter category, we have mentioned the Siberian *Claytonia* sent by Linnaeus and the rhubarb seeds sent by Collinson. Of the former there are a number of references. When he wrote to Collinson concerning Catesby's errors in describing *Zanthoxylum*, he stated "I have 4 or 5 of the trees in my garden." Again, when he took exception to Alston's views on sex in plants, he spoke of having "two female rhamnus's in my garden." On February 23, 1761, he thanked Bartram for some seed "inscribed Dracephalum, wch by the appearance & smell of the dry calyces, I take to be the same plant wch I have had several years in my Garden. It is called three leaved Moldavica with a strong scent as Balm of Gilead. I have a species of Aconite in my garden wch grows about five feet high. I found it at our little S. West mountains, the flowers are blue, & grow in the same manner as those on yr large tall Species according to yr description, in its own natural place of growth it blossoms in October, but in my garden it is about three weeks forwarder." On February 25, 1764, he wrote Bartram that "I sow always my Staresacre seed in the autumn." In the same letter he made one of a number of requests for "a little seed of the Carolina Tippitytwitchet, or Sensitive Plant, with a few directions as to the time of planting and the soil it most delights in, etc."

Clayton certainly had special associations with a great many plants in his garden: for example, *Amsonia, Claytonia, Meadia, Stuartia, Chelone,* and *Chionanthus.* The last two of these deserve special mention. Somewhere Clayton found a colored variant of the normally white-flowered fringe tree, *Chionanthus.* Long after his death, Dr. Galt saw it still blooming in what remained of his garden in 1805.[57] On February 6, 1765, Clayton wrote Bartram "I now send you the seed of the red flowered Chelone." In 1924, when Dr. Edgar T. Wherry discovered this "turtlehead" in Anne Arundel County, Maryland, it had not been reported east of the lower Ohio since Clayton's day. Wherry then made a special trip to Gloucester to look for the red chelone, and found it again just where Clayton had originally described finding it. Dr. Wherry wrote, "So we had 'the thrill that comes once in a lifetime'—we had rediscovered a plant lost to science for 175 years!"[58]

The early winter of 1765 was very severe, and Clayton wrote sadly to Bartram "My garden is intirely ruined with the cold piercing winds and frosts. All the flowers wch were in the leaf, tender, as Narcissus, Polyanthus, Ixia, Lavecodum etc. are destroyed." It is unfortunate that the only two letters of Clayton to the Nortons which mention enclosing a list of seeds and roots to be obtained from Gordon, have survived without these lists. The invoices do mention a few items other than seeds intended for the garden. These include on August 24, 1770, "1 Good Strong large Garden Spade, 1 Do Smaller," and on July 31, 1773, "a large Tin Watering pot for Gardens."

The summer of 1771 was fine for tobacco, and Clayton was able to ship more than he had for a long time. Between fourteen and fifteen hogsheads were sent to London in October, with Captain Robertson.[59] An additional nine hogsheads were shipped in Captain Archer's ship, the "Neptune," in January.[60] Clayton had other reasons to be gratified, for two of his grandsons were attending The College of William and Mary. Lucy's son, Thomas Hughes, was a student there from 1770-1773. He was quite a scholar, for in 1772 he was appointed to a "Nottoway Foundation," perhaps the equivalent of a modern student assistantship.[61] Jasper's son John, entered college in 1771.

In spite of practically grown grandchildren, John Clayton was still interested in clothes, and by the standards of the average field botanist, quite a dandy.[62] He ordered materials for suits of olive-coloured jersey and of "Iron Gray" linen. His "fine" hat was lined with silk and his wig was "fashionable." His hose, of worsted or cotton, were knitted from very fine thread. In civilized strolls about the plantation, he brandished his "closed walking cane with an amber head & black silk string." He had a weakness for snuff, and ordered great quantities. It was usually Weston's, but one order specified Brazilian snuff, which was considered much finer.

Betty Clayton must have died late in 1771, or sometime in the early part of 1772.[63] It was fortunate for Clayton that his daughter Catherine still lived at home, as well as the young Beckley. Nearby were Thomas, Lucy and her family, and Jasper and his. He was still busy as county clerk, gardener and botanist. In the fall of 1772, he made a long collecting trip to Orange County, a still fairly rugged journey for one of seventy-seven. He complained to Norton because the London merchant had charged him for insurance on his tobacco and again on his goods. He stated that he preferred, in time of peace, to risk the loss by shipwreck.[64] His eyesight had become a serious problem, so in August he had ordered a "pair of spectacles to suit a person 77 years old who can't distinguish one object from another at small distances nor read unless the book is almost to the eyes."[65] It is remarkable that his eyes had served him so well for three quarters of a century, and he still wrote many of his own letters without glasses. It took a year for the glasses to arrive. Clayton unhappily wrote Norton, "I have recd those spectacles bought of Mr. Martin but alas, to my great disappointment, they prove of no manner of use being, I imagine, designed for younger eyes than mine and if I can get an opportunity of returning these to you—beg the favour of you to prevail with Mr. Martin to change them for a pair more suitable to my eyes, which will be 79 before [long] & desire this, or a good reading glass."[66]

In order to recognize and encourage intellectual pursuits in many fields, a number of Virginians met in the spring of 1773 to found an organization similar to the American Philosophical Society in Philadelphia. The foundation for this had been laid the previous November when a smaller group had recommended the establishment of such a society, in a paper signed by Theodore Bland, Chairman, Dabney Carr, John and Mann Page, Jr., George Walker, Nathaniel Burwell, John Walker, and James McClung. As only officers were listed at the May meeting it can only be assumed that the signers of the November declaration were present. The May 13th *Gazette* duly noted: "We hear that a Philosophical Society, consisting of one hundred members, is established under the Patronage of his Excellency, the Governor,[67] for the Advancement of Useful Knowledge in this Colony, of which the following Gentlemen were elected Officers, for the year ensuing; John Clayton, Esq., author of the *Flora Virginica*, President; John Page, of Rosewell, Esq., vice-president; the Rev. Samuel

Henley, Professor of Moral Philosophy, Secretary; Mr. St. George Tucker, Assistant Secretary; David Jameson, Esq., Treasurer."[68]

It is interesting to note that in such a large and distinguished gathering that, by his election as president, recognition was given to John Clayton's distinction as a scholar, both in America and abroad. It must have been a proud moment for a student who had laboured so long far from others in his field, and far from the stimulation of the learned societies of the Old World. The vice-president was the young John Page, who eventually became governor of Virginia, and whose notes on Clayton were later used by Dr. Barton in his brief account of the botanist's life. Thus, Page was in a position to know Clayton as a scientist, as well as a neighbor. Some years later Page made the following comment on Clayton's knowledge of botany at this time:

When any one . . . described to Mr. Clayton, what he thought a newly-discovered tree, shrub, plant, or flower, he would, in a modest manner, say, "did you not find it in such a county, and in such and such a place?" On being answered that it was found in that very spot, he would add, that it was called by the Indians (I have been told) so and so; by them used for such and such purposes, and may be found described in such a class of Linnaeus. And sometimes I have heard him say, it was described by Theophrastus, and called by him, by such a name, in Greek. And such was his desire to obtain complete knowledge of the plants of Virginia, that, notwithstanding his great parsimony, he would offer a reward for any discovery of a plant unknown to him. There seemed to be no part of the learning of his day (I mean about the year 1773) unknown to him.[69]

Clayton's health failed rapidly in the year 1773. In October, he obviously suspected that his time was limited, and he wrote his will, which was witnessed on the twenty-fifth by Beckley, Michael Driskill, and Augustine Curtis. He died sometime in the week preceding January sixth, 1774. The death notice in the *Gazette* merely stated "Mr John Clayton, Clerk of Gloucester."[70] No mention is made of his funeral, and the location of his grave is unknown. It seems probable that the Claytons had their own private graveyard, as was the eighteenth-century Virginia custom. His will specified burial near the graves of his wife, and their two children, Robert and Mary. Undoubtedly, Clayton's wishes for a simple funeral and no family mourning were respected.

Rather strangely the *Virginia Gazette* took little notice of the death of Virginia's most famous botanist; perhaps it was due to the unsettled times, and the impending war with Great Britain. Only one tribute, in the form of a rather dreadful poem, appeared in 1774, with the following introduction:

In him an exalted genius, and a real regard for everything that tended to the cultivation of the human mind, intimately entered. Elogiums on the dead become insipid when heaped upon the worthless and undeserving, but when a character like his presents itself, no one should be silent in its praise. A youth who much admired the deceased sent us the following verses, which he desired may be inserted:

> 'Go, fair example of accomplish'd youth,
> Of grateful wisdom, and of courteous truth
> Mature in virtue, not advanc'd in age
> *Clayton* rejects this world's fantastic stage.
> Born to do good, and studious to excel
> Whoever knew him, knows he acted well.
> In every scene his worth confess'd appear'd.
> Beloved by good men, and by bad men rever'd.
> Malice itself on him could cast no stain
> And, if she strove to wound, she strove in vain.
> Heav'n saw such virtue unrewarded here
> And strait transferr'd to an happier sphere:
> Accept, dear shade, these lines, to friendship due,
> And may I think, and act, and die, like you!'[71]

Perhaps the sixteen-year old John James Beckley wrote this atrocity. If he did, emotion must have overcome his natural literary talent.

Clayton's will was admitted to probate on January sixth. His son William, the executor, inserted the following notice in the paper on February first: "All persons that have any demands against the estate of John Clayton, late of Gloucester County, deceased, are desired to apply for payment; and all those indebted to the said estate are desired to make immediate payment to William Clayton, Executor."[72] From William's statement, many years later, Clayton left few debts. Unlike many of his neighbors, his Norton account was in good standing, and his children were left in comfortable circumstances.

Clayton expressed his affection for William by leaving him his watch. By the agreement with his older brother, John Jr., he inherited "Morehouse." His father directed that he supervise the trust which had been set up for his sister, Lucy Hughes. Under Clayton's will, she and John Jr. shared equally the residue of the estate, after the debts and various legacies were paid. In addition, John Jr. inherited five slaves, four of which were still in the possession of his Aunt Mary, Mrs. Patrick Henry. After the crops had been harvested, Jasper became the owner of his father's plantation and twenty-one slaves. Thomas received his token inheritance of one hundred pounds, and his sister, Catherine, five hundred pounds and six slaves. Some of the grandchildren were named as beneficiaries: John Jr.'s daughter, Mildred, inherited three hundred pounds and a slave; William's daughter, Elvira, two hundred pounds and a slave; Jasper's son, John, inherited his globe and microscope and shared his grandfather's books with his cousin, Thomas Hughes. Both boys received a slave apiece. Thomas' brother, Jasper Hughes, became the owner of Clayton's "negro woman Sapho" and William Beverly Clayton of "little Jacob."

Unmentioned in his will were perhaps the most valuable items for posterity. They were described thus by Galt: "two volumes of manuscript; neatly copied and prepared for the press: and a *hortus siccus,* of folio size, with marginal notes, and directions for the engraver in preparing plates for his proposed work. Mr. Jasper Clayton, grandson of the botanist, says, that this work, which was in the possession of his father, when the revolutionary war commenced, was sent to a Mr. William Clayton, clerk of New Kent, as to a place of safety against the invading enemy. It was lodged in the office with the records of the county."[73] This may have been the manuscript of the "Flora Virginiana." When Laurens Gronovius published his edition, Collinson may have returned Clayton's unprinted book, but it is more likely that this was just a duplicate copy which Clayton had kept for his own use. There is the possibility that this may have been an entirely different flora, dealing with non-Virginian plants, collected on his northern or western trips.

On Sunday night, July 12, 1787, a man by the name of John Price Posey escaped from the jail in New Kent County. He had been sentenced for a month, for assaulting Mr. Robert B. Armistead. Enlisting the help of a laborer, Thomas Green, the two men rode down to what Posey termed "the Damn'd Prison." With the assistance of two Negroes, they placed fence rails and shingles inside the jail, to which they set fire with steel, a tinderbox and a flint. As they cantered off up the main road, they passed the clerk's office and set it ablaze. The William Claytons were not aroused from sleep until the crackling flames had become uncontrollable. Both buildings and their contents were a total loss.[74] "Thus perished, not only the records of the county, but the labours of Clayton."[75]

XI
CLAYTON'S CONTRIBUTION

Although his two unpublished manuscripts, the one in Virginia and the one in England, have been lost, John Clayton left a legacy to botanists the world over, since the products of his fifty years of collecting are still represented in several herbaria. Five years after his death, when the Gronovian collections came up for sale, Sir Joseph Banks was very much interested. Banks had employed Daniel C. Solander, for the unprecedented salary of five thousand pounds, to accompany him on his famous globe-circling trip in 1771. This was the best equipped expedition to that date, and included artists and scientists of various fields, even astronomers. They visited the South Seas and returned by way of the Cape of Good Hope, loaded with specimens of all sorts. On September first, 1778, Joseph Gaertner (1732-1791), a Leiden botanist and an F. R. S., wrote to Banks that he would inform him as to the "state" of the Gronovian herbarium, which was to be sold on October fifth.[1] A letter four days later reported that the older Gronovius' collection contained four thousand specimens, including plants from Vaillant, Miller, Houston and Clayton—all of which had been studied by Linnaeus.[2] For some reason

Banks did not acquire the herbarium at that time. Instead, it was bought by John, Earl of Bute, for the paltry sum of ninety pounds. When Bute died in 1794, Sir Joseph was able to buy it for even less, a mere forty-four pounds, two shillings. It is now in the British Museum as part of the Banks Collection. Although two hundred years have passed since these plants were collected, the specimens are in an astonishingly fresh state of preservation. Clayton's plants also appear in the herbarium of the Sherardian Museum at Oxford, and there is at least one at Cambridge University. Certainly, many of the Virginia plants among those in Linnaeus' herbarium also came from him, but they are not so identified. One plant specimen from Clayton, which was given to Linnaeus by Gronovius, was in turn given by Linnaeus to Peter Jonas Bergius. This plant, *Rudbeckia triloba,* is now in his herbarium at the Hortus Bergianus (Bergianska Tradgarden), Stockholm.[3]

The name of John Clayton has been commemorated in many ways. A number of plants bear his name: Burgess named *Aster claytoni* in 1898; Michaux, *Galium claytoni* in 1803; Clarke, *Osmorhiza claytoni* in 1879; in addition to the *Claytonia virginica,* L., Michaux named *Claytonia caroliniana;* in 1753, *Osmunda claytoniana,* L. appeared in *Species Plantarum.* In 1843, Edward Tuckerman applied the synonym *Potamogeton claytonii,* to *Potamogeton epihydrus,* Rafinesque.[4] The name *Agastache Clayt.,* as found in botanical works, indicates that the genus was first named by Clayton. A building at the Mountain Lake Biological Station, of the University of Virginia, is dedicated to him. The flora committee of the Virginia Academy of Science published for five years (1934-1939) the journal, *Claytonia.* A wrought iron marker has been placed at the supposed location of his home by the Mathews County Garden Club, and a state historical marker has been placed on a nearby highway. A "John Clayton Day" was held in his honor in Williamsburg in October, 1957, by the Garden Clubs of Virginia. In this same year, the Cape Henry Women's Club sent to the British Museum of Natural History a "beautiful cypress shadow box" containing specimens of the

American Lotus in honour of Clayton.[5] How solid, then, is Clayton's claim to fame?

It is very easy for the biographer to become so personally involved with his subject that an unprejudiced evaluation is difficult. It seems desirable, therefore, to lean heavily upon the estimates of contemporary and more recent commentators who have expressed an opinion concerning the subject's contribution. A fair appraisal, in the case of a scientist, should take into account the conditions under which his work was done, his preparation for it, the time and tools available to him, the influence of his accomplishments on others of his own day, and the continuing value of his work to those who came after him.

Although nothing is presently known as to where Clayton received his formal education, there can be no doubt that he did receive a good one. Contemporaries who knew him well, John Page for example, referred to him as a very learned man. We know that he had some knowledge of French, Greek, Latin, medicine, and law. Unfortunately, the extent of his training in any of these subjects is not clear. We can, however, conclude that he was better prepared than most of the Virginians of his day to appreciate the scientific importance of a systematic study of the native plants, and of making the results of the study available to interested persons elsewhere. We have the evidence of Gronovius that he successfully mastered the taxonomic methods of John Ray in preparing his Catalogue of Virginia plants which Gronovius published as part one of the *Flora Virginica*. We know that Clayton regularly ordered books and periodicals from London, and that he intensively studied the books of Linnaeus. His interest in the work of botanists elsewhere is emphasized by his comments to Linnaeus concerning Gmelin's expedition to Siberia, and his reply to Alston's article concerning sex in plants.

Clayton's botanic studies were presumably confined to his "spare time," since he held office as clerk of court throughout his adult life. The fact that he raised a large family and carried on farming operations as well, would seem to indicate that his spare time was distinctly limited. Although other

Virginians of his day are known to have had some interest in botany, John Mitchell seems to have been the only other man generally referred to as being a scientist. Thus, it is understandable that Clayton felt very much isolated from other botanists, and that he derived great pleasure from his correspondence with them. There seems to have been no one with whom he might confer when he encountered a botanic problem, with the possible exception of Mitchell, who returned to England in 1746. It is doubtful that he and Mitchell had very frequent contact even before that time. Urbanna is not very far from Gloucester in terms of present-day travel, but was far enough to make communication difficult at that time. Then, too, Mitchell was unwell for some years before he left Virginia.

Very little serious work in botany had been done in Virginia prior to that of Clayton. John Banister's Catalogue of Virginia Plants, published by Ray, was the most notable work, although the Reverend John Clayton, Catesby, and others had done some collecting and had published general observations. Thus, Clayton had both the opportunity and the problems presented by a largely unexplored field. Furthermore, systems of plant classification were in the midst of change in Europe during his lifetime. The system of Ray was initially used by Clayton, and the new system proposed by Linnaeus became the cause of great controversy.

Against this general background the accomplishments of Clayton must be viewed. Some writers have felt that the frequent references to the *Flora Virginica* as a publication of Gronovius rather than Clayton imply that Clayton has been credited only with the collecting of plants, and that the taxonomic treatment of them has been credited to Gronovius. Benjamin Smith Barton, in 1792, contended that the merit of the Flora was due to Clayton rather than Gronovius.[6] Francis W. Pennell cited James Greenway, of Dinwiddie County, Virginia (who was "projecting a Flora Virginica" in 1792 and 1793) as having written Barton that "Clayton . . . underwent the Labour of the Pack-Horse and Gronovius reaped the Profit and Credit of the Whole."[7] Although Greenway's comments were made only a few years after Clayton's death, he was incorrect in thinking that Clayton's contemporaries, either in America or in Europe, did not regard him as an able and serious scientist. There is very abundant evidence to the contrary. Peter Collinson wrote of him in 1764 as "My Friend Mr. Clayton the Great Botanist of America."[8] Linnaeus, certainly the foremost botanist of the eighteenth century, obtained membership for Clayton in the Swedish Academy of Sciences—a society "which has from its first institution been known for the greatest delicacy in choosing members of distinction and note," as John Bartram wrote.[9] Sir James Edward Smith corroborated Bartram's evaluation of the Society, saying "that Academy was always very select in its choice of foreign members."[10] In the list of eminent botanists given in Clement's article Gronovius is not named as one of the prominent botanic writers, but Clayton is. The fact that Peter Kalm planned to include him in his reference work of well-known botanists also established Clayton as respected in his own century. These three references, in conjunction with many others cited in earlier chapters, seem to make it abundantly clear that Clayton was considered by contemporary botanists competent to judge as one of the ablest scientists of the time. As early as November 17, 1739, Gronovius wrote to Linnaeus that "Clayton, if not unmatched, is at least the most distinguished foreign resident."[11]

The previously cited comments of those few men who saw Clayton's "Flora Virginiana" indicate that he had produced a vastly improved edition of the *Flora* on his own. The conclusion seems justified that Clayton had continued to improve and mature as a botanist, as the interest of Gronovius in the subject waned. It is altogether probable that the "Flora Virginiana" would have been an even more valuable work than the second edition of the *Flora Virginica*.

Since Clayton's death, his memory has continued to be honoured, despite expressions of concern to the effect that he has been insufficiently appreciated, and his work has continued to be useful. Jefferson, who had an intense interest in botany, expressed the prevailing opinion of him in his day in the passage previously quoted. Reference has also been made to Benjamin Smith Barton's admiration for Clayton. This was well expressed in the Preface to his own *Flora Virginica*, in which he planned to incorporate Clayton's and add to it:

> The *Flora Virginica* of Clayton and Gronovius is a work of very considerable merit. It may, with great propriety, be said to be the best foundation of our knowledge of the plants of a considerable part of the tract of country now called the United States. And although the researches and discoveries of many botanists, since the time of Clayton, have greatly extended our knowledge of the botany of these states, and have perhaps rendered the *Flora Virginica* a less indispensable work in the hands of the explorer of American plants, the work still continues to be extremely useful; and is daily sought after.[12]

He went on to refer to Clayton as "one who was an ornament and an honour to the country, at a time when Virginia was barren of men of scientific and literary merit...."

Dr. Moses Marshall, nephew of Humphry Marshall, wrote to Grimwood, Hudson and Barrit in England, December 11, 1793: "With respect to *new* things, when I consider that a KALM and a CLAYTON have been here, I have little hopes of making discoveries."[13]

Frederick Pursh, in his *Flora of North America* (1814) gave credit to assistance from Clayton's work: "Clayton's Herbarium—The whole of this interesting collection, from which the *Flora Virginica* of Gronovius was compiled, is preserved in the Banksian Museum. This has been particularly useful to me in tracing the plants which Linnaeus had adopted from this work."[14] It is true that he seems to emphasize Clayton's role as being that of the collector.

Darlington, writing in 1849, may have had comments such as that of Pursh in mind when he wrote of Clayton: "As a practical botanist he was perhaps inferior to no botanist of his time.... It is to be regretted that succeeding botanists are in the habit of referring to that *Flora,* as the work of Gronovius, though its great value is derived from the masterly descriptions communicated to the Leyden professor by Clayton."[15] We now know that Clayton sent more complete descriptions which, at least in some cases, were not used. In a second reference to the *Flora*, Darlington mentioned "that excellent pioneer of American Botany, John Clayton, of Virginia, who is entitled to more of the credit due to that work, than has generally been awarded to him."

It has been indicated that Clayton sent plants to Catesby, Dillenius, Gronovius, Linnaeus, and others, and that the *Flora Virginica* was a valuable reference work to these men as well as to Bartram, Colden, Garden, Geoffrey, and others. Probably, the greatest significance of his work, both in the eighteenth century and since that time, however, lies in its influence upon Linnaeus. Few would question that Linnaeus was the outstanding botanist of the eighteenth century and that his work has profoundly influenced the science since his time. By international agreement his binomial system of nomenclature has been adopted throughout the world, and his *Species Plantarum* has been taken as the starting point in determining priorities of nomenclature. We know that Linnaeus studied with Gronovius the earlier plants sent by Clayton and that the latter sent him plants and plant descriptions for years. We also know that the *Flora Virginica* and these plants were the chief source of his knowledge of North American plants included in the *Species Plantarum*. That this is still a matter of some importance to present day botanists was well stated by S. F. Blake (1918) in the following passage:

It should be borne in mind that Clayton's plants were worked out by Gronovius with the constant assistance of Linnaeus and that citations from the *Flora Virginica* have therefore, as represented by still extant specimens, actually seen by Linnaeus, a greater value today in the interpretation of Linnaean species than the often unintelligible descriptions and figures of earlier writers not now authenticated by specimens. The usual identity of citations of older authors in both the *Flora Virginica* and the *Species Plantarum*, is also significant in this connection and may be taken as indicating the probability that the synonymy of the earlier work was likewise due to the cooperation of Gronovius and Linnaeus, and was later adopted directly by Linnaeus for the *Species Plantarum*.[16]

Blake pointed out that Clayton's herbarium "has been frequently consulted by American workers, especially Asa Gray," but that he seems to have been the first to make a "systematic examination of the whole collection." He then went on to discuss the "rather numerous changes in nomenclature necessitated by the reidentification of Clayton's specimens. . . ."

Kenneth R. Mackenzie, writing in 1928, also stressed the present value of Clayton's work. "One of the great basic collections of American plants is the collection made by Clayton in Virginia. . . . So when we find Linnaeus in 1753 in his *Species Plantarum* constantly referring to Gronovius' *Flora Virginica,* these references are to a work in which he had assisted and to a collection with which he was personally thoroughly familiar. And these references are of the most definite nature, because they are to the specific specimens with which Gronovius and Linnaeus worked."[17] Mackenzie further points out that "not infrequently, in dealing with one of the American species of Linnaeus we are confronted with the choice of applying a name given by him either (1) to a specimen of Clayton's collecting which is definitely cited by Linnaeus and which we know he studied but which was not preserved in his own herbarium; or (2) to a specimen in the herbarium of Linnaeus but not cited by him, frequently without date and the history of which is entirely unknown, but one which bears his naming." Mackenzie then cited some examples of this situation and concluded that "in such cases it seems to me that we should apply the Linnaean names to the specimens collected by Clayton; that we should follow certainty rather than uncertainty, definitely cited specimens rather than specimens merely names in an author's 'herbarium.' "

M. L. Fernald, in 1940, two centuries after the first appearance of the *Flora,* referred to it as "one of the fundamental books upon the flora of eastern North America." After some discussion of the different parts and editions, he added: "In *Species Plantarum* (1753) and in his later works Linnaeus gave binomials to hundreds of the species which had been originally described by Gronovius from Virginia. Probably one-half of the number rest safely upon the Gronovian account and the Clayton specimens cited by him. . . . It thus results that probably 400-500 Linnean species of eastern North America rest for their typification upon the specimens described by Gronovius in the first edition of his *Flora Virginica*. Happily, the series of specimens, almost complete, is carefully preserved and quite available to students in the herbarium of the British Museum (Natural History)."[18]

A. B. Massey, in an article on the "Plant Hunters of Virginia," wrote: "With the death of Clayton went the greater part of the interest in our native plants on the part of Virginians. Dr. James Greenway of Dinwiddie and Dr. Richard Field of Brunswick and others are reputed to have studied the native plants of their sections and to have been eminent botanists. However, little or no record of their work is to be found."[19] Most of the work on Virginia plants since that time, has been done by men not resident in the state: Barton, Pursh, Gray, Britten and Brown, Small, Heller, Kearney, and others. There have been two exceptions to this rule. Professor and Mrs. Grimes, of The College of William and Mary, collected plants from much the same area as had Clayton. Dr. Paul Merriman, of the University of Richmond, published a *Flora of Richmond*. The herbaria for this, and that made by the Grimes, have both been lost, so Clayton's *Flora*, substantiated by specimens, still remains unique among the work of Virginia botanists.

It would seem to be clearly evident that Clayton earned by years of hard work and the application of sound scientific principles a secure position in the history of botany. His work was neither brilliant nor spectacular, but it was thorough and painstaking. It was of great value to other scientists of his own time and it has continued to be used by others for two hundred years. His name deserves to be honored among those who have made important contributions to science.

APPENDIX

"Flora Virginiana Claytonii"
Notes Taken on Clayton's "Flora" by John Ellis.

Classis 1
Monandria Monogynia
Salicornia

Dygnia
Corispermum
(Stellaria)

Classis 2
Diandria Monogynia
Circaea
Veronica
Gratiola
Utricularia
Dianthera
Verbena
Lycopus
Horminum   Salvia
Monarda
Collinsonia
Oleaster   Chionanthus Lin.

Classis 3
Triandria Monygynia
Valerianella
Melothria
Chamaeris   Iris Lin.
Iris
Commelina

Xyris
Gramen
  Dactyloides*   Scirpus Lin.
Scirpus
Cyperus
Gramen
  arundinaceum   Scirpus Gron.
Gramen
  Cyperoides   Scirpus Lin.
Juncus
  Bombycinus   Eriophorum Lin.
Phudatia

Triandria Dygnia
Oryza   Phalaris
                      oryzoides Lin.
Hordeum
Gramen
  Milliaceum.   Panicum Lin.
Gramen
  Phalaroides   Poa Lin.
Elymus
Hordeum
Gramen   Andropogon
  ischoemum   Linnaei
Gramen
  Alopecuroides.   Panicum Lin.
Gramen
  Dactyloides.   Panicum
Panicum.

*Many items consisting of two or more words have been placed on successive lines and indented.

Appendix

Gramen paniculatum arundinaecum		Ptelea Ludwigia Ammania	
Gramen maritimum spicatum.	Dactylis Lin.	Tetrandria Digynia	
Gramen avenaceum	Dactylis Gro. Aira Gro.	Percepier Cuscuta Hamamelis	Aphanes Lin.
Melica	Helons. Lin. [?]	Tetrandia Tetragynia	
		Agrifolium	Ilex Lin.
Poa		Ilex	Quercus Lin.
Uniola		Arbuscula	Cassine & Yaupon—foliis [?]
Bromus			
Gramen Loliaceum	Uniola Lin.	Cassinoides	Catesby Vol. 2 Tab: 57
Agrostis			Paraguay tea. foliis deciduis
Gramen Caninum.	Cynosurus Lin.		
Arundo		Potamogeton	
Millium		Sagina	
Gramen maritimum glaucum		Alsine	Sagina Lin.

Class. 5
Pentandria Monogynia

Triandria Trygynia.

Globularia affinis		Cynoglossum Anchusa Lilliospermum	Myosotis Lin.
Gramen Mari Spicatum	Proserpinaca Lin.	Cynoglossum Pulmonaria	———Lin.
Mollugo		Buglossum	Lycopsis Gron. & Lin.
Knawell			
Polygono affinis	Lechea Lin.	Lycopsis Echium	
Lechea		Anagallis	Lysimachia Lin.
		Lysimachia Nummularia.	Lysimachia Lin.

Classis 4
Tetrandria Monogynia.

		Anagallis	———Lin.
Scabiosa Dendroides.	Cephalanthus Lin.	Hydrophyllum Azalea	
Dipsacus.		Meadia	Dodecatheon Lin.
Diodia			
Houstonia		Hottonia	
Cruciata		Ophiorrhiza	Metreola Gron. Lin.
Aparine			
Sherardia		Lychnoides	Phlox Lin.
Coronopus	Plantago Lin.	Convolvusus	[?] [?]
Plantago		Polemonium	
Cornus		Campanula	
Ludwigia		Triosteum	
Ludwigia	Olden Landia Lin.	Symphoricarpus Lonicera Lin.	
Mitchella		Periclymenum	
Callicarpa	Johnsonia Miller	Lonicera Lin.	
Veronica	Polypremum Lin.	Samolus	

Appendix

Stramonium	Datura Lin.	Myrrhis	
Verbascum		Smyrnium	
Solanum		Seseli	
Alkekengi	Physalis Lin.	Chaerophyllum	
Hedera	Helia Mitch.		
Vitis		Pentandria Trygnia	
Trutex. Red			
Root inolis.	Ceanothus Lin.	Toxicodendron	Rhus Lin.
Cyclamen affinis	Claytonia Lin.	Rhus	
Galax	Gronovius	Viburnum	
Itea		Sambucus	
Celosia		Staphylodendron	Staphylea Lin.
Grossularia		Xanthoxylon	Zanthoxylon Lin.
Tritea a.	Celastrus Lin.	Centaurium	
Euonymus		luteum	Sarothra Lin.
Centaurium	Gentiana		
minus vd.	Chironia Lin.	Pentandria Pentagynia	
Calypsantha		Angelica	
Amsonia		baccifera	Aralia Lin.
Centaurium	Gentiana L.	Aralia	
Frangula	in the addenda	Limonium	Statice Lin.
		Linum	
Pentandria Digynia		Ros folis	Drosera Lin.
Apocynum	Asclepias Lin.		
Asclepias	Apocynum Lin.	Class the 6th	
Periploca		Hexandria Monogynia	
Chenopodium			
Kali	Salsola Lin.	Renealmia	
Ulmus		Burmannia	
Heuchera		Ephemerum	Tradescantia
Centaurium			Lin.
minus.	Swertia Lin.	Lilionarcissus	Amaryllis Lin.
Centaurium		Pontederia	
minus.	Gentiana Lin.	Lilium sive	
Gentiana	Lin.	Martogon	Lilium Lin.
Eryngium		Allium	
Hydrocotyle		Fritillaria	Uvularia Lin.
Hydrocotyle	Elatine Lin.	Ornithogalum	
		Polygonatum	Convallaria Lin.
Umbelliferae		Aletris	Hyacinthus
Sanicula			Gronovius
Daucus		Pancratium	
Ammi		Dens Canis	Erythronium Lin.
Ammi pliorum ?		Onitophriana [?]	
laciniis		racemosa.	Leontice Lin.
Capillaribis	Cicuta Lin.	Juncus	
Ligusticum		Gramen Eriguum	
D°.	Smyrnium Lin.	hirsutum	
Angelica		Prinos	
D°.	Cicuta Lin.	Agave	
Sium		Yucca	
Cerefolium	Scandix Lin.	Asphodelus	Anthericum Lin.
Pimpinella		Orontium	
D°.	Sium Lin.	Cepa	
Sison		Acorus	

Appendix

Hexandria Trigynia

Lapathum	Rumex Lin.
Acetosa	Rumex Lin.
Arenaria	
Medeola	
Menispermum	
Saururus	
Melanthium	
Trillium	
Helonias	

Hexandria Polygynia

Sagittaria	Alisma Lin.
Sagitta	Alisma Lin.

Class the 7th
Heptandria Mongynia

Pavia
Trientatis

Class the 8th
Octandria Monogynia

Rhexia	
Onagra	Oenothera Lin.
Gaura	
Orobanche	Monotropa
Epilobium	
Dirca	
Vaccinium	

Octandria Trigynia

Persicaria	Polygonum Lin.
Polygonum	
Helxine	Polygonum Lin.
Fagotriticum	Helxine Lin.
Fagopyrum scandens	Polygonum Lin.

Class the 9th
Enneandria Mongynia

Laurus.

Class the 10th
Decandria Monogynia

Qu: Vaccinium	
Arbor Juda	Cercis Lin.
Sena	Cassia Lin.
Clethra	
Pyrola	
Sophora	
Arenaria	
Kalmia	

Andromeda	Rhododendron Lin.
Andromeda	——Lin.
Epigaea	

Decandria Digynia

Hydrangea	
Saxifraga	
Mitella	Tiarella Lin.
Saponaria	

Decandria Trigynia

Lychnis.	Silene Lin.
Silene	
Viscago	Silene Lin.
Alsine [?]	Arenaria ? Lin.
Alsine [?]	Stellaria Lin.
Alsine	
Lychnis	

Decandria Pentagynia

Penthorum	
Oxys	
Myosotis	Cerastium Lin.
Alsine	Cerastium Lin.
Sedum	

Decandria Decagynia

Phytolacca

Class the 11th
Dodecandria Monogynia

Asarum	
Lythrum	
Salicaria	Lythrum Lin.
Portulaca	

Dodecandria Digynia

Agrimonia

Dodecandria Trigynia

Tithymalus.	Euphorbia Lin.

Class the 12th
Icosandria Monogynia

Tuna	Cactus Lin.
Prunus	
Cerasus	Prunus Lin.

Icosandria Digynia

Mespilus	Crataegus Lin.
Crataegus	

Appendix

Icosandria Pentagynia
Mespilus
Malus   Pyrus Lin.
Spiraea
Ulmaria   Spiraea
Aruncus   Spiraea

Icosandria Polygynia
Rosa
Rubus Idaeus   Rubus Lin.
Fragaria
Pentaphyllum   Potentilla Lin.
Caryophyllata   Geum Lin.

Class the 13
Polyandria Monogynia
Christophoriana   Actaea Lin.
Nymphaea
Nelumbo   Nymphaea Lin.
Glaucium   Chelidonium Lin.
Sanguinaria
Anapodophyllum   Podophyllum Lin.
Podophyllum
Tilia
Saracena
Anona
Mimosa

Polyandria Trigynia
Delphinium
Aconitum

Polyandria Pentagynia
Aquilegia
Qu: Steuartia

Polyandria Polygynia
Arbor Tulipifera.   Liriodendron Lin.
Magnolia
Anemone
Hepatica   Anemone Lin.
Thalictrum   Anemone Lin.
Clematitis   Clematis Lin.
Thalictrum   Lin.
Ranunculus
Caltha
Helleborus niger   Helleborus Lin.
Frutex Corni ⎫
   foliis   ⎬ Beureria [?]
   floribus   ⎪ Ehret
   anemones   ⎭

Class the 14th
Didynamia Gymnospermia
Chamaepitys   Teucrium Lin.
Scorodonia   Teucrium Lin.
Trichostema
Acinos
   Sylvestris   Satureia Lin.
Clinopodium   Satureia Lin.
Clinopodium   ——Lin.
Origanum
Calamintha   Melissa Lin.
Nepeta   ——Lin.
Nepeta   Hyssopus Lin.
Agastache
Pulegium   Melissa Gron.
Galeopsis   Lamium Lin.
Galeopsis   Betonica Lin.
Marrubrium
Cardiaca   Leonurus Lin.
Brunella   Prunella Lin.
Phryma   Verbena Gronovius
Cassida   Scuttellaria
Mentha

Didynamia Angiospermia
Linaria   Antirrhinum Lin.
Elatine   Antirrhinum Lin.
Gerardia
Pedicularis
Bartsia
Mimulus
Orobanche
Chelone
Penstemon   Chelone Lin.
Schwalbea
Scrophularia
Bignonia
Ruellia
Obolaria
Buchnera
Vitex

Class the 15
Tetradynamia Siliculosa
Lepidium
Thlapsi
Bursa pastoris   Thlapsi Lin.
Alysson   Cardamine Lin.
Alysson d.
   Paranochia.   Draba Gron.
Alysson.   Draba Lin.
Coronopus
   Ruellii   Cochlearia Lin.

Appendix

	Siliquosa
Hesperis	Arabis Lin.
Cardamine	
Erysimum	
Turritis	Arabis Lin.
Cakile	Bunias Lin.
Nasturtium aqu:	Sisymbrium Lin.
Dentaria	
Sophia Chirug^m.	Sisymbrium Lin.
Alysson	

Class the 16
Monodelphia Decandria
Geranium

Monodelphia Polyandria
Malvinda	Sida Lin.
Abutilon	Sida Lin.
Malva	
Ketmia	Hibiscus Lin.
Hibiscus	———Lin.

Class the 17
Diadelphia Hexandria
Fumaria

Diadelphia Octandria
Polygala

Diadelphia Decandria
Lupinus	
Crotolaria	
Anonis	Glycine Lin.
Phaseoloides.	
Pseudoacacia	Robinia Lin.
Phaseolus	Dolichos Gron. & Lin.
Dolichos	
Clitorius	Clitoria Lin.
Onobrychis	Cracca Lin.
Galega	Vicia. Gron.
Aracus.	Vicia. Gro
Vicia	
Trifolium	
Melilotus fruticosa:	Trifolium Lin.
Lagopus	Trifolium Lin.
Apios	Glycine Lin.
Phaseolus	Glycine. Lin.
Barba Jovis	Medicago. Lin.
Hedysarum	
Trifolium anonoides	Hedysarum Lin.
Melilotus	Hedysarum Lin.

Trifolium Fruticosa	Hedysarum Lin.
Astragulus	
Ervum	
Amorphia	

Class the 18th
Polyadelphia Polyandria
Hypericum	
Androsaemum	Hypericum Lin.
Ascyrum.	
Alcea Floridana.	Hypericu. Lin.

Class the 19
Syngenesia
Polygamia. equalis
Prenanthes	
Chondrilla	Sonchus Lin.
Chondrilla	——Gron.
Hieracium	
Hyoseris	
Tarraxacon	Leontodon Lin.
Tragopogon	
Sonchus	Praenanthes Lin.
Elephantopus	
Atractylis	Carlina. Gro.
Bardana.	Arctium. Lin.
Cirsium	Serratula Lin.
Serratula	
Crostum	Carduus Lin.
Carduus	
Carduus benedict^s.	Cnicus Lin.
Coma avoea	Chrysocoma Lin.
Eupatorium	
Eupatorium	Ageratum Lin.
Porophyllum	Cacalia Lin.
Bidens.	

Polygamia. superflua
Gnaphalium	
Elichrysum	Gnaphalium Lin.
Artemisia	
Conyza	Baccharis Gron.
Q: Eupatorium	
Baccharis	
Senicio arborsc:	Baccharis Lin.
Senicio.	Cacalia. Lin.
Aster vernus	Erigeron. Lin.
Erigeron.	
Doronium an	Arnica. Lin.
Virga aurea	Solidago Lin.

Appendix

Jacobaea	Senecio.	*Gynandria Pentandria*	
Baccharis seu		Granadilla	Passiflora
Conyza magna.	Senecio. Lin.		
Senecio		*Gynandria Hexandria*	
Aster.		Serpentaria	Aristolochia Lin.
Trifolium.	Aster - Lin.		
Solidago.		*Gynandria Polyandria*	
Leucanthemum.	Chrysanthemum Lin.	Arum	
		Arisarum	Arum Lin.
Asteriscus.	Buphthalmum Lin.	Calla	Dracontium Lin.
Cotula foetida	Anthemis.	Class 21	
Millefolium.	Achillea	*Monoecia Monandria*	
Helenia	Helenium Lin.	Zanichellia	
Verbesina	Sigesbeckia. Lin.		
		Monoecia Triandria	
Verbesina.		Sparganium	
Tetragonatheca		Typha	
Corona folis altiss:	Buphthalmum Lin.	Gram^n:	
		Lachryma Jobi aff:	Coix Lin.
Verbesina.		Gramen	
Tetragonatheca		Cyperoides	Coix Lin.
Corona folis altiss:	Buphthalmum Lin.	Gramen Alopocuroides	
		Arund^m.	Carex Lin.
Polygamia frustranea		Carex	
Corona solis.	Helianthus Lin.	Gramen	
Coreopsis		pratense minus.	Poa Lin.
Rudbeckia			
Calcitrapa	Centaurea Lin.	*Monoecia Tetrandria*	
Polygamia necessaria		Urtica	
Osteospermum		Betula	
Chrysogonum		Alnus	Betula Lin.
Sylphium		Morus	
Asteriscus	Sylphium Lin.		
		Monoecia Pentandria	
Monogamia		Xanthium	
Rapuntium.	Lobelia. Lin.	Ambrosia	
Viola		Partheniastrum.	Parthenium Lin.
Balsamina.	Impatiens. Lin.	Iva	
		Amaranthus	
Class 20			
Gynandria Diandria		*Monoecia Hexandria*	
Orchis		Zizania	
Neottia	Ophrys		
Arethusa.		*Monoecia Polyandria*	
{Satyrium		Acalypha	
{Limodorum	——Lin.	Quercus	
Ophrys		Juglans	
Cypripedium		Castanea	Fagus Lin.
		Carpinus	
Gynandria Triandria		Ostrya	Carpinus Lin.
Bermudiana-	Sisyrinchium Lin.	Corylus	
		Platanus	

190 *Appendix*

Liquidamber
Croton
    Monoecia Monadelphia
Pinus
Abies   Pinus Lin.
Thuja
Cupressus.   Croton Lin.
Ricinoides   Jatropha Lin.
Ricinoides   Pinus Lin.
Ricinus
Larix
Napaea
    Monoecia Syngenesia
Sicyos

    Class 22d
    Dioecia Diandria
Salix
    Dioecia Tetrandria
Myrica
Viscum
    Dioecia Pentandria
Cannabis   Acnida Lin.
Lupulus.   Humulus. Lin.
Cissaema
    Dioecia Hexandria
Smilax
Dioscorea
    Dioecia Octandria
Populus
    Dioecia Monodelphia
Juniperus
Taxus

    Class 23
    Polygamia Monoecia
Celtis
Veratrum
Lagurus   Andropogon Lin.
Cenchrus
Atriplex
Acer
    Polygamia Dioecia
Gleditsia
Fraxinus

Diospyros
Nyssa
Araliastrum   Panax Lin.

    Class 24
    Cryptogamia
      Filices
Equisetum
Osmunda
Filix florida   Osmunda
Ophioglossum
Lunaria   Osmunda
Pteris
Filix ramosa
  major
Lonchitis
Adiantum
Lonchitis   Polypodium Lin.
Trichomanes   Acrosticum Lin.
Acrosticum   Arcola Gronov.
Polypodium
Filix minor
Phyllitis
Asplenium

    Cryptogamia. Musci
Muscus   ⎰ Lichen Lin.
  pyxidatus† ⎨ Coralloides
            ⎱ Dilleni.
Lycopodium   Lin.
Marchantia   Lin.
Lichenoides   Lichen Lin.
             ⎧ Usnia, Dill.
Lichenoides ⎨
             ⎩ Lichen Lin.
Polytrichum   Dill.
Jungermannia   Lin.
Muscus Aquat.
  Thuja foliis.   Sphagnum Lin.
Coralloides   Lichen Lin.
Lichenoides
  crinitis   Lichen
Bryum
Hypnum
Lichenastrum   Jungermannia
                  Lin.
Lichen   Hepatica Mich.
Selago   Lycopodium Lin.
               (Bryum
               Roseum!)
               Ray.

† This item and the next 37 items all have check marks in the margin, except Spongia and Isis, which have plus marks, and Polypodium and Algamarina, which have dashes.

Appendix

Didynamia angiospermia. Lin.
Fungoides
Phallus
Bolitus
Agaricus
Ulva
Peziza
Lenticula   (monoecia
                  diand^{ia}.
                  Lemma [?]
                  Lin.)
Spongia
Isis
Tubera terrae.   Lycoperdon
                      Lin.
Polypodium
  (vide Filices)   Acrosticum Lin.
Conserva
               vide
Algamarina   Gynandria
  gramena   polyandria
               Zostera Lin.
Fucoides
Fucus plumerus   Sertularia Lin.
Clavaria
Ulva marina
Fungus
Tremella
Lyoperdon
Madrepora
Sphagnum
Alcyonium

            Musci
Muscus
  pyxidatus   Coralloides
Lycopodium
Polytrichium
Bryum

Hypnum
Lichenoides
Sphagnum
Coralloides

              Algae
Marchantia
Jungelmania
Lichen
Lichenoides
Lichenastrum
Fucus
Fucoides
Ulva
Conserva
Tremella

            Fungi
Fungoides   Clavaria
Clavaria
Phallus
Bolitus
Agaricus
Peziza
Tubera Terrae   Lycoperdon
                      solidum
Fungus
Lycoperdon
Fucus
  plumosus: Sertularia Gron.
Isis. Gron.
(Keradophyton?)
Madrepora
Spongia
Alcyonium

          Class 25
           Palmae
{Palma humilis   Chamaerops.
{vulgo Palmetto   Lin.

ABBREVIATIONS

The following abbreviations are used in the notes:

BM	British Museum
CLO	James Edward Smith, *A Selection of the Correspondence of Linnaeus and Other Naturalists* (London, 1821)
DNB	*Dictionary of National Biography*
EJ	*Executive Journals, Council of Colonial Virginia*, ed. H. R. McIlwaine (Richmond, 1928)
GM	*Gentleman's Magazine*
HM	*Historical Magazine*
HMC	Historical Manuscripts Commission
HSP	Historical Society of Pennsylvania
JHB	*Journals of the House of Burgesses of Virginia* (1702/3-1705, 1705-6, 1710-12), ed. H. R. McIlwaine (Richmond, 1912)
LC	Linnaean Correspondence, Linnean Society of London
LPCC	*Letters and Papers of Cadwallader Colden* (New York, 1920)
MJB	William Darlington (ed.), *Memorials of John Bartram and Humphrey Marshall with Notices of their Contemporaries* (Philadelphia, 1849)
NP	Norton Papers: John Norton and Son (1750-1795) Papers in the Archives of Colonial Williamsburg, Inc., Williamsburg, Va.
PRO	Public Record Office, London
PTRS	*Philosophical Transactions of the Royal Society of London*
VMHB	*Virginia Magazine of History and Biography*
WMQ	*William and Mary Quarterly*

NOTES

CHAPTER I

1. *LPCC*, IV, 251.
2. Thomas Jefferson, *Notes on the State of Virginia*, ed. William Peden (Chapel Hill, 1955), p. 42.
3. His letter to Samuel Durant, 21 March 1739, ed. W. G. Stanard, *VMHB*, VII (1899), 172-4. The botanist was born in 1694, and not in 1685, as has sometimes been stated. This fact is established by a letter (NP, August 2, 1773) written by Clayton, in which he says that he will soon be seventy-nine.

CHAPTER II

1. Peter LeNeve, *Pedigrees of the Knights*, ed. by George W. Marshall, London, 1873, *Harleian Society*, VIII, 186-87.
2. Joseph L. Chester and George J. Armytage, *Allegations for Marriage Licenses Issued by the Bishop of London 1611-1828* (London, 1887), p. 138.
3. *Old Lombard Street*, Notes by the Royal Insurance Co., Ltd. (London, 1912), p. 5. Reference is made to these two houses in the wills of Sir Jasper and his wife (P.C.C. 180 NABBS and P.C.C. COKER 75, respectively); also in a lawsuit in 1707, Clayton vs. Clayton & Boteler, PRO, C9/318/30.
4. LeNeve states the former, and Chester and Armytage the latter.
5. Joseph Foster (ed.), *Alumni Oxonienses: The Members of the University of Oxford 1500-1714* (London, 1891); Jasper Thomson was mentioned in Dame Mary's will.
6. The Poor Rate and Churchwardens' Account, Fulham Public Library, London.
7. The Honourable Henry Sidney, *Diary of the Times of Charles the Second*, ed. R. W. Blencowe (London, 1843), I, lxvii.
8. Edward Hasted, *The History and Topographical Survey of the County of Kent* (London, 1798) III, 95; V, 126-36; Thomas Philipott, *Villare Cantianum* (London, 1776), p. 156.
9. David Jennings, *Hawkhurst* (London, 1792), pp. 5-6; Richard Kilburne, *Survey of the County of Kent* (London, 1659).

10. 24 April; *Acts and Ordinances of the Interregnum 1642-1660*, ed. C. H. Firth and R. S. Railt (London, 1911) I, 1131.

11. Alfred B. Beaven, *The Aldermen of the City of London* (London, 1913) II, 78.

12. Chancery Proceedings in PRO: Clayton vs. Clayton, C9/82/131, 1681; Clayton vs. Clayton, C9/265/6, 1693; Clayton vs. Clayton, C9/296/32, 1706; Clayton vs. Clayton & Boteler, C9/318/30, 1707. See also "Manuscripts of the House of Lords, #1493, New Series IV (1699-1702)" London, 1908, in publications of HMC. Among the "Tracts relating to Law Cases, etc." in the British Museum, there is one of the botanist's father, John Clayton, "Executor of Dame Mary Clayton, Executrix of Sir Jasper Clayton, Appellant; Prudence Clayton, Respondent," dated 22 February 1699. This last reference gives a summary of the case to that date.

13. William Brigg, *The Parish Registers of St. Edmund the King, Lombard Street, London 1670-1812* (London, 1892), p. 89.

14. John Venn and J. A. Venn (eds.), *Alumni Cantabrigienses: A Biographical List . . . from the Earliest Times to 1900* (Cambridge, 1922) Part I, III.

15. Wasey Sterry (ed.), *The Eton College Register* (Eton, 1943), p. 74, quoting from the Repertory Book of the Court of Aldermen, 1660-1662, p. 63.

16. F. A. Inderwick, *A Calendar of the Inner Temple Records* (London, 1901) III, 320.

17. Paston represented Castle Rising in Parliament for twelve years (1661-1673). He was succeeded by Samuel Pepys when he was raised to the peerage as a baron and viscount, eventually becoming Earl of Yarmouth in 1679. As early as 1664 he was working towards these goals when he was a Gentleman of the Privy Chamber. He wrote to his wife: "This morning I took my leave of the King, who above 20 times the day before repeated it to my friends that none was nearer his heart than myself, that he intended to mend my honour and fortune, the which I had this day from his own mouth in his bedchamber, viz. that he will speedily make me a nobleman of England." ("Letters of Sir Robert Paston in the Sir H. Ingilby, Bart., Manuscripts, Ripley Castle, County York," HMC, *Appendix to the 6th Report*, p. 364b.)

18. The second earl was born in 1652.

19. John Evelyn, *The Diary of John Evelyn*, ed. E. S. deBeer (Oxford, 1955) III, 186.

20. Henshaw later accompanied the Duke of Richmond, as Secretary of the Embassy, when the Duke became Ambassador to Denmark. He also served as French Secretary under Charles II, James II, and William III. (*DNB*)

21. E. S. deBeer, "Earliest Fellows of the Royal Society," *Notes & Records of the Royal Society of London*, VII (April, 1950).

22. *Ibid.* The formal beginning of the Society, which was composed of several groups, is dated from the granting of the Charter of Incorporation, the 15th of July, 1662. The following May, one hundred and fifteen persons were named as Original Fellows.

23. "Ingilby Papers," HMC, *Ap. to the 6th Report*, p. 363.

24. *Ibid.*, "Epistre Generale de Villa Cary a nos tres cher amis a Oxnet." Evelyn called Lady Mordaunt "the most virtuous Lady in the world." (Evelyn, *Dairy*, III, 469.)

25. HMC, *Ap. to the 6th Report*, p. 364. The Breams were likely "Sir Richard Breames" and his wife, to whom Evelyn refers, although the name was actually spelled Braham: Richard Braham (1613-1675/6) knighted 1645, baronet, 1662. Likewise, the "Boye's" were probably the Bowyers, Sir John's future in-laws. Charles Stuart (1639-1672) was the third Duke of Richmond.

Notes to pages 11-15

26. LeNeve, *Pedigrees*, pp. 186-7.

27. The botanist wrote to his English steward, at his father's death, "he dyed Nov. 18th, 1737, in the 72nd year of his age." (*VMHB*, VII [1899], 172-4.)

28. The botanist's father corresponded with his first cousin, Cecil Bowyer and his letters included orders for picture frames and coats of arms to be engraved on silver plate. His son, Thomas, when a medical student at Cambridge, was the subject of some. Copies of these letters were in the letter-book belonging to Jasper S. Clayton; see W. G. Stanard, "The Clayton Family," *HM*, II (October, 1891), pp. 26-27.

29. From 1664 on, Dame Mary had paid the taxes; then, in 1670, Sir John did (Charles James Feret, *Fulham Old and New* [London, 1900] II, 188). Also see the Poor Rate & Churchwardens' Accounts 1637-1675, Fulham.

30. Feret, *Fulham*, II, 188.

31. There is a rather detailed account given in an inventory of "Oxnead" in the Paston Letters in the British Museum, Add. Mss. 36,988, f. 264.

32. HMC, *Ap. to the 6th Report*, p. 366.

33. Copies of his letters to the Duke of Richmond in which he referred to a law case coming up in court, were made by Sir John, and are now in the British Museum, Add. Mss. 21,948, f. 103.

34. Osborne was the second baronet. He was raised to the peerage in 1673; after receiving various titles, he finally became the Duke of Leeds in 1694, having served as Lord High Treasurer for six years, 1673-1679. HMC, *Ap. to the 6th Report*, p. 366.

35. Feret, *Fulham*, II, 158; HMC, *Ap. to the 6th Report*, p. 366; King of England, *Miscellaneous Publications*, Document II, Charles II, British Museum; HMC, *Ap. to the 8th Report*, p. 257.

36. Letters of Dr. William Aglionby in The Paston Letters, Dd.11.57, Cambridge University Library.

37. Robert Paston to his wife, B. M. Add. Mss. 27,447, f. 370.

38. Inderwick, *Inner Temple*, III, 101.

39. Evelyn, *Diary*, IV, 96.

40. "The Manuscripts of the House of Lords 1690-1" 12, Ms. Min. L. J., XIV, 441; 232-33, 26 Dec. L. J. XIV, 605: HMC, *13th Report, Ap. Part V*.

41. Edward Chamberlayne, *Present State of England* (London, 1694, 1, 2.), p. 231.

42. Hargreaves' Manuscript, Letter L, February 23, 1779, 211-12, Virginia State Library, Richmond.

43. The Admission record was kindly sent to us by Mr. E. A. P. Hart, Librarian of the Inner Temple Library.

44. Venn, *Alumni Cantabrigienses* (1922) Part I, I.

45. Indewick, *Inner Temple*, III, 274.

46. *Ibid.*, 306, February 1 & 3, 1693.

47. Stanard, "The Clayton Family," p. 26.

48. According to Peter Walne, County archivist.

49. A. A. Shaw (ed.), *Calendar of Treasury Books and Papers* (London, 1903); "Promotions" in *GM*, IX (July, 1739) 384; (Nov. 1739) 606. B. M. Add. Mss. 23,643 gives some account of his problems at Gibraltar.

50. *GM*, XIII (July, 1743), 383-84.

51. P.C.C. BOYCOTT 224, f. 1643 (July).

52. "The Wren Mss. Court Orders," *Wren Society*, Vol. 18 (Oxford, 1941).

53. At Henry Symonds's death at the end of the seventeenth century, Sir Christopher Wren wrote the following letter to Sir John Clayton: Sir, it is noe surprise to mee to hear the ill news of my dear Nephew's death, having but little reason to expect his recovery when I last saw him. I am much

afflicted for his family and am not a little afraid it will not be in my power to serve the poor children in the way I had projected for them. for it is not an hour since a servant neer the King's person came to me with a sort of mandamus, if I can weather this point, the best I can doe, will be that a friend and not a stranger should succeed; I heartily lament his Death and his being long so dangerously ill hath created once not a little Trouble to answer the sollicitations of great persons whom I must and will disoblige. I wish the best comfort to the good widdow, who hath shown herself a tender nurse and infinitely deserved the good opinion of all his Relations, and particularly of

                    Sr.,
              Y^r very humble Servant
                  Chr. Wren

(Ernest Law, *The History of Hampton Court Palace* [London, 1891] II, 83, quoting a letter in Treasury Papers, LXIII, #46.) Alice Symonds had wanted her husband's clerkship for her son, the botanist's first cousin, but as Wren stated, his influence had waned and he was unable to obtain this appointment for him.

54. The genealogies are taken from G. E. C[ockayne], *The Complete Peerage of England, Scotland, Ireland, Great Britain and the United Kingdom, Extant, Extinct, or Dormant* (new ed.; London, 1910-), and L. G. Pine (ed.), *Burke's . . . Landed Gentry* (17th ed.; London, 1952).

55. *Documents Relating to Colonial New York*, ed. J. R. Broadhead (Albany, 1855), V & VI; *GM*, IX (June 1739), 327; *GM*, XV (February 1745), 94; *GM*, XIX (April 1749), 188.

56. PRO, C9/319/22: "The answer of John Clayton Esq. one of the Defds to the Bill of Complt of Prudence Clayton Spinster Compt." (Oct. 3, 1693).

57. Maryland was sometimes used in a generic sense and could equally well have meant Virginia.

58. P.C.C. TENISON 125.

59. *EJ* III, 125-26.

60. *DNB*.

61. Her will was proved in that year.

62. Record of her son's (Thomas') baptism at St. Mary's Church, Walton-on-Thames.

63. Miss Edith Andrews, Clerk to the Church-wardens, kindly searched the parish registers for us.

64. A fourth brother, Samuel, has been invented at least once.

65. *Calendar of Virginia State Papers*, ed. Wm. P. Palmer (Richmond, 1875), I, 94.

66. *EJ*, III, 69-70 (Jan. 23, 1705/6).

67. *Ibid.*, p. 163 (Oct. 30, 1707).

68. *JHB*, November 10, 1710, 262-63.

69. PRO, C. O. 5/1316, f. 284 (o.99).

70. PRO, C. O. 5/1316, f. 503.

71. *Virginia Gazette* (Parks), 18 November 1737; *JHB, passim.*

72. *The Official Letters of Alexander Spotswood*, ed. R. A. Brock (Richmond, 1882), II, 353-54.

73. Letter book of Robert Carter in the Alderman Library, University of Virginia.

74. Stanard, "The Clayton Family," p. 26.

75. There are two of these documents in PRO: C. O. 5/1318, f. 134; C. O. 5/1319, f. 258.

76. "Letters of William Byrd and Sir Hans Sloane Relative to Plants and Minerals of Virginia," ed. E. G. Swem, *WMQ* (2), I, 186.

77. Elizabeth Donnan, "Eighteenth Century English Merchants: Micajah Perry," *Journal of Economic and Business History*, IV (November 1931), 70-98.
78. *James City County* (Colonial Abstracts, Ser. 2, IV, 32, MS 101). He was given a power of attorney by Micajah Perry.
79. *EJ*, III, 125-26 (Aug. 30, 1706).
80. Most of these occur in Louis B. Wright and Marion Tinling (eds.), *The Secret Diary of William Byrd of Westover 1709-1712* (Richmond, 1941). There are a few references in Louis B. Wright and Marion Tinling (eds.), *William Byrd of Virginia: The London Diary (1717-1721) and other Writings* (New York, 1958).
81. J. S. Bassett (ed.), *The Writings of Colonel Byrd* (New York, 1901), p. 361.
82. Original letter-book of Custis in the Library of Congress, typescript by Dr. Maude H. Woodfin in the Virginia State Library, Richmond.
83. E. G. Swem (ed.), *Brothers of the Spade: Correspondence of Peter Collinson of London, and of John Custis, of Williamsburg, 1734-1746* (Barre, Mass., 1957), p. 14.
84. *Ibid.*, pp. 23-24.
85. This practice was started under his predecessor, Steven Thomson.
86. The ownership and occupancy of this house between 1718 and 1749 have not been authenticated, but there are reasons for believing it to have been owned for a part of that time by Colonel Grymes. It would be interesting to establish this point beyond speculation since Colonel Grymes' house seems to have been the one which Mr. Clayton occupied, as is indicated by the following items from the *Virginia Gazette*: "George Charleton, Taylor, lately arrived from London, now lives in Williamsburg, at the next house to Colonel Grymes (late Mr. Clayton's) by whom Gentlemen may have Cloaths made after the newest and most fashionable manner." (Sept. 6, 1738.) "For Sale: The House which formerly belong'd to Col. Jenings, in which the Bristol Store was lately kept, being the next house to John Clayton's Esq. in Williamsburg. It is a large commodious House with Two Lots, a Garden, Coach House, Stables and Other Outhouses and Conveniences. Enquire of Captain William Rogers in York, or of William Parks, Printer, in Williamsburg." (Sept. 10, 1736.) One additional reference to the house is in connection with preparations for the celebration of the King's birthday in 1727. Robert Carter, acting lieutenant-governor until Gooch arrived, sent instructions: "The Governour's House to be Illuminated Mr. Clayton also and likewise the Capitol if it was so before. I believe the Colledge and all the houses in Town will be Illuminated bonnfires to be made as before." (From his letter-books in the Alderman Library.)

CHAPTER III

1. Clayton to Carolus Linnaeus, October 10, 1748, Linnean Society of London.
2. Venn, *Alumni Cantabrigienses*.
3. *The Eton College Register 1698-1752*, ed. with biographical notes by Richard Arthur Austen-Leigh (Eton, 1927).
4. Letter to Samuel Durant. See Note 3, Chapter I.
5. Reference to Clayton's Pteridophyta are in J. S. L. Gilmour and T. G. Tutin, *A List of the More Important Collections in the University Herbarium, Cambridge* (Cambridge, 1933).
6. Payments to "Cap. Clayton" for tithing lists are recorded in C. G. Chamberlayne (ed.), *The Vestry Book of Petsworth Parish, Gloucester,*

Virginia (Richmond, 1933). This title, no doubt, derived from his rank in the county militia.

7. Peter Collinson to Cadwallader Colden, May 19, 1756, *LPCC*, V, 81-82.
8. *EJ*, IV, 284.
9. Chamberlayne, *Vestry Book of Petsworth Parish*, p. 154.
10. Anne Maury, *Memoirs of a Huguenot Family*, transcribed and compiled from the manuscripts of James Fontaine, etc. (New York, 1853). This contains the only known account of the Spotswood expedition as well as the earlier one undertaken by John Fontaine.
11. Beverly became a member of the Council July 12, 1720.
12. C. G. Chamberlayne (ed.), *The Vestry Book of St. Paul's Parish, Hanover County, 1706-1786* (Richmond, 1940), pp. 94-95.
13. *Statutes at Large*, ed. W. W. Hening (Philadelphia, 1823), p. 63.
14. John Clayton to John Norton, London, August 31, 1768, NP.
15. Governor Drysdale's report on the "State of Virginia," 1726, PRO, C. O. 5/1320.
16. According to the tablets on the present buildings.
17. "A Few Things About Our County" in *WMQ*, III (July 1894), 20-21. General Taliaferro refers to Clayton as "The Linnaeus of America."
18. See various issues of *The Virginia Gazette*.
19. From a talk given by Mr. Webster S. Rhoads, of Richmond, Virginia, at the "John Clayton Day," in Williamsburg, October 1957, in Phi Beta Kappa Hall. A copy of this is deposited in the Alderman Library, University of Virginia.
20. W. H. Whiting, Jr.: "Notes on Major Henry Whiting," *WMQ*, X (1930), 47-51.
21. "John Clayton & Elizabeth Whiting both of Ware Parish, were married J—— 2, 1723." This was taken from a remnant of the Ware parish records according to the Rev. W. T. Williams, "Notes on Clayton-Davies," *Tyler's Quarterly*, IV (1927), 163-4, and VII (1931), 209.
22. Barton is quoting from John Page's letter of January 18, 1805. Benjamin Smith Barton, "Memorandums of the Life and Writings of Mr. John Clayton, the Celebrated Botanist of Virginia," *Medical and Physical Journal*, II (1805), 139-45.
23. Whiting, "Notes on Major Henry Whiting," pp. 47-51.
24. All of these orders are from the Clayton correspondence in the Norton Papers, Archives of Colonial Williamsburg, Inc.
25. According to Francis Hargreaves.
26. Jessie Hopkins and A. B. Massey, "In Memory of John Clayton, Botanist of Colonial Virginia," *The Virginia Journal of Science, News and Notes* (new series) II (July, 1951), 222.
27. D. D. Johannes Claytonus and D. Joh. Fred. Gronovius, *Flora Virginica* (Leiden, 1762), p. 143.
28. Clarence R. Williams, "Dr. John Dunn as a Virginia Botanist," *WMQ*, XV (1935), 115.
29. Hargreaves' Manuscript, Letter L, February 23, 1779, 211-212.
30. Bartram Papers, I, 14, Historical Society of Pennsylvania, Philadelphia. Probably written July 1739.
31. Marriage contract of Mary Berkeley and Clayton's great-grandson, Jasper Clayton, in 1808. Berkeley Manuscripts, Alderman Library, University of Virginia.
32. Polly Cary Mason, Records of Colonial Gloucester County (typescript printed at Newport News. First volume, 1946; second volume [completed by her husband] printed in 1948), II, 34.
33. About a third of these were edited by Frances Norton Mason in *John*

Notes to pages 31-42 199

Norton & Sons, Merchants of London & Virginia (Richmond, 1937). All Clayton letters to the Nortons, except for two, which appear in this book are from unpublished correspondence in the Archives of Colonial Williamsburg, Inc.

34. Clayton's letter to Durant, *VMHB*, VII (1899), 172-4.
35. Clayton to Norton, January 25, 1773, NP.
36. August 31, 1768. Pale Catechu, or Terra Japonica—an extract prepared from the leaves and twigs of the Ancaria Gambir (Hunter) Roxburg., a plant which grows in the Dutch East Indies, and the Malay Archipelago (H. W. Youngken, *Pharmacognosy* [Philadelphia, 1936]). Samuel Dale mentions Terra Japonica in an article on "Materia Medica" in *PTRS*, XVII, 933. Dale described it as "condensed Juice of the Fruit of the Fausel."
37. August 31, 1772. Anderson pills were also favorites of Robert Carter. He mentioned them in a letter to William Byrd II, March 3, 1721, in the William Byrd Papers (1711-1757) in the Huntington Library.
38. Letter LI, February 26, 1779.
39. The bulk of Bishop Clayton's estate went to a niece, who married Dr. Barnard, Dean of Derry. The Dean considered that his wife's uncle had been a controversial figure, and rather than revive old arguments, suppressed the bishop's manuscripts. (Kipp's *Biographica Botanica*, III, 620-28. Manuscript copy of a Memoir of Bishop Robert Clayton in Trinity College Library, Dublin.)
40. Alexander Garden to John Ellis, February 17, 1759: *CLO*, I, 428.
41. Clayton to Linnaeus, October 10, 1748, LC.
42. "I ask Pardon if I did not *before now*, acknowledge the favour of Flora orientalis Rau. which Mr. Hook [?] carefully Deliver'd, & those copies for Mr Clayton and for John Bartram were forwarded to them." Collinson to J. F. Gronovius, October 18, 1756. Ward Mss., 1874, Linnean Society of London.
43. Governor Page to Dr. Barton, quoted in the latter's "Memorandum."
44. August 2, 1773, NP.
45. August 15, 1769, NP.
46. September 27, 1773, NP.
47. *GM*, VI (August 1736), 487.
48. *GM*, IX (June 1739), 327.
49. *GM*, XIII (July 1743), 383-84.
50. *GM*, XV (August 1745), 444.
51. From John Custis' letter-book in the Library of Congress.
52. Swanskin was a type of flannel, either woolen or cotton; tabby was usually a taffeta; shalloon, a French twill made of wool.
53. Gloucester County Tax Accounts, 1770-1772, #21341, Virginia State Library, Richmond.
54. Mason, *John Norton & Sons*, p. 293, n.
55. According to Nott in a letter to the Board of Trade, September 22, 1705, PRO, C. O. 5/1314.
56. John Jr. ran an advertisement in the *Virginia Gazette* (Purdie Dixon), July 11, 1766, of one hundred acres of land for sale in Hanover County, called "Horseshoe" and another tract in New Kent County "To be sold (during the life of John Clayton of Henrico County, who is very healthy and about 40 years of age)."

CHAPTER IV

1. Charles E. Raven, *John Ray, Naturalist, His Life and Works* (Cambridge, 1950); Marie Boas, *Robert Boyle and Seventeenth Century Chemistry*

(Cambridge, 1958). Basil Willy has written a pertinent essay on the subject, "Seventeenth Century Background" in Louis Trenchard Morse, *The Life and Works of the Honourable Robert Boyle* (Oxford, 1944).

2. Grew's *The Anatomy of Plants* was published in 1682.
3. Raven, *John Ray*, p. 229.
4. Walter T. Layton, *The Discoverer of Gas Lighting, Notes on the Life and Work of the Reverend John Clayton, D.D. 1657-1725* (London, 1926), p. 12.
5. B. M. Birch Collection 4437, f. 398.
6. "Anatomical Observations in the Heads of Fowel at several times," Allen Moulen, M.D., S.R.S., *PTRS*, XVII (April, 1693), 711-16.
7. For much information and a delightful visit, the authors are indebted to Mr. W. G. McKenzie. According to him, the garden bordered the Thames before the Embankment was filled in. A small canal ran up the main path and formed a water garden. When the street was made, the old buildings were torn down and more land was given for the garden on the Embankment side. There is one original green-house. Philip Miller lived nearby at 1 Swan Walk and Sir Joseph Banks on neighbouring Tite Street.
8. A most complete account of his life is given in E. St. John Brooks' *Sir Hans Sloane* (London, 1954). Sloane's obituary appeared in *GM*, XXIII (January, 1753), 52.
9. Brooks, *Sir Hans Sloane*, p. 203.
10. Hans Sloane, *A Voyage to the Ilands Madera, Barbados, Nieves, S. Christophers and Jamaica with the Natural History of the Herbs and Trees, Four-footed Beasts, Fishes, Birds, Insects, Reptiles, Etc. . . .* (London, 1707-1725).
11. *GM*, XVIII (July, 1748), 301.
12. Brooks, *Sir Hans Sloane*, p. 192.
13. Collinson to Linnaeus, May 8, 1753, LC.
14. Raymond Phineas Stearns, "James Petiver, Promoter of Natural Science," *Proceedings of the American Antiquarian Society*, LXII (October, 1952), 243-365.
15. Banister's letters from Virginia to Bishop Compton are in the Sloane Collection (3321) in the British Museum.
16. Sloane wrote in 1721 that he and his friends had been disappointed by the results of Mr. Vernon's and Mr. Jones' trips. (Brooks, *Sir Hans Sloane*, p. 182.)
17. E. G. Swem (ed.), "Letters of William Byrd II and Sir Hans Sloane," *WMQ*, 2s., I (1921), 186-200.
18. Sloane 4063 f. 79; 4064, f. 214, 249, 271; 4067, f. 10, British Museum.
19. When it was republished in 1714, the title was changed to *The History of Carolina: Containing the Exact Description and Natural History of that Country; Together with the Present State Thereof.* Percy G. Adams gives an interesting sidelight on this book in "The Real Author of William Byrd's *Natural History of Virginia*," *American Literature*, XXVIII (1956-7), 211-20.
20. *VMHB*, V (June, 1898), 15-17.
21. Sarah P. Stetson, "Traffic in Seeds and Plants from England's Colonies in North America," *Agricultural History*, XXIII (January 1949), 45-56.
22. From Peter Collinson's notes in his books in the library of John Cator of Buckingham Place. This library had been left to him by his uncle, who had married Collinson's daughter. The notes were copied by Mr. Ayler Bourke Lambert, and are now in the library of the Linnean Society of London. These notes have been published in the Society's *Transactions*, X (1811), 270-82.

23. William Sherard was the English consul at Smyrna for many years and later became one of England's outstanding botanists. His collections are now in the Sherardian Museum at Oxford. He bought Sebastian Vaillant's papers and worked on them with Dr. Herman Boerhaave. The results of their studies were published in 1727 as the *Botanicum Parisienne*.

24. From a sketch of Dillenius by Collinson on a loose sheet in the back of one of his Common Place Books in the Linnean Society of London. Under "Deaths" in *GM*, VIII (February, 1738), 109: "James Sherard, M.D. (formerly an Apothecary) worth upwards of 150,000 £ at Eltham, Kent."

25. There is a lengthy description of Miller among the Collinson notes copied by Ayler Bourke Lambert.

26. George Frederick Frick and Raymond Phineas Stearns: *Mark Catesby, the Colonial Audubon* (Urbana, Ill., 1961). In the library of the Linnean Society of London is a copy of a biographical sketch of Catesby by Collinson, found in his copy of *The Natural History of Carolina*.

27. Louis B. Wright and Marion Tinling (eds.), *The Secret Diary of William Byrd, 1709-1712* (Richmond, 1941), p. 194. Frick and Stearns (*Mark Catesby*, p. 11) state that Cocke arrived in Virginia "apparently shortly after 1700," but Byrd's entries for June 22, 1710; April 22, 25 and 30, 1712, make it clear that Mrs. Cocke came with Catesby in 1712, and her husband in 1710.

28. Wright and Tinling, *Secret Diary of William Byrd*, p. 585.

29. Dawson Turner (ed.), *Extracts from the Literary and Scientific Correspondence of Richard Richardson* (Yarmouth, 1855), p. 371.

30. Richard Pulteney, *Historical and Biographical Sketches of the Progress of Botany in England* (London, 1790), p. 224.

31. List in Frick and Stearns, *Mark Catesby*, pp. 109-11.

32. *Ibid.*, p. 37.

33. Catesby to Bartram, 1740, *MJB*, pp. 319-20.

34. Collinson's sketch of Catesby, Linnean Society of London.

35. "Magnolia flora albo folio majore accuminato haud albicanto Clayt. Specimens of this Tree were first sent me in the year 1736, by my worthy friend, John Clayton, Esq. of Virginia and from the only Tree known in that country." Catesby added that Bartram had found it in Pennsylvania. (Catesby, *The Natural History of Carolina, Florida & the Bahama Islands* [London, 1771] I, 115.)

36. *Ibid.*, p. 13.

37. *Ibid.*, p. 2.

38. Mark Catesby, *Hortus Europae Americanus* (London, 1767), p. 30.

39. Catesby, *Natural History of Carolina*, II, Appendix, 116.

CHAPTER V

1. His father, Jacob, and his grandfather, for whom he was named, had taught at the University of Leiden.

2. A dissertation on the camphor tree, his doctor's thesis, published in 1715; a publication on geological subjects, 1750; and *Flora Orientalis*, a book on Rauwolff and his collections, 1755. There is a short article on "The Life of Gronovius," by Dr. H. J. Lam, in *Chronica Botanica*, VI, #2, 28-30.

3. Introduction to the *Flora Virginica* (1739) Part I.

4. Dawson Turner, *Extracts from the Literary and Scientific Correspondence of Richard Richardson*, pp. 343-44. Dr. Richardson (1663-1741) was an English naturalist, whose specialty was corals. He had received a bachelor of Physik degree from the University of Leiden. Gesner (1516-1565) was a

Swiss naturalist who published five over-sized volumes entitled *Historiae Animalium*. His work has been regarded as the beginning of modern zoology. He was also a botanist, but his two books on the subject were not published until 1751 and 1771.

5. Dr. Arvid HJ. Uggla, "Linnaeus," translated by Alan Blair under the auspices of the Swedish Institute, Stockholm (Uppsala, 1957); D. H. Stoever, *The Life of Sir Charles Linnaeus*, translated by Joseph Trapp (London, 1794); Miss Brightwell, *A Life of Linnaeus* (London, 1858); Norah Gourlie, *The Prince of Botanists* (London, 1953). For a guide to some of the literature relating to Linnaeus see W. T. Stearn, *An Introduction to the Species Plantarum and Cognate Botanical Works of Carl Linnaeus* (London 1957).

6. Albrecht Haller (1708-1777), a student of Boerhaave, was versatile in many fields: a public health official, a member of the Swiss council, an economist, a founder of a philological seminary and an orphan asylum, president of the Royal Academy of Gottingen.

7. *CLO*, II, 258.

8. Boerhaave (1668-1738) was often called "The Common Teacher of all Europe," as so many of his students became teachers themselves, and were famous in their own fields. He founded the Leiden Botanical Garden, and wrote many books. Five of Boerhaave's pupils were on the University of Edinburgh faculty, which may have influenced Clayton's choice of that University for his son, Thomas.

9. Sloane Mss. 4054, f. 154, BM.

10. *CLO*, II, 179. The 12th ed. (1766-8) had 2500 pages.

11. George Clifford was an Amsterdam banker and merchant of English descent. Linnaeus acted as his personal physician while cataloguing his remarkable garden. The results of his study were published under the title *Hortus Cliffortianus*.

12. No date, but thought to be October 1, 1737. Alston Letters, La. III, 375, Library of the University of Edinburgh.

13. Turner, *Correspondence of Richardson*, p. 348, n.

14. Letter to Richardson, July 22, 1738: C. 10, f. 44 Ms. Radcliffe Trust, Bodleian Library, Oxford.

15. Dr. E. Hulsjoff Pol, Classics Archivist of the University of Leiden, has recently completed an article on Abraham Gronovius. She kindly allowed the authors to study microfilms of the Gronovian correspondence in the library of the University of Munich.

16. September 7, 1735: LC, V, 365.

17. LC, V, 378.

18. Introduction to the *Flora Virginica* (1739).

19. Samuel Doody, an apothecary, was a "demonstrator" at Chelsea Garden, according to Pulteney (*Historical and Biographical Sketches . . . of Botany*). *Vernonia*, or "iron-weed," was named for Vernon, and *Krigia* (Adopogoi) was named for David Krieg.

20. *CLO*, II, 300.

21. Michel, *Nova Plantarum Genera* (Florence, 1729); Plukenet, *Almagestum Botanicum* (London, 1696), *Amaltheum Botanicum* (London, 1705), and *Amalthei Botanici mantissa* (London, 1700); Morison, *Plantarum Historia Universalis* (Oxon, 1679).

22. LC, V, 530.

23. July 12, 1739: LC, V, 444.

24. November 17, 1739: LC, V, 442.

25. April 22, 1740: LC, V, 450.

26. December 24, 1736: LC, V, 405.

27. November 11, 1738: LC, V, 443.

28. March 26, 1743: LC, V, 467.
29. November 11, 1738: LC, V, 443.
30. September 2, 1738: Turner, *Correspondence of Richardson*, p. 179.
31. January 23, 1738: *CLO*, II, 314-15.
32. December 24, 1736: LC, V, 405.
33. "Secundum Leges Linnai sunt sequentia Gronovii Flora Virginica . . . Lugdb. 1739 Oct." This pamphlet is in the library of the Linnean Society of London.
34. Gronovius to Colden, July 9, 1745: *LPCC*, VII, 125-26.
35. Gronovius to Linnaeus, September 4, 1739: LC, V, 445.
36. September 26, 1740: Turner, *Correspondence of Richardson*, p. 190.
37. January 28, 1743: Bäck Correspondence in the library of the Karolinska Institute, Stockholm. Dr. Bäck was the royal physician and a close friend of Linnaeus.
38. Bartram to Colden, April 29, 1744: Autograph Collection Simon Gratz. Case 7, Box 21, Historical Society of Pennsylvania.
39. July 26, 1740: LC, V, 454.
40. There are a great number of these among the Gronovian letters in the Linnaean Correspondence.

CHAPTER VI

1. *EJ*, p. 22.
2. *Ibid.* Sir John Randolph, born 1693, admitted to the bar in November 1717, knighted 1732, married Susannah, daughter of Peter Beverly and aunt of the botanist's wife.
3. Administration Book 1725, 116 (June) Somerset House, London. A brief statement in Latin and very difficult to read. Although Prudence died in 1711, her will was not actually administered until June 1726, probably when Mr. Clayton returned to England. This was due to the death of her executrix, Elizabeth Nourse, a niece, prior to 1711.
4. Deodans goods forfeited to the Crown.
5. M. E. Sorley, *Lewis of Warner Hall* (Missouri, 1935).
6. According to Mr. Clayton's will.
7. Court records of Hanover County, 1733-1735, and Juliana's tombstone at Warner Hall.
8. He came to this country from Scotland in 1733, and became rector of St. George's Parish, Spotsylvania. In 1737, he moved to St. Paul's Parish, Hanover, where he met and married Arthur Clayton's widow. Mr. Henry was a very learned man, and defended with vigor the Established Church against his famous nephew. The date of the death of Arthur Clayton's widow is not known, but she was still living in October, 1773, since she is mentioned in John Clayton's will on that date.
9. "Letters of William Byrd 2nd of Westover to Sir John Randolph, Jan. 21, 1735," *VMHB*, IX (January, 1902), 239.
10. *Virginia Gazette* (Parks) November 11, 1737.
11. *Ibid.*, November 18, 1737.
12. *Ibid.*, November 25, 1737.
13. The Reverend W. A. R. Goodwin, *The Record of Bruton Parish Church* (Richmond, 1941), p. 143.
14. *Virginia Gazette* (Parks) October 26, 1739.
15. W. G. Stanard, "The Clayton Family," *HM*, II (October, 1891), 236. The inscription on the botanist's brother's tombstone is as follows:

Here beneath are the remains of Dr. Thos Clayton Bachelor of Medicine, youngest son of John Clayton, esq. former graduate of Pembroke College Cambridge; who broken in health by studies and the toil of his profession in the thirty-eighth year of his age on the seventeenth day of October In the year of our salvation by Christ 1739 Fell asleep devoutly and sweetly in the Lord. His most loyal widow Isabella with copious tears has most devoutly set up this marble as her last service. You will not see here any stately columns of his or blocks of stone bidden to come alive by the hand of the artist. Nor do I rejoice that lofty pyramids here rise by skill made equal to those on the plains of Isis. Doubtless let him seek that form of monument who is unable to win renown by his desserts.

This inscription is in Latin, and the above was taken from the translation given in the glass case on the wall of the graveyard. The translator's name is not given.

16. Deed #759. This book is in the Virginia State Library.
17. York County Deeds, Bonds, 1713-1729, Volume III, 513. A second deed the following year (p. 525) records the sale of 20 acres of the same land by John Clayton to Mann Page. No reference to the remaining 180 acres has been found.
18. *WMQ* (1) XXI, 51.
19. Clayton versus Clayton and Boteler, PRO, C9/318/30.
20. *VMHB*, VII, 172-74.
21. Perry gave Mr. Clayton a power-of-attorney, November 6, 1710. This was used to sell certain lands September 1, 1721 (James City County, Virginia Colonial Abstracts, Series 2, Volume 4, 32-Mss. 101).
22. Elizabeth Donnan, "Eighteenth Century English Merchants: Micajah Perry," *Journal of Economic and Business History*, IV (November, 1931), 70-98.
23. "The younger Micajah stated in 1723 that his father paid to the Crown duties on tobacco amounting to £80,000 and £100,000 per annum." *Ibid.*, p. 91.
24. *Ibid.*, p. 79.
25. *GM*, XXIII (January, 1753), 53, in the list of deaths.
26. Robert W. Hill, Keeper of Manuscripts, New York Public Library, very kindly sent this item.
27. Porcupines seem to be unknown in Virginia today although Catesby also mentioned them.
28. Brants are small geese, similar to Canadian geese.
29. Kildees and sandpipers, still often called plover.
30. *Porzana caroliniana*, a fat, gray-brown rail, sometimes known as a "rice bird."
31. Fieldfare (*Turdus pilaris*), a European thrush with pale gray head and chestnut coloured wings, according to Webster's Dictionary: could be any one of several American birds.
32. *Philohela minor.*
33. Wilson's snipe (*Capellas gallinago delicata*).
34. Bartram's first draft of a report of his trip, Bartram Papers, I, 14, HSP.
35. July 12, 1739, LC, V, 444 and November 17, 1739, LC, V, 442.
36. Richard L. Morton, *Colonial Virginia* (Chapel Hill, 1960), II, 545.
37. November 17, 1739, LC, V, 442.
38. "Amicus noster D. J. Mitchel . . ." *Flora Virginica* (1762), p. 23.
39. Collinson to Bartram, May 16, 1742—Bartram Papers, II, 67, HSP. Darlington's Copy of this letter (p. 156) differs from the original.
40. It was published under the title of "Nova Genera Plantarum Virginiensium" in the *Act. Phys. Med. Acad. Caes. Leopold*, VIII.

41. Bartram to Colden, January 25, 174-, Simon Gratz Autograph Collection, Case 7, Box 21, HSP.
42. Swem, *Brothers of the Spade*, 51; *MJB*, p. 113.
43. Collinson to Blackburn October 20, 1742, Ms. Radcliffe Trust c. 11, f. 28-29. Bodleian Library, Oxford.
44. A copy of one of these is among the Bartram Papers in the HSP. Ernest Earnest says "The catalogue of the Bartram garden issued in 1801 mentions Clayton's garden as existing first." (*John and William Bartram* [Philadelphia, 1940], p. 20.)
45. July 19, 1740/1, La. III. 375, Alston Letters, University of Edinburgh. John Fothergill wrote the well-known account of his friend: *Some Account of the Late Peter Collinson* (London, 1770).
46. LC, XVII (Supplement).
47. *Gordonia lasianthus* (L.) Ellis. "Tan-Bay, Black laurel" (John Kunkel Small, *Manual of the Southeastern Flora* [New York, 1903], p. 794).
48. *MJB*, p. 276.
49. From James Manson, Kennington-Gore, July 12, 1768. BPL 1900, Library of the University of Leiden. A list of the stolen plants was given in *The Daily Advertiser*, July 4, 1768. John Ellis wrote to Solander "You may let Mr Collinson & Dr. Fothergill know that Mr. Webb will assist them in getting a clause put into an act of parliament to make it transportation to steal curious plants." BM 29533, undated.
50. *MJB*, p. 250.
51. William Bennett ("Bisket Baker & Corn-factor") of London to David van Royen, undated. BPL 1900, Library of the University of Leiden.
52. Collinson to Blackburn, MS Radcliffe Trust c. 11, f. 28, Bodleian Library, Oxford.
53. February 25, 1764, *LPCC*, VI, 290.
54. The following quotations are all from L. W. Dillwyn: *Hortus Collinsonianus* (Swansea, 1843) "Not published," 58, 12, 13, 5, 9, 20.
55. Collinson to Bartram, December 14, 1737, *MJB*, p. 106.
56. January 18, 1743; LC, XVII.
57. Collinson to Linnaeus, April 1, 1757, *CLO*, I, 40. Miss Colden published a Latin botanic dissertation in two volumes of the *Edinburgh Essays*.
58. May 13, 1739; LC, XVII.
59. Collinson to Bartram, June 10, 1740; *MJB*, p. 135.
60. Loose sheet in Peter Collinson's Common Place Books, Linnean Society of London.
61. Swem, *Brothers of the Spade*, p. 51. Collinson letter in the library of the American Philosophical Society.
62. Swem, *Brothers of the Spade*, p. 89. The umbrella tree was probably the *Magnolia tripetala* L. (sometimes known as *M. Umbrella* L. and named in honour of Pierre Magnol (1638-1715) botany professor at Montpelier) since Clayton refers to its "stink" in *Flora Virginica* (1762), p. 83, and Small, *Manual of the Southeastern Flora*, p. 536, says "flowers scented, but not pleasantly."
63. Swem, *Brothers of the Spade*, p. 50. Written December 24, 1737.
64. J. W. Campbell, *A History of Virginia* (Philadelphia, 1813), p. 240.
65. From a Russian's account of his visit and interview with Bartram, in the Preface to *MJB*, p. 52.
66. Collinson to Bartram, December 20, 1740: HSP, Bartram Papers, II, 55.
67. *MJB*, p. 162.
68. January 18, 1743; LC, XVII.

69. Collinson to Bartram, July 21, 1741: HSP, Bartram Papers, II.
70. *MJB*, pp. 319-20.
71. Undated letter from Catesby to Bartram in HSP, Simon Gratz Autograph Collection, Case 12, Box 6.
72. *MJB*, p. 170.
73. *Ibid.*, pp. 224-25.
74. *Ibid.*, p. 202.
75. *GM*, XXVIII (October 1758), 479.
76. *MJB*, p. 304.
77. *Ibid.*, p. 89.
78. *Ibid.*, p. 114.
79. Isham Randolph was Thomas Jefferson's maternal grandfather, and lived at "Dungeness" on the James River in Goochland County.
80. Probably written July, 1739, but torn and in poor condition: HSP, Bartram Papers, I, 19. See also Bartram's letter to Dr. Mitchell, June 3, 1744, "in the year 1738, when I lodged in Fredericksburg, from whence I traveled near sixty miles down Rappahannock & hence over Dragon Bridge to John Claton's (where I was disappointed of seeing him, he being gone towards the mountains)." (*MJB*, p. 363.)
81. Swem, *Brothers of the Spade*, p. 64.
82. Bags or sacks; probably referred to saddlebags in this case.
83. *MJB*, p. 113.
84. HSP, Bartram Papers, I, 19.
85. *MJB*, p. 138. Dated October 20, 1740.
86. *Ibid.*, pp. 162 and 165.
87. *Ibid.*, p. 155.
88. *Ibid.*, p. 173.
89. *Dicentra eximia* (Ker) Torr. or "staggerweed," pink or purple-flowered. (Gray, *Manual of Botany*, p. 682).
90. *Napaea dioica* L. or "glade-mallow" (Gray, p. 1003).
91. *Polygala Senega* L. ? Name from the use of this plant by the Seneca Indians, according to Gray, p. 955.
92. "Prickly-ash."
93. *Seneair L.* (?) "Groundsel," or "ragwort."
94. *Abies balsamea* (L.) Mill. See Peter Kalm's "Account of Use and care of Some North American Plants; Sugar from trees," translated by Esther Louise Larsen in *Agricultural History* (1939) 13, 33-64 & 149-156.
95. *Sorbus* (Tourn.) or "Mountain ash."
96. Bartram wrote to Jared Eliot: "I am obliged to thy son-in-law Doctor Gale for his very kind letter. The specimen he sent me is called in Parkinson Christophoriana or herb Christopher it differs a little from the Europian & not much our common call black snake root or as some call it rich weed is near A kin to it in form & virtue see Parkinsons figure but thine is A true Christophoriano A churlish but good medicine judiciously used." 30 January ——. Yale University Library.
97. *Aralia spinosa*, L., "tooth-ache tree."
98. Gin-zeng or Ginseng.
99. One of the trilliums; see Bartram to Mitchell, June 3, 1744; *MJB*, p. 364.
100. Salamander.
101. HSP, Bartram Papers, I, 28.

CHAPTER VII

1. *Early Proceedings of the American Philosophical Society 1744-1838* (Philadelphia, 1884) by one of its secretaries, pp. 1-2. The original of the letter on the proposal is in the Yale Library.
2. Bartram to Colden, April 29, 1744; HSP, Autograph Collection of Simon Gratz, Case 7, Box 21.
3. Colden to Collinson, June 1744; *LPCC*, III, 60.
4. Franklin to Colden, April 5, 1744, "MSS. Minutes of the A. P. S.," 2.
5. Gronovius to Bartram, June 2, 1745: "Pray acquaint me in your next, how it goes with your learned newly erected Society, and what improvements they have made." (*MJB*, p. 357.)
6. Clayton's cognizance of the Society is mentioned in a letter of Thomas Penn in the Library Company of Philadelphia, according to Brooke Hindle, *The Pursuit of Science in Revolutionary America* (Chapel Hill, 1956).
7. Bartram to Colden, October 4, 1745; *LPCC*, III, 159-60.
8. *Ibid.*
9. April 17, 1745; LC, V, 484.
10. Bartram to Colden, November 2, 1744; *LPCC*, III, 79. When Mitchell visited Bartram, he introduced him to Franklin.
11. Collinson to Colden, August 23, 1744; *LPCC*, III, 69.
12. Mitchell to Franklin, September 12, 1745; *ibid.*, p. 152.
13. Franklin to Colden, November 28, 1745; *ibid.*, p. 182.
14. Franklin to Colden, August 15, 1745; *ibid.*, p. 143.
15. Colden to Bartram; *MJB*, p. 330.
16. Kalm, *Travels in North America*, I, 43.
17. For a more complete account of the Society, see Carl Van Doren, "The Beginnings of the American Philosophical Society," *Proceedings of the A. P. S.*, LXXXVII, 277-89.
18. Colden to Fothergill, October 18, 1757; *LPCC*, V, 203.
19. Colden to Gronovius, October 1, 1755; *ibid.*, p. 29.
20. Anna Murray Vail, *Jane Colden, An Early New York Botanist* (Catalogue from the New York Botanical Garden, 1907).
21. "Nature printing" had been first used in the fifteenth century in Germany, and was used there rather extensively in the eighteenth century as well as by Hessel in America in 1707, according to Linnaeus in his *Philosophia Botanica*. See Wilfred Blunt, *The Art of Botanical Illustration* (London, 1950), p. 139.
22. Collinson to Colden, March 5, 1740/1; *LPCC*, II, 207-8.
23. Colden to [Dr. Whytte?] February 15, 1758; *ibid.*, V, 216.
24. Gronovius to Colden, August 6, 1743; *ibid.*, III, 31.
25. Colden to Collinson, November 13, 1742; *ibid.*, II, 283.
26. Gronovius to Colden, April 3, 1744; *ibid.*, III, 55.
27. Colden's place is usually spelled "Coldengham."
28. Colden to Gronovius, December, 1744; *LPCC*, III, 91. A footnote says that this type was much more efficient than the one we know today as the "Franklin" stove.
29. LC, V, 488.
30. Bartram to Collinson; *MJB*, p. 161.
31. Bartram to Colden, April, 1745; *LPCC*, III, 179-180.
32. Bartram to Colden, January 25, 17-; HSP, Autograph Collection of Simon Gratz, Case 7, Box 21.
33. Bartram to Colden, July 9, 1745; *LPCC*, III, 126.
34. Colden to Bartram, December, 1744; *ibid.*, pp. 94-95.
35. See also note 36. Peter Collinson, in an article on the white pine

(*GM*, XXV [November 1755], 503) quotes a Dr. Douglas' book on New Hampshire. This book is not given in the bibliography of the *Flora Virginica* (1762), although Paul Dudley's manuscript, "A Description of the Evergreens of New England" is listed as "presented to Peter Collinson," who seemed to have been the recipient of many such treatises, and may have also possessed Douglas' "book," of whose publication the authors have found no notice.

36. Bartram to Colden, November 2, 1744; *LPCC*, II, 78-79. It was published under the title of "Nova Genera Plantarum Virgiensium" in the *Act. Phys. Med. Acad. Caes. Leopold*, VIII.

37. Dr. Alexander Garden (1730?-1791) of Charleston, South Carolina.
38. The Russians.
39. Collinson to Colden, May 19, 1756; *LPCC*, V, 81-82.
40. Collinson to Colden, March 27, 1746/7; *ibid.*, III, 369.
41. Collinson to Colden, December 11, 1751; *ibid.*, IX, 109.
42. Collinson to Bartram, October 2, 1760; *MJB*, p. 234. Bill of lading for Colden's "Chariot"; *LPCC*, VII, 108-10.
43. Collinson to Colden, June 24, 1765; *ibid.*, VII, 44.
44. As Linnaeus named this for John Stuart (1713-1792), third Earl of Bute, whose surname was sometimes spelled "Stewart," two different versions appear.
45. April 16, 1745; LC, V, 483.
46. Catesby, *Natural History of Carolina*, II, App. 13.
47. LC, III. The authors are indebted to Dr. Gustaf Holmgren (Keeper of MSS at the University Library, Uppsala) for information concerning this enclosure, which he had obtained from Dr. Arvid Hjalmar Uggla.
48. Ms. 61, library of the Karolinska Institute, Stockholm. Ehret's drawing is now in the British Museum (Natural History).
49. William Gordon "At James Gordon's Gardener Bow Road near London" to Van Royen, October 15, 1777; BPL 1900, Library of the University of Leiden.
50. July 20, 1746, Ms. 61, Library of the Karolinska Institute, Stockholm.
51. March 27, 1747/8; LC, III.
52. Miss Brightwell of Norwich, *A Life of Linnaeus* (London, 1858), p. 99, quoting Linnaeus' Autobiography. Dr. John Fothergill wrote Alston, January 20, 1740, "Linnaeus is fix'd at Stockholm, made prof: of Botany there and Physician to the navy." (Alston Letters, La. III, 375, Library of the University of Edinburgh.)
53. Donald Culross Peattie in *Green Laurels* (New York, 1936) gives a vivid description of Linnaeus' field trips.
54. Dr. A. Holmberg, Director of the Library of the Swedish Academy, wrote that he was unable to find any papers or letters written by Clayton in the Academy's archives. This was confirmed by a visit of the authors there in the summer of 1961. From Dr. Holmberg's letter of May 30, 1958, in regard to the May 3, 1747 election: "At the same time and in the same 'class' (for botany and natural history) were chosen the following scientists: Iussieu proposed by Bäck; Gesnerus, by Linnaeus; Raben, by The Secretary (at that time Elvius); Reaumur, by DeGeer; Clayton, by Linnaeus; Gleditsch(?), by (name not readable); and Collinson, by Bäck."
55. Milk-wort.
56. Spring Beauty.
57. A Swedish clergyman who came to North America in 1747.
58. In 1767, Gmelin was chosen by the Empress of Russia to travel extensively in the interests of science (GM, XXXXIV [November, 1774]).

59. LC, III. Transcribed in the original Latin by Dr. W. A. Montgomery of The College of William and Mary, in *WMQ*, (2) IV, 246-248. This translation was made by Mrs. Robert H. Davis, Jr.
60. Letter to [?] from Collinson, March 31, 1748 (the date is written in another hand), Wellcome Library, Wellcome Trust, London.
61. *GM*, XVIII (March 1748), 130.
62. *Ibid.*, p. 540.
63. Gmelin to Linnaeus, February, 1745; LC, V.
64. July 20, 1746, Collinson to Bäck, Ms. 61, Library of the Karolinska Institute, Stockholm.
65. Gronovius to Linnaeus, April 16, 1750; LC, V, 507.
66. *MJB*, p. 371, gives this letter as "not dated." In the library of The Linnean Society of London, in a box labelled "Additions to Linnaean Correspondence" in a folder marked "Transcripts of Letters from English Correspondents," this letter is to be found under the date of March 20, 1753.
67. LC, XVII.
68. Box marked "Varia Linn. Pater, Miscell. Anon." in the Linnean Society of London.
69. Donald Culross Peattie gives a short biography of Kalm in an introduction to his *Travels*, transcribed and edited by Adolphe B. Benson (New York, 1937).
70. Gronovius to Linnaeus, August 27, 1748; LC, V, 502.
71. *Travels*, ed. Benson, I, 154.
72. *LPCC*, III, 251.

CHAPTER VIII

1. *GM*, XXVI (1756), 278-79.
2. March 24, 1747, Gronovius to Linnaeus; LC, V, 492.
3. Morton, *Colonial Virginia*, II, 535.
4. Barton, "Memorandums of the Life and Writings of Mr. John Clayton," *Phila. Med. & Phys. Journ.* II (1805), Part I, 139-45.
5. "Meadia" was *Dodecatheon* (L.) or "Shooting Star." *MJB*, p. 254.
6. *Flora Virginica* (1762), p. 102.
7. Bartram to Jared Eliot, December 1, 1762; Yale University Library.
8. August 27, 1748; LC, V, 502.
9. Morton, *Colonial Virginia*, II, 610-11. Also see Salling's Journal edited by Fairfax Harrison, "The Virginians on the Ohio and the Mississippi," *VMHB*, XXX, 203-22. The Reverend John Clayton had sent the Batts and Fallam journal to the Royal Society where it was read August 1, 1688. (This is printed in *The First Exploration of the Trans-Allegheny Region by the Virginians, 1650-1674*, by Clarence Walworth Alvord and Lee Bidgood [Cleveland, 1912] 181-95.) This expedition took place in September of 1671, and refers to an earlier exploration by Colonel Wood.
10. *Executive Journals of the Council of Virginia*, ed. Wilmer L. Hull (Richmond, 1945), p. 258.
11. Collinson to Bäck, November 3, 1747; Ms. 61, Karolinska Institute, Stockholm.
12. Gronovius to Linnaeus, May 5, 1748; LC, V, 498.
13. Clayton may have read the news in the December, 1749, issue of *GM*, XIX, 573, before he heard it from his English friends.
14. G. F. Frick and R. P. Stearns, *Mark Catesby* (Urbana, 1961), p. 37.
15. Note by Dawson Turner, *Correspondence of Richard Richardson* (Yarmouth, 1835), p. 401.

16. Knowlton to Richardson; *ibid.*, p. 400.

17. From the Journal Books of the Royal Society of London, Collinson's active role in the Society and his varied interests are obvious.

18. This appears in the Journal Book of the Royal Society, Volume 21 (1751-54) 47. "A Letter from Mr. John Clayton of Virginia to Mr. Peter Collinson F R S containing an extract from a Manuscript in Mr. Clayton's possession concerning the Smoaky Weather in Virginia, and a remark concerning an uncommon kind of humming Bird, together with Mr. Collinson's Observations upon that Weather were read."

19. The quotations are from the *GM* (June, 1752), 262-63. The account in the Journal Book is merely a brief summary, but does identify Clayton as Collinson's correspondent, which the *GM* does not.

20. He remains unidentified.

21. December 24, 1751; Yale University Library.

22. Yale University Library.

23. March 28, *GM*, XXIII (April, 1753), 200.

24. LC, III. This was not printed in *CLO*.

25. John Ellis to Alexander Garden, April 8, 1761; *Correspondence of Richardson*, I, 507.

26. Notes written by Peter Collinson in his Common Place Book, September 2, 1763, page 4, Linnean Society of London.

27. NP.

28. Collinson to Bartram, February 10, 1756; *MJB*, p. 203.

29. *GM*, XXIV, 465-66.

30. Grew, in his *Anatomy of Vegetables*, made observations later confirmed by microscopical investigations by Lister and Leeuwenhoek. Richard Bradley (d. 1732), botanist, F. R. S., became professor of botany at Cambridge in 1724, on Dr. Sherard's recommendation. Pulteney says he was the author of twenty books on gardening and horticulture, including one on *Succulent Plants*. James Logan (1674-1751), an Anglican clergyman turned Quaker, was William Penn's secretary. Logan became a Council member in Pennsylvania, a representative and a judge. He invested in land, and with the fortune he made, accumulated a personal library of 3,000 books, which he left to Philadelphia at his death. Linnaeus named Loganiaceae (the family which included *Gelsemium Juss.*, or "yellow Jessamine," and *Spigelia L.*, or "Pink root," etc.) for him. Logan's treatise, *Experiments concerning the impregnation of the Seeds of Plants*, sent to the Royal Society in 1736, was published in Leyden in 1739. It was translated by Dr. Fothergill and published in London in 1747. The Logan manuscripts are now in the library of the Historical Society of Pennsylvania. James Parsons (d. 1770) was a member of the College of Physicians and the Royal Society. In April, 1752, he published a book, *Philosophical Observations on the Analogy between the propagation of Animals and Vegetables*.

31. *Rhamnus L.* or "Buckthorn," shrubs and small trees with a black berry-like fruit.

32. Possibly *Ipomoea Quamoclit L.*, or "cypress vine," a type of morning glory.

33. *GM*, XXV (1755), 407. This letter was brought to the attention of the authors by Dr. Conway Zirkle.

34. Conway Zirkle, "John Clayton and our Colonial Botany," *VMHB*, LXVII (July, 1959), 292.

35. See also Conway Zirkle, *Beginnings of Plant Hybridization* (Philadelphia, 1935) and his "A Possible Early Eighteenth Century Record of Introgression in Oaks," *Journal of Heredity*, XLI (1950), 315-17, for a discussion of John Lawson's use of the word "bastard." Collinson's use of the

expression "bastard species" of rhubarb was probably with the same connotation, as he was certainly familiar with this meaning from his experiments on "mule plants." (Journal Book XVIII, 474, Royal Society of London.)

36. September 27, 1754, Gloucester County Surveyor's Book 1733-1810, p. 32. A photostat of this book is in the Virginia State Library.

37. June 30, 1754, Gloucester County Surveyor's Book, p. 31.

38. *A Provisional List of Alumni, Grammar School Students, Members of the Faculty and Members of the Board of Visitors of the College of William and Mary in Virginia* from 1693-1888 (Richmond, 1941).

39. Governor Gooch wrote on May 28, 1731 that Fox had been sent to receive Holy Orders. He had sent six hams by him. Typescript of Gooch papers from the originals PRO C.O.S/324, in the library of The Virginia Historical Society.

40. *Virginia Gazette* (Parks) January 21, 1736/7.

41. *Ibid.*, February 17, 1738.

42. *Tyler's Quarterly Magazine* (April, 1940).

43. "Memoir of Colonel John Page of Rosewell," *Virginia Historical Register*, VIII (1850), 142-51.

44. Clayton to Bartram, June 30, 1764; Library of the College of Physicians, Philadelphia.

45. March 30, 1756; Archives of the American Philosophical Society.

46. *The Life and Writings of Benjamin Franklin*, ed. Albert Henry Smyth (New York, 1905), III, 381.

47. Dr. Whitfield J. Bell, Jr. (Associate Editor of *The Papers of Benjamin Franklin*) wrote June 26, 1958: "I can tell you that we have turned up no Franklin-Clayton correspondence nor has our indexing caught significant references to Clayton in other Franklin letters."

48. Faculty Minutes of The College of William and Mary, April 2, 1756; from the library of the college.

49. Bernard de Jussieu (1699-1777), French botanist of the Jardin du Roi.

50. From the Laing Manuscripts in the library of the University of Edinburgh, through the kindness of Mr. C. P. Finlayson, Keeper of the Manuscripts.

51. Garden to Linnaeus, March 15, 1755; *CLO*, I, 284.

52. Garden to Colden, November 4, 1754; *LPCC*, IV, 472.

53. Garden to Linnaeus, March 25, 1755; *CLO*, I, 345.

54. Collinson to Colden, May 19, 1756; *LPCC*, IV, 81-82.

55. Garden to Ellis, February 17, 1759; *CLO*, I, 434.

56. Garden states twenty-five pounds but Raymond Phineas Stearns in "Colonial Fellows of the Royal Society, 1661-1788" (*Notes and Records of the Royal Society of London*, VIII, 178-261) says that after 1753 the exemption of dues for Colonial fellows was withdrawn, and they paid twenty-one pounds in lieu of dues.

57. Volume XXII (p. 630) of the Journal Books of the Royal Society notes that on November 24, 1757, Franklin signed the obligation as a duly elected member. His name had already been ordered to be printed on the list of fellows "without Fee or other payment to the Society, on account of his having deserved highly of it."

58. August 31, 1760; Letters of Ellis, Francillon, etc. to Solander, 1760-63. BM 29, 533, f. 8.

CHAPTER IX

1. *MJB*, p. 192.
2. April 16, 1754; LC, V, 507; *MJB*, pp. 360-61.

3. Ward Mss., 17, Linnean Society of London.
4. Written on the back of Bartram's letter, which he was forwarding to Gronovius. Ward Mss., Linnean Society of London.
5. Dreer Collection of Scientists, HSP.
6. Ward Mss., 18, Linnean Society of London.
7. Mss. 61, Library of the Karolinska Institute, Stockholm.
8. LC, V, 491.
9. LC, V, 496.
10. LC, V, 498.
11. LC, V, 502.
12. Mss. 594, #2244, National Library of Scotland.
13. LC, V, 328.
14. LC, XVII, and *CLO*, I, 42. Smith has corrected Collinson's colorful spelling.
15. LC, V, 330.
16. *CLO*, I, 93-94.
17. John Ellis' Letter Book #1, Letter to "Sir Charles Linnaeus," Linnean Society of London.
18. John Ellis' Letter Book #1, Linnean Society of London.
19. Ehret to Bäck, December 26, 1743; Library of the Karolinska Institute, Stockholm.
20. Wilfred Blunt, *The Art of Botanical Illustration*, pp. 143-45; see also Richard Pulteney, *Historical and Biographical Sketches*. The British Museum and the Victoria and Albert Museum both have large collections of Ehret's drawings.
21. Garden to Ellis, April 27, 1759; *CLO*, I, 395.
22. Garden to Colden, March 31, 1759; *LPCC*, V, 299. Millar was sometimes spelled with an "e" rather than an "a."
23. *GM*, X (April, 1740), 208.
24. Ehret Mss., Trewes' Life of Ehret, 26f19, page 47, British Museum (Natural History).
25. LC, XIV, 212. *Tabernamontana Amsonia* in *Species Plantarum* (1762) 308. Philip Miller said that Clayton had first discovered it in Virginia and named it. Later, Walter had raised it to a genus. Dr. John Amson practised in Williamsburg in 1751 (Wyndham Blanton, *Medicine in Virginia in the Eighteenth Century* [Richmond, 1931], p. 324). Aside from that fact, little seems to be known of Dr. Amson. There is one other reference, in a letter to John Norton from William Nelson September 4, 1769: "how they will relish it I know not; but that's neither here nor there; as Dr. Amson used to say, that is, who cares." (Mason, *John Norton & Sons*, p. 105.) Clayton had found *Amsonia* on the shady and marshy banks of the Appomatox River. (LC, XIV, 152.)
26. This book is in the library of the Linnean Society of London.
27. LC, V, 341.
28. LC, V, 343. From the English translations of the Latin introductions of both editions of the *Flora*, we are indebted to Mrs. Robert H. Davis, Jr., and Dr. Bayly Turlington.
29. At complete variance with J. F. Gronovius' statement to Linnaeus, January 6, 1747, "Now I have completed into readiness the second edition of the Flora Virginica." (LC, V, 491.)
30. April 4, 1762, Letters of Ellis, Francillon, etc. to Solander, BM #29,533, f. 371.
31. Collinson to Bartram, May 22, 1762; *MJB*, p. 236.

32. Bartram to Collinson, December 3, 1762, *ibid.*, p. 243.
33. Gronovius to Linnaeus, July 26, 1740, quoting Clayton; LC, V, 454.
34. Journal Book of the Royal Society, XXII (1754-57), 70.
35. Dr. John Huxham, a well known English physician. Garden to Ellis, February 17, 1759; *CLO*, I, 433. Garden later published "An Acc't of the Medical Properties of Pink Root." He even considered exporting it to England as a commercial enterprise, but never carried through with the project.
36. *Ibid.*, p. 540.
37. Paul Dudley (1675-1751) F. R. S. and a frequent contributor to the *Transactions*.
38. Commercial supplies are now gathered in Virginia, North Carolina, and Tennessee, for use as a uterine sedative. Herbert W. Youngken, *Textbook of Pharmacognosy* (Philadelphia, 1948), p. 207.
39. Now used as an aromatic, a stimulant, and a carminative. (Youngken, *Pharmacognosy*, pp. 623-34.) Bartram wrote Collinson, June 24, 1760: "Those [seeds] that I sowed, are come up as close as they can grow, except the Mountain *Angelica*, which Clayton tells me will never come up: but I hope yet to find him mistaken, though he is a worthy, ingenious man." *MJB*, 224.
40. *Cassia occidentalis* L. (Gray, 886). Youngken, *Pharmacognosy*, pp. 469-70.
41. Youngken, *Pharmacognosy*, p. 764. He says this plant is not native but rather has been naturalized in the United States.
42. It is collected in Virginia, North Carolina, Kentucky, Indiana and Tennessee. Youngken, *Pharmacognosy*, pp. 347-51.
43. There are many other such items. Three, in particular, are of interest: *Melissa* (*Flora Virginica*, p. 91) "It is for [treatment] of the uterus and sets in motion the monthly periods."; *Oenothera* 3 (p. 59) "The crushed leaves are used outside, placed close together, for wounds."; and *Andromeda* 3 (p. 67) "A decoction of the leaves soothes a fever and allays thirst."
44. Dr. Lee was one of the Virginia members of the American Philosophical Society, and had won the prize for the best Hortus Siccus at the University of Edinburgh in 1763. BPL 1900, Library of the University of Leiden.
45. In his Preface, after a glowing account of the earlier *Flora Virginica*, Barton wrote: "But the work is not to be procured. It is nearly out of print, and unless some pains were taken to preserve it, in less than half a century, copies of it would not be found in the libraries of one botanist in one hundred." It is supposed that Barton took his own book to England when he went there in 1813. Dr. Pennell listed three known copies, all in Philadelphia libraries: the American Philosophical Society, the Academy of Natural Sciences, and the Library Company of Philadelphia; see Francis W. Pennell, "Benjamin Smith Barton as a Naturalist," *Proceedings of the American Philosophical Society*, 86, #1 (September, 1942) 108-22. The Library of Congress also has a copy of Barton's *Flora*.
46. C. R. Williams, "Dr. John Dunn as a Virginia Botanist," *WMQ* (2), XV, 114-15. Dr. Dunn received an M.A. from the Medical College of Virginia, and his M.D. from the University of Virginia. He also studied in Paris and in London.

CHAPTER X

1. Accounts of this visit are from Clayton's letters to Bartram, July 23 (Bartram Papers, II, 1, HSP; *MJB*, pp. 406-7); August 30 ("Manuscripts

1660-1855," Yi2,7301F, Archives of the Library Company of Philadelphia; *MJB*, pp. 407-8); and September 1, 1760 (Collections of Arnold Arboretum, Cambridge, Massachusetts; *MJB*, p. 408).

2. Clayton to Bartram, February 23, 1761; Bartram Papers, II, 2, HSP; *MJB*, pp. 408-9.

3. *Ibid.*

4. "Letters of the Byrd Family," *VMHB*, XXXVIII (1930), 53.

5. Clayton to Bartram, February 25, 1764; Bartram Papers II, 4, HSP; *MJB*, p. 411.

6. "Highly" according to *MJB*, p. 410, but now undecipherable in the original.

7. *Gymnocladus* Lam., "Kentucky Coffee-tree"; *ibid.*, p. 233. Collinson also desired the seeds of this tree.

8. March 16, 1763; Bartram Papers, II, 3, HSP; *MJB*, p. 410.

9. Clayton to Bartram, February 25, 1764. See Note 5.

10. Notebook #2, 38, Ellis Mss., Linnean Society of London.

11. April 8, 1761; *CLO*, I, 508.

London Dec 12 1760
Sent Tea Seeds preserved in wax to the following Gentlemen.

Gave Mr B. Franklin for the Northern Provinces	5 balls
Doctor Garden for South Carolina	2 balls
Arthur Dobbs Esqr for North Carolina	1 ball
James Wright Esqr for Georgia	1 ball
Pickering Robinson Esqr Georgia	1 ball
Hon'ble John Clayton Esqr Gloucester County Virginia	1 ball
Mr John Bartram Philadelphia	1 ball
Cadwallader Colden Esqr N York	1 ball

Addressed to, with Letter to Each describing from whence they came. Mr Alexander Colden Esqr Postmaster at N York & franked by the favr of Hampden Esqr Post Master Genl Delivered to Mr Solander 1 ball of Tea Seed for Dr Linnaeus

(Note book 2, 38, Ellis Mss., Linnean Society of London.)

12. Mrs. Gertrude D. Hess, Assistant Librarian of the American Philosophical Society library, wrote the authors that this letter had been found during a study of the holdings of The College of Physicians in Philadelphia, by the A.P.S. It was tipped in a copy of Carson's *History of the Medical Department of the University of Pennsylvania*. Dr. W. B. McDaniel, 2d, Curator of the Historical Collections there, was most helpful in having a photostat made and identifying the "Walch Tract" as a parcel of 40,000 acres of high ground between Derby Creek and the Schulkyll River, purchased from William Penn by the Welsh settlers. Young Fox's inheritance also included a 3,000 acre estate by the name of "Greenwich," in Gloucester County, Virginia.

13. *GM*, XXIV (December, 1754), 558.

14. LC, XVII.

15. Clayton to Bartram, February 6, 1765; Bartram Papers II, 5, HSP; *MJB*, p. 412.

16. May 22, 1765; *WMQ* (2) VI, 325; Ferdinand J. Dreer Autograph Collection, HSP.

17. Affidavit of William Clayton before John Bacon, Magistrate of New Kent County, May 1, 1790. Manuscript in the Collections of the Virginia Historical Society.

18. *Virginia Gazette* (Purdie & Dixon), July 11, 1766.

19. These copies of the Clayton wills are among the Jennings Papers in the library of the Virginia Historical Society, Richmond.

Notes to pages 152-67 215

20. *Journals of the House of Burgesses, 1766-69, 1770-72*, ed. John Pendleton Kennedy (Richmond, 1906).
21. *Ibid.*, IV, 163.
22. In the land grants (Book 24, 446, Virginia State Library) William Clayton of "East Greenwich," was allowed privileges of hunting, hawking, fishing, and fowling on two hundred acres of the upper part of Beaver Pond in Prince George County.
23. Mason, *Records of Colonial Gloucester*, p. 71.
24. Gloucester County Tax Accounts, 1770-71. #21341, Virginia State Library.
25. Hargreaves' Letterbook, Letter LI, February 26, 1779. The books were left to Jasper's son, John, who died a year after his grandfather.
26. Theses 1758, 59-60, Library of the University of Edinburgh.
27. Collinson wrote this extract from Thomas Clayton's letter on the back of one he had received from Garden April 20, 1759; LC, XVII.
28. March 6, 1762; BPL 1900, library of the University of Leiden.
29. LC, XVII.
30. *Virginia Gazette* (Purdie & Dixon), July 17, 1769.
31. Gloucester County Tax Accounts (1770-1772), Virginia State Library.
32. Barton, "Memorandums of . . . Mr. John Clayton," *Phila. Med. & Phys. Journ.*, II (1805), 139-145.
33. *WMQ* (2), I, 119.
34. *Virginia Gazette* (Purdie & Dixon), June 2, 1768.
35. *Ibid.*, June 9, 1768.
36. *Ibid.*, June 16, 1768.
37. Clayton to John Norton, August 31, 1768; NP.
38. David Jennings, *Hawkhurst*, pp. 22-23.
39. *GM*, XXXVI, 579; XXXVII, 70, 343-438; defence, XXXVII, 101, 285.
40. August 31, 1768; NP.
41. William Clayton to George Flowerdewe Norton, London, November 5, 1774, June 2, 1775, June 9, 1775, April 1, 1777; NP.
42. Under Hundred of Gt. Barnfield, County Kent Tax records.
43. NP.
44. T. Collinson to [?], August 13, 1768; Ms. Montagu, d. 12, Bodleian Library, Oxford University.
45. Edmund and Dorothy S. Berkeley, " 'The Ablest Clerk in the U.S.,' John James Beckley," *VMHB*, LXX (October, 1962), 434-46.
46. Clayton to John Norton, August 3, 1769; NP.
47. August 15, 1769; NP.
48. August 3, 1769; NP.
49. John Page to William Blackburn, May 29, 1797; Alexander R. Boteler Collection, Duke University Library, Durham, North Carolina.
50. Kennedy, *Journals of the House of Burgesses*, VIII, 13.
51. June 7, 1770; NP.
52. May 5, 1770; *ibid.*
53. August 24, 1770; *ibid.*
54. March 18, 1771; *ibid.*
55. October 5, 1771; *ibid.*
56. Williams, "Dr. John Dunn," *WMQ* (2), XV, 114-15.
57. Barton, "Memorandums of . . . Mr. John Clayton," *Phila. Med. & Phys. Jour.*, II (1805), 139-45.
58. "Chasing Chelones," Proceedings of the Philadelphia Botanical Club, No. 10 (1927-28), p. 4.
59. October 5, 1771; NP.
60. Invoice January 17, 1772; *ibid.*

61. Minutes of the Faculty, from the library of The College of William and Mary.
62. See invoices in the Norton Papers.
63. The orders for "B.C." cease after this date.
64. August 31, 1772; NP.
65. Invoice of August 31, 1772; *ibid.*
66. August 2, 1773, *ibid.*
67. John Murray, Fourth Earl of Dunmore.
68. *Virginia Gazette* (Purdie & Dixon), May 13, 1773. The following year, the Society elected corresponding members, including such well-known Philadelphians as Benjamin Franklin, Dr. Benjamin Rush, and David Rittenhouse. The famous Dr. Lettson of London was also extended an invitation. *Ibid.*, June 16, 1774.
69. Barton, "Memorandums of . . . Mr. John Clayton," pp. 139-45.
70. *Virginia Gazette* (Purdie & Dixon), January 6, 1774.
71. *Virginia Gazette* (Pinkney), October 13, 1774.
72. *Virginia Gazette* (Purdie & Dixon), February 10, 1774.
73. Barton, "Memorandums of . . . Mr. John Clayton," p. 145.
74. William Clayton to the governor, July 20, 1787, *Calendar of Virginia State Papers*, IV, 321; and W. Clayton to Lt. Gov. Randolph August 8, 1787, enclosing a confession, 329.
75. Barton, "Memorandums of Mr. John Clayton," p. 145.

CHAPTER XI

1. *The Banks Letters*, A Calendar of the Manuscript correspondence of Sir Joseph Banks preserved in the British Museum (Natural History) and other collections in Great Britain. Ed. Warren R. Dawson (London, 1958), p. 351.
2. *Ibid.* Jean Nicolas Sebastien (1713-1787) F.R.S., in writing Banks the same day (p. 14) said that several plants were believed to have been lost from the herbarium. Dryander (1748-1810) who was Banks' librarian, referred to Clayton as "Medicus in Virginia" in the Index of Volume II, 186, of *Catalogus Bibliothecae Historico Naturalis Josephi Banks* (London, 1800).
3. W. T. Stearn, Introduction to A Facsimile of the first edition of Linnaeus' *Species Plantarum, 1753* (London, 1957), pp. 113-14.
4. This list of plants named for Clayton was based largely on one kindly sent the authors by Dr. A. B. Massey, Blacksburg, Virginia.
5. Louisa Venable Kyle, "Clayton was Virginia Gentleman Botanist," *Norfolk Virginian-Pilot* and *The Portsmouth Star*, October 6, 1957.
6. "A Botanical Description of the *Podophyllum Diphyllum* of Linnaeus," *Transactions of the American Philosophical Society*, III (1793), 335.
7. "Benjamin Smith Barton as a Naturalist," *Proceedings of the American Philosophical Society*, 86 (September, 1942), 119, n.
8. Collinson to Colden; *LPCC*, VI, 291.
9. Bartram to C. M. Wrangel, July 2, 1769; Bartram Papers, IV, 114, HSP.
10. Foot-note to DaCosta's letter to Linnaeus, February 27, 1759; *CLO*, II, 495.
11. Gronovius to Linnaeus; LC, V, 442.
12. Preface to Barton's incomplete *Flora Virginica.*
13. *MJB*, p. 581.
14. Frederick Pursh, *The Flora of North America* (London, 1814) I, xvi. Samuel Miller wrote in his *Brief Retrospect of the Eighteenth Century* (London, 1803): "Dr. John Mitchell, who resided some time in Virginia, and Dr.

John Clayton, a native of that country, both rendered important services in investigating the botanical treasure of America."

15. *MJB*, pp. 407 and 19.
16. S. F. Blake, "Notes on the Clayton Herbarium," *Rhodora*, XX (February, 1918), 21-28.
17. Mackenzie, "Concerning the Proper Identification of Linnaean Species, Especially those Based on Material Collected by Clayton," *Rhodora*, XXX (December, 1928), 232-37.
18. "The *Flora Virginica* of Gronovius," *Chronica Botanica*, VI (1940), 27-28.
19. *The Commonwealth* 64 (1939), 15.

BIBLIOGRAPHY

Primary Sources

Alvord, Clarence Walworth and Lee Bidgood. *The First Exploration of the Trans-Allegheny Region by the Virginians, 1650-1674*. Cleveland, 1912.

American Philosophical Society. *Early Proceedings of the American Philosophical Society 1744-1838* by one of its secretaries. Philadelphia, 1884.

Anonymous, *A Provisional List of Alumni, Grammar School Students, Members of the Faculty and Members of the Board of Visitors of The College of William and Mary in Virginia from 1693-1888*. Richmond, 1941.

Bartram, John. *Observations Made by Mr. John Bartram in his Travels*. Preface by Mr. Jackson of the Temple. London, 1751.

———. *John and William Bartram's America*, ed. Helen G. Cruikshank. New York, 1957.

Batts, Thomas and Robert Fallam. Journal from Virginia to the Apalachin Hills. Copy by the Reverend John Clayton, Sloane Mss. 4432, f. 9, BM.

Beverly, Robert. *The History and Present State of Virginia* [1705], ed. Louis B. Wright. Chapel Hill, 1947.

Boyle, Robert. *The Life and Works of the Honourable Robert Boyle*, ed. Louis Trenchard Morse. Oxford, 1944.

Brigg, William, ed. *The Parish Registers of St. Edmund the King and Martyr Lombard Street, London 1670-1812*. London, 1892.

Burnaby, Andrew. *Travels Through the Middle Settlements in North America, 1759 and 1760*. London, 1798.

Byrd, William. *Another Secret Diary of William Byrd of Westover, 1739-1741*. Ed. Maude H. Woodfin, transcribed and collated by Marion Tinling. Richmond, 1942.

―――. "Letters of William Byrd 2nd of Westover to Sir John Randolph," *Virginia Magazine of History and Biography,* IX (January, 1902).

―――. "Letters of William Byrd II and Sir Hans Sloane Relative to Plants and Minerals of Virginia," ed. E. G. Swem. *William and Mary Quarterly* (2) I, 186.

―――. *The London Diary 1717-1721 and Other Writings,* ed. Louis B. Wright and Marion Tinling. New York, 1958.

―――. *William Byrd's Natural History of Virginia, or the Newly Discovered Eden.* Berne, 1737. Ed. and trans. by R. C. Beatty and W. J. Mulloy. Richmond, 1940.

―――. *The Secret Diary of William Byrd of Westover, 1709-1712,* ed. Louis B. Wright and Marion Tinling. Richmond, 1947.

―――. *The Writings of "Colonel William Byrd of Westover in Virginia, Esqr.,"* ed. J. S. Bassett. New York, 1901.

Carter, Robert. Letter book, Alderman Library, University of Virginia.

―――. *Letters of Robert Carter, 1720-1727,* ed. Louis B. Wright. San Marino, 1940.

Catesby, Mark. *The Natural History of Carolina, Florida & the Bahama Islands.* London, 1771.

―――. *Hortus Britanno-Americanus.* London, 1763.

Chamberlayne, C. G., ed., *Vestry Book of Petsworth Parish, Gloucester, Virginia.* Richmond, 1933.

―――. *The Vestry Book of St. Paul's Parish, Hanover County, 1706-1786.* Richmond, 1940.

―――. *The Vestry Book and Register of St. Peter's Parish, New Kent and James City.* Richmond, 1937.

Chamberlayne, Edward. *Present State of England.* London, 1694.

Chester, J. L., and Armytage, George J. *Allegations for Marriage Licenses Issued by the Bishop of London 1611-1828.* London, 1886.

Clayton, John. "Letter of John Clayton to Mr. Samuel Durrent at Hawkhurst in Kent, March 21, 1739." *The Virginia Magazine of History and Biography,* VII (October, 1899).

―――. "Letter to Linnaeus," trans. and ed. W. A. Montgomery. *William and Mary Quarterly* (2) IV.

―――. "Letter from a Gentleman in Virginia," *Gentleman's Magazine,* XXII (June 1752) 262-63.

―――. "Some Remarks Made on Dr. Alston's Dissertation on the Sexes of Plants by Two Celebrated Botanists of North America, both dated June 10, 1755." *Gentleman's Magazine,* XXV (1755) 407.

Clayton, John and John Frederick Gronovius. *Flora Virginica,* Part I. Leiden, 1739.

——. *Flora Virginica*, Part II. Leiden, 1743.
——. *Flora Virginica*. Leiden, 1762.
Cl——t, B. "Essay on the History of Botany," *Gentleman's Magazine*, XXVI (June, July, August, 1756).
Colden, Cadwallader. *Letters and Papers of Cadwallader Colden*. New York, 1920.
——. *The History of the Five Indian Nations*. London, 1727, 1747. Cornell University Press, 1958.
Darlington, William. *Memorials of John Bartram and Humphrey Marshall*. Philadelphia, 1849.
des Cognets, Luis, Jr. *English Duplicates of Lost Virginia Records*, Princeton.
Dillenius, J. J. *Historia Muscorum*. Oxford, 1741.
Dillwyn, L. W. *Hortus Collinsonianus*. Swansea, 1843. "Not published."
Dodson, Leonidas. *Alexander Spotswood*. Philadelphia, 1932.
Evelyn, John. *The Diary of John Evelyn*, ed. E. S. de Beer. Six volumes. Oxford, 1955.
Firth, C. H. and R. S. Railt. *Acts and Ordinances of the Interregnum 1642-1660*. Three volumes. London, 1911.
Fothergill, John. *Some Account of the Late Peter Collinson*. London, 1770.
Franklin, Benjamin. *Benjamin Franklin's Autobiographical Writings*, ed. Carl Van Doren. New York, 1945.
——. *The Life and Writings of Benjamin Franklin*, ed. Albert Henry Smyth. New York, 1905.
——. *The Papers of Benjamin Franklin*, ed. Leonard W. Labaree. Volumes I and II. New Haven, 1959.
Gentleman's Magazine, I-XLV (1730-1775).
Gray, Asa. ed. "Selections from the Scientific Correspondence of Cadwallader Colden with Gronovius, Linnaeus, Collinson and other Naturalists." *American Journal of Science and Arts*. XLIV (1845).
"Hanover County Small Book," *William and Mary Quarterly* (1), XXI, 51.
Hasted, Edward. *The History and Topographical Survey of the County of Kent*. London, 1798.
Hening, W. W. ed. *The Statutes at Large: Being a Collection of All the Laws of Virginia From the First Session of the Legislature in the Year 1619*. Thirteen volumes. Richmond and Philadelphia, 1809-1823.
Historical Manuscripts Commission [Great Britain]. New Series, IV.
——. Appendix to the Sixth Report.
——. Thirteenth Report, App. Part V.

Hull, Wilmer L., ed. *Executive Journals of the Council of Virginia.* Richmond, 1945.
James City. *James City and James City Island Landowners,* Comp. George C. Gregory. Richmond, 1935.
——. *James City County,* Virginia Colonial Abstracts, Series 2, IV.
Jefferson, Thomas. *Garden Book 1766-1824,* ed. Edwin Morris Betts. Philadelphia, 1944.
——. Memoir, *Correspondence and Miscellanies from the Papers of Thomas Jefferson,* ed. Thomas Jefferson Randolph. Charlottesville, 1827.
——. *Notes on the State of Virginia,* ed. William Peden. Chapel Hill, 1955.
——. *The Papers of Thomas Jefferson,* ed. Julian P. Boyd Princeton, 1950.
Jennings, David. *Hawkhurst.* London, 1792.
Jones, Hugh. *The Present State of Virginia,* ed. Richard L. Morton. Chapel Hill, 1956. [First ed. London, 1724.]
Kalm, Peter. "Account of Use and Care of Some North American Plants: Sugar from trees." Trans. Esther Louise Larsen. *Agricultural History* XIII (1939).
——. *Travels into North America.* Trans. F. R. Forster, London, 1772.
Kilburne, Richard. *Survey of the County of Kent.* London, 1659.
Lawson, John. *The History of Carolina: Containing the Exact Description and Natural History of that Country: Together with the Present State Thereof.* London, 1714.
Linnaeus, Carolus. *Linnei Species Plantarum 1753,* A Facsimile, ed. W. T. Stearn. London, 1957.
McIlwaine, H. R. *Executive Journals, Council of Colonial Virginia.* Richmond, 1928.
——. *Journals of the House of Burgesses.* Richmond, 1912.
Mason, Frances Norton, ed. *John Norton & Sons, Merchants of London & Virginia.* Richmond, 1937.
Mason, Polly Cary, ed. *Records of Colonial Gloucester County,* Newport News, I, 1946; II, 1948.
Maury, Anne, ed. *Memoirs of a Huguenot Family,* New York, 1853.
Miller, Philip. *Gardener's Dictionary.* London, 8th Ed.
Mitchell, John. *American Husbandry.* Attributed to Arthur Young. Two volumes. London, 1775.
——. "Essay on the causes of the Different Colour of People of Different Climates." *Transactions of the Royal Society of London.* (1743).
New York. *Documents Relating to Colonial New York,* ed. J. R. Broadhead. Albany, 1855.
North, The Hon. Roger, ed. *The Lives of Francis North, Baron*

Guildford, The Hon. Sir Dudley North & The Hon. & Rev. Dr. John North, London, 1828. Originally published, 1740.

Palmer, Wm. G., ed. *Calendar of Virginia State Papers and other Manuscripts Preserved in the Capitol at Richmond.* Richmond, 1875.

Philpott, Thomas. *Villare Cantianum.* London, 1776.

Richardson, Richard. *Extracts from the Literary and Scientific Correspondence of Richard Richardson,* ed. Dawson Turner. Yarmouth, 1835.

Sidney, Henry. *Diary of the Times of Charles the Second,* ed. R. W. Blencowe, two volumes. London, 1843.

Smith, Sir James Edward, ed. *A Selection of the Correspondence of Linnaeus and other Naturalists.* London, 1821.

Spotswood, Alexander. *The Official Letters of Alexander Spots-Wood,* ed. R. A. Brock, two volumes. Richmond, 1882, 1885.

Spotsylvania. *Spotsylvania County Records 1721-1800,* ed. W. A. Crozier, Baltimore, 1855.

Sterry, Sir Wasey. *The Eton College Register.* Eton, 1943.

Stith, William. *The History of the First Discovery and Settlement of Virginia.* Williamsburg, 1747.

Swem, E. G. ed. *Brothers of the Spade*—Correspondence of Peter Collinson of London, and of John Custis, of Williamsburg: 1734-1736. Barre, Mass., 1957.

Venn, John and J. A. Venn. *Alumni Cantabrigienses.* Cambridge, 1922.

Virginia Almanac 1751. William Hunter. Williamsburg.

Virginia Gazette. Williamsburg, 1736-1775.

———. *Virginia Gazette Index,* for the Years 1736-1780, eds. Lester J. Cappon and Stella M. Duff. Two volumes. Williamsburg, 1950.

Walker, Thomas. *Journal of an Exploration in the Spring of the Year 1750,* ed. William Cabell Rives. Boston, 1888.

Williamsburg. *Williamsburg Wills,* ed. W. A. Crozier. Baltimore, 1954.

This list does not include the many unpublished manuscripts consulted, but the foot-notes refer to those which the authors found most important to this study.

Secondary Sources.

Abernethy, Thomas Perkins. *Three Virginia Frontiers.* Baton Rouge, Louisiana, 1940.

Adams, Percy G. "The Real Author of William Byrd's *Natural History of Virginia.*" *American Literature* XXVIII (1956-1957) 211-20.

Anonymous. *Memoirs of the Celebrated Persons Composing the Kit-Cat Club.* London, 1821.

———. *Old Lombard Street.* London, 1912.
Barton, Benjamin Smith. "A Botanical Description of the Podophyllum Diphyllum of Linnaeus." *Transactions of the American Philosophical Society,* III, 334-48.
———. *Collections for an Essay towards a Materia Medica.* Philadelphia, 1810.
———. *Elements of Botany.* London, 1804.
———. "Memorandums of the Life and writings of Mr. John Clayton, the Celebrated Botanist of Virginia." *Philadelphia Medical and Physical Journal,* Part I, II (1805) 139-45.
Barton, Sir D. Plunket, Charles Benham, Francis Watt. *The Story of the Inns of Court.* Boston, no date.
Bartram, William. "Some Account of the Late John Bartram of Pennsylvania," *Philadelphia Medical and Physical Journal,* Part I, I.
Beaven, The Reverend Alfred B. *The Aldermen of the City of London.* Two volumes. London, 1913.
Berkeley, Edmund and Dorothy S. "The Ablest Clerk in the U.S.," *Virginia Magazine of History and Biography,* LXX (Oct., 1962), 434-46.
Blake, S. F. "Notes on the Clayton Herbarium." *Rhodora* XX (February, 1918) 21-28.
Blanton, Wyndham B. *Medicine in Virginia in the Eighteenth Century.* Richmond, 1931.
Blunt, Wilfred. *The Art of Botanical Illustration.* London, 1950.
Boas, Marie. *Robert Boyle and Seventeenth Century Chemistry.* Cambridge, 1958.
Brendel, Frederick. "Historical Sketch of the Science of Botany in North America from 1635-1840," *The American Naturalist,* XIII (1879) 754-61.
Brightwell, Miss. *A Life of Linnaeus.* London, 1858.
Britten, James. "John Clayton," *Journal of Botany, British and Foreign,* XLVII, 297-301.
———. *The Sloane Herbarium.* Revised and ed. J. E. Dandy. London, 1958.
Britten, James and G. S. Boulger. *British and Irish Botanists.* London, 1931.
Brooks, E. St. John. *Sir Hans Sloane.* London, 1954.
Burk, John. *The History of Virginia.* Four volumes. Petersburg, 1805.
Burke's *Genealogical and Heraldic History of the Peerage and Baronetage.* Various Editions.
Butterfield, Lyman H. *Williamsburg's First Institute.* Williamsburg, 1954.
Campbell, J. W. *A History of Virginia.* Petersburg, 1813.

Carrier, Lyman. "Dr. John Mitchell, Naturalist, Cartographer, and Historian," *Annual Report of the American Historical Association* (1918) 199-219. Washington, 1921.

Castiglioni, Arturo. *A History of Medicine*. New York, 1941.

Cheston, Emily Read. *John Bartram, His Garden and His House*. Ambler, 1953.

Cockayne, G. E. *The Complete Peerage*, Rev. and much enlarged by H. H. Doubleday and Lord Howard de Walden. London, 1932.

Cook, John Esten, *Virginia, A History of the People*. Boston, 1887.

Cover, Carol Minor (Tanner), John Page, 1743-1808. Unpublished Master's Thesis, University of Virginia, Archives #1337.

Dabney, Mary Howard. "John Clayton of Windsor," *Garden Gossip*, XXXII (Sept.-Oct., 1957).

Dawson, Warren R. *The Banks Letters*. London, 1958.

DeBeer, E. S. "Earliest Fellows of the Royal Society," *Notes and Records of the Royal Society of London*, VII, No. 2.

Dictionary of American Biography, ed. Allen Johnson, Dumas Malone, et als. 22 volumes. New York, 1943.

Dictionary of National Biography, ed. Sir Leslie Stephens and Sir Sidney Lee. London, 1917.

Dodson, E. Griffith. *Speakers and Clerks of the Virginia House of Delegates 1776-1955*. Richmond, 1956.

Donnan, Elizabeth. "Eighteenth Century English Merchants: Micajah Perry," *Journal of Economic and Business History*, IV (November, 1931), 70-98.

Dryander, Johann. *Catalogus Bibliothecae Historico Naturalis Josephi Banks*. London, 1800.

Dugdale, Arthur A. "Williamsburg Remembers John Clayton," *Richmond News-Leader*, October 4, 1957.

Dugdale, Elizabeth. "In Honour of John Clayton," *The Garden Club of Virginia Journal*, II, No. 5 (September-October 1957).

Earnest, Ernest P. *John and William Bartram*. Philadelphia, 1940.

Eddy, Clyde. "John Clayton, Virginia Botanist," *The Garden Journal of the New York Botanical Garden* (May-June 1951) 85-87.

Eggleston, Edward. "Husbandry in Colonial Times," *Century Magazine*, XVII (January, 1884).

Ewan, Joseph. "Analytical Index to Darlington's *Memorials of Bartram and Marshall* (1849)," *Journal of the Society of Bibliographical Natural History*, III part 5, 1957, 263-72.

Featherstonhaugh, G. W. "On the Comparative Encouragement Given to the study of Natural History in Europe and North America," *Monthly American—Journal of Geology and Natural Science*, I (March, 1832) 391-407.

Bibliography

Fernald, M. L. "The Flora Virginica of Gronovius," *Chronica Botanica*, VI, No. 2 (1940) 27-28.
Fox, R. H. *Dr. Fothergill and His Friends.* London, 1919.
Frick, George Frederick and Raymond Phineas Stearns. *Mark Catesby, the Colonial Audubon.* Urbana, 1961.
Gilmour, J. S. L. & Tutin, T. G. *A List of the More Important Collections in the University Herbarium, Cambridge.* Cambridge, 1933.
Goode, George Brown. "The Origin of the National Scientific and Educational Institutions in the United States," *Annual Report of the Historical Asociation* (1899), 53-161.
Goodwin, the Reverend W. A. R. *The Record of Bruton Parish Church.* Richmond, 1941.
Gordon, Armistead C. *Men and Events.* Staunton, 1923.
Gourlie, Norah. *The Prince of Botanists.* London, 1953.
Gray, Asa. *Manual of Botany*, ed. M. L. Fernald. New York, 1950.
Green, J. Reynolds. *A History of Botany in the United Kingdom.* London and Toronto, 1914.
Hawks, Ellison. *Pioneers of Plant Study.* New York, 1928.
Hepburn, Henry F. "The Clayton Family," *Papers of the Historical Society of Delaware*, XLI.
Herbst, Josephine. *New Green World.* New York. 1954.
Hindle, Brooke. *The Pursuit of Science in Revolutionary America, 1735-1789.* Chapel Hill, 1956.
Hopkins, Jessie. "Botany's Debt to John Clayton," *Garden Gossip*, XXX (August, 1955).
Hopkins, Jessie and A. B. Massey. "In Memory of John Clayton, Botanist of Colonial Virginia," *The Virginia Journal of Science, News and Notes* (new series) II (July, 1951).
Howe, Henry. *Outline History of Virginia.* Charleston, 1849.
Inderwick, F. A. *A Calendar of the Inner Temple Records.* Three volumes. London, 1901.
Kelly, Howard A. *Some American Medical Botanists.* New York, 1929.
Lam, H. J. "The Life of Gronovius," *Chronica Botanica*, VI, No. 2, 28-30.
Law, Ernest. *The History of Hampton Court Palace.* Three volumes. London, 1888-1891.
Layton, Sir Walter T. *The Discoverer of Gas Lighting.* London, 1926.
LeNeve. *Pedigrees of the Knights*, ed. George A. Marshall. London, 1873.
Levin, Bernard S. *Guide to the Manuscript Collections in the Historical Society of Pennsylvania.* Philadelphia, 1940.

Lonn, Ella. *The Colonial Agents of the Southern Colonies.* Chapel Hill, 1945.
Mackenzie, Kenneth R. "Concerning the Proper Identification of Linnaean Species, Especially those Based on Material Collected by Clayton," *Rhodora,* XXX (December, 1928) 232-37.
Martin, Eleanor Field. "John Clayton, Tidewater Gentleman," *Garden Club of Virginia Journal,* II, No. 5.
Mason, Polly Cary. "The Story of Elmington," *William and Mary Quarterly* (3) LV (July, 1947).
Massey, A. B. "Plant Hunters of Virginia," *The Commonwealth,* 64 (1939).
Meade, Bishop William. *Old Churches, Ministers and Families of Virginia.* Two volumes. Philadelphia, 1861.
Meade, Robert Douthat. *Patrick Henry, Patriot in the Making.* Philadelphia, 1957.
Meisel, Max. *A Bibliography of American Natural History.* Three volumes. Brooklyn, 1924-1929.
Middleton, M. S. "John Bartram, Botanist," *Scientific Monthly,* XXI (1925) 191-216.
Miller, Samuel. *A Brief Retrospect of the Eighteenth Century.* Two volumes. New York, 1803.
Morison, Samuel Eliot. *The Intellectual Life of Colonial New England.* New York, 1936.
Morton, Richard L. *Colonial Virginia.* Two volumes. Chapel Hill, 1960.
Munk, William. *The Roll of the Royal College of Physicians.* London, 1818.
Packard, Francis R. *History of Medicine in the United States.* Two volumes. New York, 1931.
Page, R. C. M. *Genealogy of the Page Family in Virginia.* New York, 1893.
Peattie, Donald Culross. *Green Laurels.* New York, 1936.
Pennell, Francis W. "Benjamin Smith Barton as a Naturalist," *Proceedings of the American Philosophical Society,* 86 (September, 1942), 108-22.
Price, F. G. Hilton. *The Signs of Old Lombard Street.* London, 1904.
Pulteney, Richard. *Historical and Biographical Sketches of the Progress of Botany in England.* Two volumes. London, 1790.
Pursh, Frederick. *Flora Americae Septentrionalis.* Two volumes. London, 1814.
Raven, Charles E. *John Ray, Naturalist, His Life and Works.* Cambridge, 1942.
Reed, Howard S. *A Short History of the Plant Sciences.* Waltham, 1942.

Rhoads, Webster S. Talk given on John Clayton Day, Williamsburg, October 1957. Deposited in the Alderman Library, University of Virginia.
Scott, Edward J. L. *Index to the Sloane Manuscripts in the British Museum.* London, 1904.
Sherborn, Charles Davies. *An Account of the Various Natural History Collections.* Cambridge, 1940.
Singer, Charles J. *A History of Biology.* New York, 1959.
Smallwood, William Martin and Mabel Sarah Coon Smallwood. *Natural History and the American Mind.* New York, 1941.
Sorley, M. E. *Lewis of Warner Hall.* Missouri, 1935.
Stanard, Mary Newton. *Colonial Virginia.* Philadelphia, 1917.
Stanard, W. G. "The Clayton Family," *Historical Magazine* (October, 1891).
Stearn, William T. "Botanical Exploration to the Time of Linnaeus," *Proceedings of the Linnean Society of London.* (December, 1958).
Stearns, Raymond Phineas. "Colonial Fellows of the Royal Society 1661-1788," *Notes and Records of the Royal Society of London,* VIII, 178-261.
———. "James Petiver, Promoter of Natural Science," *Proceedings of the American Antiquarian Society,* LXII (October, 1952) 243-365.
Stetson, Sally. "John Clayton," *Garden Club of Virginia Journal,* II (September-October 1957).
Stetson, Sarah P. "Traffic in Seeds and Plants from England's Colonies in North America," *Agricultural History,* XXIII (January, 1949) 45-56.
Stoever, D. H. *The Life of Sir Charles Linnaeus.* Trans. Joseph Trapp. London, 1794.
Swem, Earl G. *Virginia Historical Index.* Two volumes. Roanoke, 1934, 1936.
Taliaferro, William B. "A Few Things About our County," *William and Mary Quarterly* (1) III (July, 1894).
Thacher, T. C. *American Medical Biography.* Boston, 1826.
Thatcher, Herbert. "Dr. Mitchell, M.D., F.R.S. of Virginia," *The Virginia Magazine of History and Biography,* XXXIX (1931) 126-35, 206-20; XL (1932) 48-62, 97-110, 268-79, 335-46; XLI (1933) 59-70, 144-56.
Toner, Joseph M. *Contributions to the Annals of Medical Progress and Medical Education in the United States.* Washington, 1874.
Tyler, Lyon G. *Williamsburg, The Old Colonial Capitol.* Richmond, 1907.
———. "Virginia's Contribution to Science," *American Antiquarian Society Proceedings,* XXV (1915) 364.

Turner, Dawson. "Remarks upon the Dillenium Herbarium," *Transactions of the Linnean Society of London,* VII, 101-15.
Vail, Anna Murray. *Jane Colden, an Early New York Botanist.* Publication of the New York Botanical Garden, No. 88, New York, 1907.
Van Doren, Carl. "The Beginnings of the American Philosophical Society," *Proceedings of the American Philosophical Society,* LXXXVII, 277-89.
Whiting, W. H., Jr. "Notes on Major Henry Whiting," *William and Mary Quarterly* (2) X, 47-51.
Williams, Clarence R. "Dr. John Dunn as a Virginia Botanist," *William and Mary Quarterly* (2) XV.
Williams, The Rev. W. T. "Notes on Clayton-Davies," *Tyler's Quarterly,* VIII, 209; IX, 163-64.
Wilson, Gen. James Grant. "Lord Lovelace and the Second Canadian Campaign," *Annual Report of the Historical Association, 1891.* Washington, 1892.
Wren Society, Volume 18 (Oxford, 1941).
Wright, Louis B. *The Atlantic Frontier.* New York, 1947.
――――. *The Cultural Life of the American Colonies 1607-1763.* New York, 1957.
Youngken, H. W. *Pharmacognosy.* Philadelphia, 1936.
Zirkle, Conway. "A Possible Early Eighteenth Century Record of Introgression in Oaks," *Journal of Heredity,* XLI (1950) 315-17.
――――. *The Beginnings of Plant Hybridization.* Philadelphia, 1935.
――――. "John Clayton and our Colonial Botany," *The Virginia Magazine of History and Biography,* LXVII (July, 1959).

INDEX

Abies balsamea, 92, 218
Acacia triacanthos, 141
Aconitum, 166
Acrostichum, 144
Adanson, Michael, 36
Agastache, 144-45, 174
Alchemy, 11, 12
Aletris, 143, 225
Algae, 85, 143
Alston, Charles, 61, 78, 81, 97, 120-21, 125, 131, 154, 166, 175
Althaea, 92
Amman, John, 80
American Lotus, 174
American Philosophical Society, 94-97, 125, 168, 219
Amson, John, 135-36, 139, 224
Amsonia, 3, 135-36, 139, 147, 166, 224
Anderson Pills, 33, 211
Andromeda, 225
Angelica, 143, 225
Anne, Queen, 16, 46
Apothecaries, Society of, 44-45, 53
Aralia spinosa, 91, 92, 218
Araliastrums, 92, 218
Arbor vitae, 91, 147
Artists, botanical, 52, 54-55, 132, 133-35
Arum, 131
Asclepias, 83, 143
Asparagus, 124
Aster claytoni, 174

Atamasco lilies. *See* Zephyranthes
Azalea, 83, 120

Bäck, Abraham, 69-70, 103, 105, 130, 215, 221, 224
Balm of Gilead Fir. *See* Abies balsamea
Baker, Sir John, 8
Banks, Sir Joseph, 173-74, 212
Banister, the Rev. John, 42, 43, 48, 49, 65, 145, 176
Barton, Benjamin Smith, 4, 111-12, 145, 169, 176, 178, 225
Bartram, John, and Kalm, 3, 108-9; and Clayton, 30, 90, 91-93, 94-97, 112, 113, 124, 146-51, 165, 166, 167; and Catesby, 55, 88, 213; and *Flora Virginica*, 70, 140-41; and Collinson, 78-91 *passim*, 112, 120-21, 128-30, 140, 225; garden of, 81, 86, 126, 217; life, 86-93; and the American Philosophical Society, 94-99; and Colden, 95-97, 100-1; and J. F. Gronovius, 91, 100, 129, 140; travels of, 77, 86, 88, 89-91, 110-11, 112, 149; and Garden, 126-27, 142, 148; mentioned, 36, 79, 99, 118, 130, 139, 150, 160, 177
Bartram, John, Jr., 82
Bartram, Moses, 89
Bartram, William, 79, 89, 129-30
Bartramia, 88

Bastard plants. *See* Plants, hybrid
Batts & Fallam expedition, 113, 221
Beauclerk, Lord Henry, 15, 37
Beauclerk, (Martha Lovelace) Lady, 15, 37
Beckley, John James, 161-63, 167, 169, 170
Belly-Ache-Root. *See* Angelica
Bergius, Peter Jonas, 174
Betula, 92, 93, 143
Beverly, Peter, 24, 27, 210, 215
Beverly, William, 76, 77
Birches. *See Betula*
Blue Ridge Mountains, 24, 78, 111-12, 139-40
Boerhaave, Herman, 60, 64, 78, 120, 213, 214
Boswell, Thomas, 122, 156-58
Bowyer family, 11, 14, 206, 207
Bowyer, Sir William, father of Alice Clayton, 10, 12
Bowyer, Sir William, brother of Alice Clayton, 14, 15
Boyle, Robert, 41, 43
British Museum, 3, 46, 133, 174, 175, 179-81
Byrd, William, II, 17, 19-20, 41, 72, 75, 78, 79, 85, 90-91, 117, 151; and the Royal Society, 47-48; and Catesby, 53-54
Byrd, William, III, 148

Calla, 141
Callicarpa, 130
Cambridge, University of, 10, 14, 22, 23, 42, 174
Canadian Bonduc Tree. *See Gymnocladus*
Carnations, 115
Carolina Tippity Twitchet. *See Dionaea muscipula*
Carter, Robert ("King"), 17, 18, 19, 25, 209, 211
Cassia, 143, 225
Catesby, Mark, and Clayton, 20, 54, 55-57, 58, 63, 64, 79, 88, 114-15, 118-19; life of, 53-57, 114; and Collinson, 55, 108, 114-15; and Bartram, 55, 88, 213; and J. F. Gronovius, 58, 63-69 *passim*, 102-3; mentioned, 3, 5, 44, 46, 68, 95, 108, 110, 142, 151, 176
Catochu, 33, 211
Cator, John, 82, 212
Cat-tail. *See Typha*

Channel buoys, 12
Charles II, 8, 13, 15
Chelone, 71, 83, 139, 145, 149, 166
Chelsea Physik Garden, 44-45, 61, 212
Cherry trees, 92
Chionanthus, 70, 83, 128, 139, 166
Christophoriana, 92, 218
Clayton family, arms of, 74; lawsuits of, 9, 15-16, 206
Clayton, Alice Bowyer, 10-17 *passim*, 71
Clayton, Andrew, 8, 10
Clayton, Arthur, 17, 22, 23, 25, 72, 215
Clayton, Catherine, 40, 171
Clayton, Charlotte, daughter of Gen. Jasper Clayton, 14
Clayton, Charlotte. *See* Lady Lovelace
Clayton, Cleverine Knight, 6
Clayton, Elizabeth, 12, 15
Clayton, Elizabeth Whiting, 27, 28-29, 40, 77, 167, 170, 215
Clayton, Elizabeth Willis, 151
Clayton, Elvira, wife of Wm. Clayton, botanist's son, 152
Clayton, Elvira, daughter of above, 152, 171
Clayton, George, 8
Clayton, Isabella Lewis, 72, 73-74
Clayton, Sir Jasper, 7-10, 11, 205, 206
Clayton, Gen. Jasper, 12, 14-15, 37, 71, 72
Clayton, Jasper, son of the botanist, 30, 40, 153, 157, 167, 171
Clayton, Jasper S., 5, 6, 207
Clayton, Jasper, son of botanist's son Jasper, 153, 171
Clayton, Jasper, son of botanist's son John, 152
Clayton, Sir John, 4, 8-16 *passim*, 22, 35-36, 42, 207-8
Clayton, the Rev. John, 4, 35-36, 43, 48, 75, 176, 221
Clayton, John, father of the botanist, life of, 14-21, 49, 71-73, 74-75, 206, 207, 209; will of, 6, 74-75; mentioned, 4, 11, 22, 23, 25, 34, 36, 53, 54, 215, 216
Clayton, John, the botanist, herbaria of, 3, 146, 171, 173-74, 178; recognition of, 4, 29, 30, 68-69, 70, 94, 174-82; and J. F. Gronovius, 4, 58, 62-70, 77, 78, 95-96, 102, 107, 111,

128, 130, 131, 136-45, 173, 175, 177, 178; early life in England, 5, 14, 22, 51, 105, 175, 205; will of, 6, 30, 152, 170-71; and Wm. Byrd, II, 19, 117; and Catesby, 20, 54, 55-57, 58, 63, 64, 79, 88, 114-15, 118-19; and Linnaeus, 22, 36-37, 62-68 passim, 70, 84, 102-8 passim, 121, 124, 135-37, 174, 177, 179-81; clerk of court, 23, 24, 25-26, 30, 40; titles of, 23, 27, 111; and Collinson, 23, 36-37, 38, 64, 79, 82, 83-86, 107-8, 115-21, 124, 131-37 passim, 148-55 passim, 160, 171-72, 177; travels of, 24, 77-78, 110-14, 131, 139-40; marriage and children of, 27-28, 40, 151-56, 210; home of, 29-31, 33-40, 122; garden of, 30, 90, 146-48, 149-51, 164-67, 217; Norton orders of, 31-40, 160-68 passim; library of, 33, 35-38, 68, 119, 211; and Garden, 36, 124, 125, 126-27, 135, 142, 148; zoological interests of, 56-57, 76-77, 78; plants named for, 70; executor of father's will, 74; and Durant, 75, 76-77; letters of, 76-77, 105-7, 116-17, 119; and Mitchell, 78-79, 130; and Dillenius, 84-85; and Bartram, 90, 91-93, 94, 113, 124, 146-51, 160, 165, 166, 167; and the American Philosophical Society, 94-97, 219; and Franklin, 97, 123-25, 148, 149, 223; and Perry, 103, 132, 133, 134-35; and Swedish Royal Academy of Science, 105-6, 220; and Gentleman's Magazine, 110, 116-17, 120-21; and Gordon, 119, 120, 164-65, 167; and Ellis, 132-33, 138-39, 142, 149-50; grandchildren of, 151-53; and Beckley, 160-63; death of, 169-70
Clayton, John, Jr., son of botanist, 22, 40, 113-14, 151, 171
Clayton, John, son of botanist's son Jasper, 152, 156, 167, 171
Clayton, John III, son of botanist's son John, 151-52
Clayton, Juliana, wife of Gen. Clayton, 14, 72
Clayton, Juliana, daughter of Gen. Clayton, 14, 15
Clayton, Juliana, daughter of Dr. Thomas Clayton, botanist's brother, 72

Clayton, Lucy, 17, 40
Clayton, Lucy. See Hughes, Lucy Clayton
Clayton, Mary Thomson, 7, 9, 13, 15, 206, 207
Clayton, Mary, daughter of Sir Jasper Clayton, 8
Clayton, Mary, daughter of Sir John Clayton, 12, 15
Clayton, Mary, daughter of botanist, 40, 170
Clayton, Mildred, 152, 171
Clayton, Prudence, 8, 15-16, 71, 206, 215
Clayton, Rebecca. See Yarmouth, Countess of
Clayton, Robert, Bishop of Clogher and Cork, 35-36, 211
Clayton, Robert, son of botanist, 40, 170
Clayton, Dr. Thomas, brother of botanist, 17, 22, 71, 72, 73-74, 207, 215-16
Clayton, Dr. Thomas, son of botanist, 40, 153-56, 167, 171, 214
Clayton, William, of Oakenshaw, 7, 22
Clayton, William, son of botanist, 40, 152, 160, 171-72, 227
Clayton, William Beverly, 152, 171
Claytonia, iii, 3, 58, 70, 105, 106-7, 165-66, 174
Claytonia (journal), 174
Clement, Benjamin, 110, 177
Clifford, George, 52, 61, 68, 214
Cocke, Elizabeth, 53, 213
Cocke, William, 53, 54, 213
Colden, Cadwallader, and Collinson, 79, 81, 83, 95-102 passim, 126-27, 132; and Bartram, 95-97, 100-1; life of, 97-102; mentioned, 3, 79, 83, 84, 108, 109, 120, 126, 127, 130, 135, 150
Colden, Jane, 84, 98, 99, 126, 217
College of William and Mary, 17, 27, 75, 122, 123, 125, 167, 209
Collinson, Peter, and Clayton, 23, 36-37, 38, 64, 79, 82, 83-86, 107-8, 115-21, 124, 131-37 passim, 148-55 passim, 160, 171-72, 177; introduction of plants by, 50, 80; on nursery-gardens, 50-51; and Catesby, 55, 108, 114-15; and J. F. Gronovius, 67, 91, 128-32, 137, 142; and Bartram, 78-91 passim,

Index

112, 120-21, 128-30, 140, 225; and Colden, 79, 81, 83, 95-102 *passim*, 126-27, 132; and Franklin, 79, 81, 95, 96, 102, 115, 118, 124, 132, 140; life of, 79-84; garden of, 20, 81-84, 217; and Linnaeus, 81, 84, 88, 103-8 *passim*, 118, 131-32; and Mitchell, 85-86, 88-89, 102; and Eliot, 117-18; mentioned, 3, 63, 68, 106, 107, 159, 212, 219-20
Collinsonia, 84, 94
Compton, Henry, Bishop of London, 42-43, 44-45, 48, 49, 51
Conserva, 144
Convolvulus, 144
Corispermum. See *Stellaria*
Cotton, 45
Cristophoriana. See *Christophoriana*
Cupressus, 143
Cuscuta Gronovii, 110
Custis, John, 17, 20, 38, 72, 78, 79, 85, 86, 90

Dale, Samuel, 47, 211
Datura Stramonium, 143, 225
Davies, Nicholas, 113
Desmodium Dillenii, 146
Digitalis, 145
Dillenius, Johan Jakob, 52-53, 61, 66, 84-85, 88, 92
Dionaea muscipula, 149, 151, 166
Dodecatheon, 112, 139, 150, 151, 166, 193
Doody, Samuel, 47, 64, 214
Douglas, Dr., New England physician, 101, 115, 219-20
Dracocephalum, 166
Dudley, Paul, 142, 220, 225
Dunn, John, 30, 145, 165, 225
Durant, Samuel, 75, 76-77, 158, 159

"East Greenwich," 152, 227
Edinburgh, University of, 61, 78, 97, 120, 121, 125, 131, 153-54, 214, 225
Ehret, George Dionysius, 52, 55, 103, 133-35, 138; and Clayton, 103, 132, 133, 134-35
Elephantopus, 83
Eliot, Jared, 79, 117-18, 124, 125
Ellis, John, 98, 127, 132-33, 149-50; and Clayton, 132-33, 138-39, 142, 149-50
Ellisia, 22, 127
"Elmington," 27

Eton School, 10, 14, 22, 153
Eupatorium, 144
Eutoca parviflora, 83
Evelyn, John, 10, 13

Fairchild, George, 51, 114
Firr-pines, 92
"Flora Virginiana," 131-42 *passim*, 146, 171, 177
Flora Virginica, 3, 4, 78, 83, 100, 142, 168, 176, 178, 179; Part I, 64-67, 69, 87, 91, 99, 125, 175; Part II, 65, 66, 69-70, 94, 99, 125, 130; second edition, 23, 107, 112, 129-32, 136-45, 177
Fontaine, the Rev. James Maury, 37, 156
Fontaine, John, 24, 156
Fothergill, John, 81, 106, 217
Fox, the Rev. John, 122-23, 150, 156, 223
Fox, John, son of the above, 123, 150-51
Franklin, Benjamin, and Collinson, 79, 81, 95, 96, 102, 115, 118, 124, 132, 140; and the American Philosophical Society, 95-97; and Clayton, 97, 123-25, 148, 149, 223; mentioned, 3, 46, 99, 108, 117-18, 150, 219, 223, 228
Fringe tree. See *Chionanthus*
Fulham Palace, 43, 51
Fungi, 143

Galium claytoni, 7, 174
Galt, J. M., 25, 166, 171
Garden, Alexander, 36, 79, 101, 120, 133, 134, 141-42, 150; and Clayton, 36, 125, 126-27, 135, 142, 148; life of, 125-27; and Bartram, 126-27, 142, 148
Gardenia, 103, 119, 127
Gardens, eighteenth century, 50-53, 81-84
Gentleman's Magazine, 37-38, 89, 106, 109, 110, 116-17, 120-21, 151, 158-59
Gentlemen of the Privy Chamber, 13, 16
Gerardia, 145
Gesner, Conrad, 59, 213-14
Gilly flower, striped stock, 147
Ginseng. See *Araliastrum*
Glade-mallow. See *Napaea dioica*
Gladiolus, 63-64

Index

Gleditsch, Johann Gottlieb, 107
Gleditsia, 107, 141
Gloucester County, 6, 23, 26, 30, 122, 163-64; courthouse of, 26, 155
Gloucester Court House, 26-27, 30, 157
Gmelin, George, 80, 105-7, 110, 175
Goosley, George P., 161-62
Gordon, James, 82-83, 119-20, 135, 164-65, 167
Greenway, James, 145, 176-77, 181
Grew, Nehemiah, 41, 42, 43, 47, 120, 121, 222
Gronovius, Abraham, 62
Gronovius, J. F., and Clayton, 4, 58, 62-70, 77, 78, 95-96, 102, 107, 111, 128, 130, 131, 136-45, 173, 175, 177, 178; and Catesby, 58, 63-69 *passim*, 102-3; and Richardson, 58-59, 61, 69; life of, 58-63, 128-31, 140; and Linnaeus, 59, 60-70 *passim*, 77, 99, 102-3, 104, 111, 113, 129, 131, 173, 179-80; and *Flora Virginica*, 3, 64-70, 83-84, 87, 129-32; and Collinson, 67, 91, 128-32, 137, 142; and Bäck, 69-70; and Bartram, 91, 100, 129, 140; mentioned, 36, 55, 80, 98, 99-100, 108, 109, 114, 125, 173, 213
Gronovius, L. T., 3, 23, 131-32, 136-37, 171
Gymnocladus, 149, 226

Halesia, 83
Haller, Albrecht, 59, 65, 69, 214
Hamamelis, 56
Hampton Court, 13, 15, 207-8
Hanover County, 25, 211
Hargreaves, Francis, 30, 35
Harlow, James, 44
Harrison, Benjamin, 17, 18, 73
Hawkhurst, 5, 8, 159
Helleborus, 144
Henry, Mary Clayton, 72, 74, 171, 215
Henry, the Rev. Patrick, 72, 215
Henshaw, Thomas, 10, 12, 13, 206
Herb paris. See *Trillium*
Hercules Club. See *Aralia spinosa*
Holloway, John, 18, 20, 23
"Horseshoe," 152, 211
Houston, William, 63, 173
Howard, John, 113, 114
Hughes, Jasper, 153, 171
Hughes, John, 153

Hughes, Lucy Clayton, 40, 153, 167, 171
Hughes, Thomas, 153, 156, 167, 171
Humming-bird, 117
Hunter, Col. William, 123, 124, 147
Huxhamia, 142

Indian Physik, 144
Indians, 17, 43, 56-57, 92, 116, 143, 144, 169
Inner Temple, 7, 13, 14
Ipecac, 99
Ipomoea Quamoclit, 121, 222

Jefferson, Thomas, 4-5, 23, 111, 163, 177-78, 218
Jimson weed. See *Datura Stramonium*
Jones, the Rev. Hugh, 48, 212
Jussieu, Bernard de, 105, 126, 133, 223

Kalm, Peter, 3-4, 96-97, 108-9, 110, 125, 177, 178
Kalmia, 82, 83, 120, 144
Kneller, Sir Godfrey, 13, 34
Knights of the Golden Horseshoe, 24, 210
Krieg, David, 42, 48, 64, 214

Lady's bower. See *Trillium*
Larch, 93
Lawson, Isaac, 55, 59, 60, 62, 63, 67, 102-3, 111, 114, 115, 140
Lawson, John, 49
Lawsonia, 114
Lee, Arthur, 96, 145, 225
Leeds, Thomas Osborne, Duke of, 12, 207
Leiden, Botanical Gardens, 214
Leiden, University of, 62
Lewis, John, 72
Library Company of Philadelphia, 87-88
Lighthouses, 12
Lilium Catesbaei, xi
Limnia. See *Claytonia*
Linnaea borealis, vii, 104
Linnaeus, Carolus, and Clayton, 22, 36-37, 62, 64, 65, 66-68, 70, 84, 102-8 *passim*, 121, 124, 135-36, 136-37, 174, 177, 179-81; and Clifford, 52, 61; life of, 59-62, 104-5; and J. F. Gronovius, 59-70 *passim*, 77, 99, 102-3, 104, 111, 113, 129, 131, 173, 179-80; classification sys-

tem of, 60-61, 84, 98, 121, 176;
and *Flora Virginica*, 64, 66-68; and
Collinson, 81, 84, 88, 103-8 *passim*,
118, 131-32; herbarium of, 83, 180;
mentioned, 3, 55, 120, 126, 127,
133-34, 135, 149-50
Linnean Society of London, 138
Liquidambar, 141
Lister, Martin, 41, 47, 222
Loblolly-bays, 82, 120, 147
Logan, James, 121, 125, 132, 222
London, George, 43, 49
Lonicera, 142
Lovelace, (Charlotte Clayton) Lady, 12, 15, 71
Lovelace, John, Baron, of Hurley, 15, 37
Lovelace, Martha. *See* Lady Beauclerk
Lovelace, Lord Nevill, 15, 37
Lupines, 147
Lythrum, 144

Magnol, Pierre, 45, 217
Magnolia, 45, 55, 82, 86, 88, 213, 217
Marchantia, 143
Marrubium, 139
Mathews County, 29, 30; Garden Club of, 29, 174
May-apple. *See Podophyllum*
Meadia. *See Dodecatheon*
Melissa, 225
Mentha, 144
Milkwort. *See Polygala*
Miller, Philip, 45, 53, 55, 61, 63, 133, 135, 212, 213, 224
Mimulus, 144
Mississippi River, 113, 131
Mitchell, John, life of, 78-79, 95-96, 102, 113, 120, 130; and Virginia plants, 84-89 *passim*, 101, 103, 131, 228-29; and Collinson, 85-86, 88-89, 102; and Bartram, 91, 96, 101, 218; mentioned, 96, 108, 145, 176
Mitchella repens, 79, 205
Moldavica, 166
"Morehouse," 8, 33, 74, 152, 158-60, 171
Mosses, 84-85, 143
Mountain ash. *See Sorbus*
Mulberry, 121
Mule plants. *See* Plants, hybrid

Narcissus, 167

Napaea dioica, 92, 112, 218
Nelson-Galt House, 20, 209
Neottia, 144
New River, 112-113
Nickar tree. *See Gymnocladus*
Nomenclature, binomial system of, 59-60, 66, 67
Norton, John, 31-32, 35, 36-37, 159-68 *passim*
Norton, John, & Sons, 31-40, 162, 171
Norton, John Hatley, 31, 35
Nott, Edward, 16, 17, 20
Nott, Sir Thomas, 11, 16
Nursery-gardens, 50-51, 119-20, 135

Oaks. *See Quercus*
Oenothera, 225
Oleaster. *See Chionanthus*
Ornithogalum, 83
Orobanche, 143
Osborne, Sir Thomas. *See* Duke of Leeds
Osmorhiza claytoni, 173, 174
Osmunda claytoniana, ii, 174
Oxford, University of, 8, 42, 52-53, 174, 213
"Oxnead," 12, 206, 207

Page, Gov. John, 28, 156, 163, 168, 169, 175
Page, Mann, 74, 168, 216
Palmettos, 133, 139
Palms, 133, 139
Parson's Green, 8, 11, 12, 13, 43, 50, 51
Parsons, James, 121, 222
Partridge-berry. *See Mitchella repens*
Paston, Robert. *See* Yarmouth, Earl of
Peach tree, 124
Penstemon, 139
Perry, Micajah, I, 17, 18, 20, 76, 216
Perry, Micajah, II, 31, 75-76, 216
Perry and Lane, 19, 75-76
Persimmons, 121
Petiver, James, 47-49
Petre, 8th Lord, 53, 80
Philosophical Society for the Advancement of Useful Knowledge, 168-69, 228
Pianketank River, 30, 90
Pig Nut, 83
Pink root. *See Spigelia*
Plants, classification of, 42, 59, 60-61, 65, 84, 138-39, 145, 175, 176;

Index

sex of, 42, 59, 120-22, 125, 166, 175; ecology of, 51, 144; hybrids, 115, 121-22, 222-23
Plukenet, Leonard, 47, 66
Podophyllum, 144, 225
Pole-cat weed. *See Calla*
Polemonium dubium, 84
Polyanthus, 167
Polygala, 92, 105, 218
Polypremum, 130
Postage, 107-8, 123-24, 128, 130, 148-49
Potamogeton claytonii. 174
Prickly ash. *See Xanthoxylum*
Proserpinaca, 130
Pulteney, Richard, 54
Pyrethrum, 147

Quarnoclif. *See Ipomea Quamoclit*
Quercus, 129-30, 144
Quicken trees. *See Sorbus*

Randolph, Isham, 90, 91, 218
Randolph, Sir John, 20, 71, 72, 73, 157, 215
Ranunculus, 145
Ray, John, 41-49 *passim*, 53, 65, 66, 120, 175, 176
Redford, Thomas, 158-60
Rhamnus, 121, 166, 222
Rhododendron, 83, 120
Rhubarb, 101, 165, 166
Richardson, Richard, 58-59, 61, 69, 213
Richmond, 3rd Duke of, 11, 206, 207
Royal Society of London, 41-42, 44-45, 50, 54, 106, 115-17, 141, 206, 221; members of, 4, 19, 46, 47, 55, 79, 81, 115, 118, 127, 132-33, 134, 223; Original Fellows of, 10-11, 16, 206; mentioned, 35-37, 38, 94, 135
Rudbeckia, 143, 174
Rush, Benjamin, 96, 228

Saling, John Peter (Salling, Salley), 113-14, 152
Sandin, J., 105, 107
Seneca. *See Polygala*
Senecio, 144
Sherard, James, 52-53
Sherard, William, 47, 49, 52, 54, 62, 213
Shooting star. *See Dodecatheon*
Sloane, Sir Hans, 19, 44-47, 49, 54, 55, 60, 81, 118, 124, 133, 134, 212

Smoaky weather, 116-17, 22
Solander, Daniel, 127, 135, 173
Solanum, 142
Sorbus, 92, 218
Spigelia, 41, 141-42, 222, 225
Spotswood, Col. Alexander, 17, 18, 19, 24, 49, 53, 54, 56
Spring Beauties. *See Claytonia*
Spruce, 92
Spruce Firr, 147
Staggerweed, 92
Stargrass. *See Aletris*
Stavesacre (Staresacre), 150-51, 166
Stellaria, 139
Stuartia (Stewartia) Malachodendron, 56, 83, 102-3, 130, 141, 166, 220
Sumac, 85
Swedish Royal Academy of Science, 60, 99, 104-5, 106, 108, 177, 220
Sweet Gum. *See Liquidambar*
Sweet William, 115
Symonds, Alice Clayton, 12, 15, 208
Symonds, Henry, 15, 207

Tea seeds, 149-50
Temple Coffee House Botany Club, 46-47, 48, 62
Terra Japonica. *See* Catochu
Theophrastus, 36, 169
Thomson, Jasper, 8, 205
Thomson, Steven, 18, 73, 209
Tobacco, 25-26, 32, 33, 40, 75, 161-62, 163-64, 167, 216
Tooth-ache tree. *See Aralia spinosa*
Trillium, 92, 218
Typha, 143

Umbrella tree. *See Magnolia*
Uppsala, Royal Society of. *See* Swedish Royal Academy of Science
Uppsala, University of, 59, 108, 134

Vaillant, Sebastian, 66, 173, 213
Valley of Virginia, 24, 28, 112-13
Van Royen, David, 70, 82, 145, 154
Venus Fly-trap. *See Dionaea muscipula*
Verbena, 144
Vernon, William, 42, 48, 64, 212, 214
Viburnum, 92
Violet, 121
Virginia Gazette, 38, 73, 123, 152, 154, 157-58, 169-70, 228
Virginia Moley. *See Ornithogalum*

Ware Church, 27-28, 122, 156, 210
"Warner Hall," 74, 215-16
Washington, Catherine Whiting, 28, 40
Washington, George, 28, 124, 157
Washington, John Augustin, 28
Watts, John, 44, 47
"Westover," 20, 54, 148
Whip-poor-Will, 56-57
Wheat, 118
White pine, 115, 142, 219-20
Whiting, Anne Beverly, 27
Whiting, Beverly, 28
Whiting, Francis, 28, 31, 157
Whiting, Major Henry, 27
Whiting, Kemp, 113-14
Whiting, Thomas, 28
William III, 13, 15, 16

Willis, Francis, Jr., 32
"Windsor," "Windsor Castle," "Windsor Farms," 29-31
Witch Hazel. See *Hamamelis*
Withers, James, 161, 162
Wood, General Abraham, 113, 221
Wren, Sir Christopher, 11, 15, 41, 207-8

Xanthoxylum, 92, 118-19, 166, 183, 218

Yarmouth, Rebecca, Countess of, 8, 10, 11, 12-13, 14, 206
Yarmouth, Robert Paston, Earl of, 10, 11, 12-13, 16, 206
Yew, dwarf, 92

Zephyranthes atamasco, 83

www.ingramcontent.com/pod-product-compliance
Lightning Source LLC
Chambersburg PA
CBHW021401290426
44108CB00010B/329